THE
SWEET SPOT

how to accomplish more
by doing less

CHRISTINE CARTER, Ph.D.

BALLANTINE BOOKS
NEW YORK

2017 Ballantine Books Trade Paperback Edition

Copyright © 2015 by Christine Carter, Ph.D.
Preface copyright © 2017 by Christine Carter, Ph.D.
Foreword copyright © 2017 by Brigid Schulte

Published in the United States by Ballantine Books,
an imprint of Random House, a division of
Penguin Random House LLC, New York.

BALLANTINE and the HOUSE colophon are
registered trademarks of Penguin Random House LLC.

Originally published in hardcover and in slightly different form in the United States
by Ballantine Books, an imprint of Random House,
a division of Penguin Random House LLC, in 2015.

Library of Congress Cataloging-in-Publication Data
Carter, Christine (Sociologist)
The sweet spot : how to find your groove at home and work / Christine Carter, Ph.D.
pages   cm
Includes bibliographical references and index.
ISBN 978-0-553-39204-3 (hardback)—ISBN 978-0-553-39206-7 (trade paper)—
ISBN 978-0-553-39205-0 (ebook)
1. Happiness   2. Self-actualization (Psychology)   I. Title.
BF575.H27.C387 2015
650.1—dc23
2014032772

Printed in the United States of America on acid-free paper

randomhousebooks.com

246897531

Book design by Elizabeth A. D. Eno

For Amalia, Fiona, Macie, and Tanner
Life is about learning how to get into a
great groove, so that when you (inevitably)
lose it, you know how to find it again.

CONTENTS

FOREWORD

Brigid Schulte

When I look back on my life and how I've spent my time, two scenes immediately come to mind.

One: My kids are little. They're bouncing gleefully on the trampoline in our backyard, giggling and calling out to me, "Mom! Come bounce with us!" Over and over they call. "In a minute!" I respond, with, I'm ashamed to say, increasing irritation. I was weeding the gravel. The backyard looked furry and overgrown and I just wanted to get something *done* and crossed off a to-do list that was always so jammed that items seemed to fall off the bottom, roll around the floor and constantly trip me. I had a million things on my mind. I was worried about something I can't remember now—something I hadn't done, or done well enough, at work; something that needed fixing, or arranging; some decision I was putting off that had to be made. By the time I looked up, the sun was setting, the kids were gone, the silent yard was still covered in weeds, and I was alone in the dark.

Two: I've decided to leave my job as a reporter at *The Washington Post* after nearly seventeen years. It's been a good run. I've done a lot of good work. Won awards. Made some difference. But there was a *lot* of busywork, too. A raft of forgettable stories done to please some editor or other. Less ambitious stories chosen in a panic out of fear that I'd be seen as unproductive or couldn't pull it off if I chose a harder course. I'm cleaning out my filing cabinet. I pull out folder after folder of half-reported stories, story lists, tips, hunches, inklings and ideas. "That would have made a great story," I say to myself wistfully. Over and over. Thunk. And toss each folder into the trash.

I have long regretted each of those moments. I missed the moment in the first—my kids are teens now and, understandably, no longer want much to do with their mother. And I missed the opportunity to more regularly connect my everyday work with what moved my soul in the second.

And I suspect I'm not alone.

You don't need to go very far to find the latest poll, or study, or article that shows how so many of us feel as if we're drowning—in information overload, in overwork or unpredictable, erratic work, and in crowded calendars stuffed with obligations we're not even sure why we said yes to. As if we're living our own lives on the sidelines, watching them fly by, too distracted and frantic to fully inhabit them. We live in an era where long work hours, busyness, sleeplessness, burnout, the "work martyrdom" of never taking a vacation, or taking work along if we do, and the stress of overscheduling ourselves and our kids are seen not only as badges of honor, but the price of admission. Anything less and you're a loser. We get so caught up in the swirl of just trying to make it to the end of the day, running farther and faster, that we can often lose sight of just where it is we're going. Or even want to go. Behavioral scientists call that "tunneling."

That feeling, that we're trapped, endlessly digging in that dark tunnel, missing our lives even as we're living them, is what can jolt us awake in the middle of the night in a funk of guilt, anxiety and even despair.

That's where Christine Carter's *The Sweet Spot*, blessedly, comes in.

Read this book, and, like a smart, warm friend, who's read all the research, knows all the science, and who's been there herself, Carter not only explains why it's important to change, why finding your own groove and your own *flow* matters, but also takes our hand

and shows us the way out and how even small steps can lead to bigger ones.

I think I'd stayed up too late trying to once again clean out the overflowing email inbox that always makes me feel scattered and behind when I first talked to her about the ideas in *The Sweet Spot*.

She spoke about the power of "strategic slacking"—that neuroscience and neurobiology show we're wired to actually do better work and have more time for life when we get in the habit of taking time to first set our big picture priorities, work in concentrated bursts, take regular breaks, get a good night's sleep, focus on being grateful for what *is* going well in our lives, and instead of berating ourselves for not being perfect, embracing our imperfection with compassion.

She learned the hard way. She's a happiness expert. And yet she found herself constantly sick and stressed out. One day, she wound up in the ER and was seized by hospital fantasies about how nice it would be to stay there overnight and, at least for a while, not have to live her exhausting life.

"The irony was not lost on me," she told me. "Here I was, deep in the research and methods of well-being, elite performance, the ability to sustain elite performance and productivity, *and* really sick. People would say, 'When are you going to learn you just can't have it all? You're going to have to slow down. You're going to have to make some choices.' Yet everything in my life was so hard-won, I just didn't want to give it up. I didn't want to spend less time with my children. I loved my career. Then I thought, 'If I can't figure this out, nobody can. I've been studying this stuff for ten years, I really need to road test it all.' I started applying all the lessons to my own life. I feel like I wrote *The Sweet Spot* so I could just hand all these tactics to other people like myself, so they wouldn't have to go through the period of getting sick like I did."

She started small. Getting her addiction to email under control by taking it off her phone. Scheduling time on her calendar for her top priority: concentrated writing, and taking it as seriously as she would a day full of back-to-back meetings on other people's and institutions' priorities. And, my personal favorite and something I use to this day, micro workouts that are better than nothing: twenty push-ups, twenty squats, twenty sit-ups. Maybe a one-mile run. That's it. That's enough.

There are larger cultural, institutional, economic and structural forces at work that conspire to knock us out of our sweet spot. And big change can be glacial and beyond our control. But what makes *The Sweet Spot* so hopeful is that Carter shows how there are a host of things we *can* do to find our groove, and if enough of us put on our own oxygen masks first, we can help others do the same, and together, hasten that big change toward a more joyful, authentic and meaningful time.

And the most powerful tool for change, she points out, is our own mind. "Our beliefs have the power to change more than just our physiology or our health. They also dramatically change our overall happiness levels and our performance," Carter writes. Do we believe we can never change, that we are who we are? Or do we believe that we can, and that effort, not innate ability, is what matters in the end?

If we believe we can change, we will. If we believe we are enough, right here, right now, we are.

The power of belief Carter writes about so powerfully hit home when Carter helped inspire the Timehacker Project that I ran at *The Washington Post*. We matched people who were unable to find time for an important goal with coaches like Carter, had them work together for twenty-one days, and then I wrote about what happened. Over time, I found a distinct pattern emerged: In every case, no matter who the person, their goal, or their life circumstance, what had prevented them from making time for what mattered was the belief that maybe their goal wasn't that important after all. Or the belief that they didn't really deserve it. In the end, the coaching strategies for finding and organizing time were helpful. But only those people who came to believe that their goal mattered were able to finally make time for it, and find their sweet spot.

That's perhaps what has changed most profoundly for me. I have hope. I pause more often to check in about what's really important. I catch myself sooner when I begin to mindlessly head down that dark tunnel. I'm still very much a work in progress. My sweet spot continues to come and go. But, as Carter writes, finding it takes practice. And the more we try, the better we get at it. The difference is that, now, I believe it.

Award-winning journalist Brigid Schulte is the author of the *New York Times* bestseller *Overwhelmed: How to Work, Love, and Play When No One Has the Time,* and director of The Better Life Lab at New America.

PREFACE

Dear Reader,

In the months since this book was first released, I've had lots of conversations with sheepish readers. "I bought your book," they confess, "but I haven't read the whole thing."

"That's great news!" I'll reply. Why? You don't actually need to read all of this book to get a lot out of it. And you certainly don't need to read it all at once. Think of it like a recipe book for making your life better, happier, and easier. Many of the recipes will be very appealing to you, others not so much. Your life is unique and your struggles are personal; I appreciate that.

To you I would also say: Please take the strategies I recommend in this book *one at a time*. Try them out and make them your own. But just like you wouldn't try to make every recipe in a cookbook (much less in a single season), you don't need to try out every tip or technique in this book. In fact, if you try only *one* of the hundreds of strategies in this book, you'll end up better off. Why do I believe that to be true? Because all the strategies in *The Sweet Spot* are science-based; they've proven to be empirically useful with large populations of people.

Here are some ideas about how to begin accomplishing more by doing less:

If you're struggling to "have it all"—like so many of my readers—take heart. It is entirely possible to raise children well and still have a successful career! Begin at the beginning, with the Introduction (p. xix).

If things are pretty good for you, but you are ready to make them even better—if you are interested in elite performance and talent development—start with Chapter 8: Making Hard Things Easy (p. 179).

If you are exhausted and time-starved, start with Chapter 5: Easing "The Overwhelm" (p. 79). You might also be interested in my free ebook, *How to Gain an Extra Day Each Week*, which you can find on my website, christinecarter.com.

If you are stressed, depressed, or anxious, start with Chapter 2: The Stress/Success Tipping point (p. 15).

If you want better relationships—perhaps your friendships or marriage is suffering at the hands of your career or busy life—start with Chapter 6: How to Die Happy, Giving, and Beloved (p. 117).

If you are having a hard time doing something good for yourself, like exercising or meditating or getting enough sleep—or if self-care always comes last for you—consider making self-care habitual. You'll never have to will yourself to do it ever again! Begin with Chapter 3: Doing Without Trying (p. 39), and be sure to get the companion worksheets for your new habit from my website, christinecarter.com/resources.

If you've recently been through a tough time, like a divorce or a difficult move, begin at the end with Chapter 10: A Short Guide to Getting Your Groove Back (p. 213).

Above all, have fun with this book!
May you be happy,

Christine Carter, PhD

INTRODUCTION: STEPPING OFF THE TREADMILL

We all have a sweet spot where everything seems to flow; where we feel happy, competent, in sync with everything around us, uniquely talented, and predictably successful. It feels like magic, but it's not.

—Peter Bregman

This book arose, like a phoenix, as an experiment in having it all. Could I fulfill my career potential and have a fulfilling family life? Could I be a great parent and still attend to my own needs? Could I be successful and happy without also feeling stressed and anxious?

Having studied well-being and elite performance for the past decade, I've long known what to do to be both happy and successful; after all, I coach people from all over the world on these topics. But to be totally honest, in my day-to-day life, I used to struggle to walk the talk. Five years ago, I was a single mother holding down three demanding part-time jobs, and my life was a blur. Yes, our family did find a way to eat dinner together most nights, and we talked about what we were grateful for. In some ways, I practiced what I preached. But in other ways, I was caught up in the busyness of modern life—winded, running on a hamster wheel, afraid to slow down. I'd lost my groove.

Life today is a pressure cooker. Even the most talented—and privileged—people are struggling to "balance" relentless work with family commitments, to manage a constant flood of information and emails, to cope with extraordinary stress levels. Only 17 percent of the adult population is said to be flourishing, fulfilling their potential for happiness, success, and productivity.

Consider this description of a working American's life, written by futurist and philosopher Sara Robinson, in an essay about the disappearance of the forty-hour workweek:

> If you're lucky enough to have a job right now, you're probably doing everything possible to hold on to it. If the boss asks you to work 50 hours, you work 55. If she asks for 60, you give up weeknights and Saturdays, and work 65.
>
> Odds are that you've been doing this for months, if not years, probably at the expense of your family life, your exercise routine, your diet, your stress levels, and your sanity. You're burned out, tired, achy, and utterly forgotten by your spouse, kids, and dog. But you push on anyway because everybody knows that working crazy hours is what it takes to prove that you're "passionate" and "productive" and "a team player"—the kind of person who might just have a chance to survive the next round of layoffs.

And think about the fact that: 66 percent of working parents say they aren't getting everything done that they want to, 57 percent feel like they don't spend enough time with their families; and 46 percent feel they have no time for leisure. Most people have actually lost time for pleasure compared to our ancestors a hundred years ago—despite the fact that in the olden days, they had to hand-wash their laundry.

Here's the strange thing: For most of the twentieth century, the broad consensus was that "working more than 40 hours a week was stupid, wasteful, dangerous, and expensive—and the most telling sign of dangerously incompetent management to boot," Robinson writes. Further, more than a hundred years of research shows that "every hour you work over 40 hours a week is making you less effective and productive over both the short and the long haul." Really! Even though most people think this makes intuitive sense, they are still surprised to hear that it is actually true.

This common sense is so widely ignored that overwork—and the problems with health, happiness, and productivity that it brings—is epidemic. At the same time that our lives have gotten easier in many ways—with devices to wash the dishes, learn just about anything, have our groceries delivered—it has also gotten easier to work more. We communicate with our co-workers at all hours of the day and night in person, by phone, text, and email. Instead of starting work at 8:00 a.m., we start at 6:00 a.m., when we switch off the alarm on our smartphones and check the emails that came in overnight.

While it's true that new technologies can save us a lot of time, often it doesn't matter, because we fill "found" time in ways that heighten neither productivity nor happiness. I understand this paradox both intellectually and personally, especially when I look back a few years.

I had work I really loved—as a parenting and life coach, as a sociologist at UC Berkeley's Greater Good Science Center, and as a keynote speaker, author, and blogger—but the sheer logistics of my single-parent triple-job life were leaving me dead tired, and, if I'm honest, often snappish with the people I loved the most. It seemed like I never rested anymore, never just sat down to watch a movie or read for pleasure, and I never saw my friends during the week. Every minute of every day, I needed to make progress answering emails, checking things off of lists, driving the kids around, and arranging things on one of my multiple task lists and Google calendars.

The low point for me came at a time when my business was really picking up and my life as a single mother was changing. I was launching an online class platform, had just moved to a new town, and was traveling a lot for speaking engagements. Constantly crisscrossing time zones (and arranging care for my children while I was gone) left me beyond exhausted.

I caught every virus on every airplane, and one autumn morning I found myself in the ER, dehydrated, in excruciating pain, with a 103 degree fever and a kidney infection. To make matters worse, I was scheduled to deliver a keynote address at a large conference in Atlanta at the end of the following week. I knew I couldn't do it. I found myself hoping that the doctor would insist I stay the night in the hospital. I was having my first "hospital fantasy," something I'd heard other women had.

(Not familiar with the concept of hospital fantasies? I was nearly as tired as this woman, who wrote on Katrina Alcorn's "Working Moms Break" blog: "I stumbled back to work when my son was 6 weeks old. He had colic and chronic ear infections, so I really didn't sleep for a year. No exaggeration. I would fantasize about having a minor car accident on the way to work. Nothing serious—just enough to lay me up in the hospital for a few days so I could sleep!")

I knew I'd be okay soon, but I had simply been too tired for too long. I emailed the conference organizers once the IV antibiotics kicked in. They were furious that I'd emailed instead of calling, that I hadn't given them more warning, that I hadn't called before I was so sick that I needed hospitalization. They would not be booking me in the future.

I was devastated. As a lifelong perfectionist and overachiever, I found that disappointing the conference organizers was in many ways as painful for me as the infection.

That short stint in the hospital (in the end, I didn't even spend the night) prompted me to begin the series of life experiments that led to this book. Could I bring joy and rest back into my life? This felt risky, as though I would have to give up financial reward and professional success for time to rest and play. But I wanted a life where I had enough ease in my day that I could stop and chat with my neighbor, throw a ball for my dog and delight in his joy (and not be simultaneously on the phone taking care of business), spend entire weekends making art and reading for pleasure and hanging out with my kids. I wanted to go back to cooking as a hobby, making real food for my family, rather than just warming up frozen stuff.

I needed to get my groove back, to live in my sweet spot rather than on a hamster wheel of busyness. The sweet spot is that point of optimum impact that athletes strike on a bat or racket or club, that place where an athlete has both the greatest power and the greatest ease. Playing tennis, I can feel it when I hit the ball in the racket's sweet spot—the ball launches easily and powerfully over the net. When I hit the ball out of the sweet spot, my hit doesn't have as much strength and there is an element of strain. I can feel the resistance—the bump or the friction created by missing the sweet spot—in my body. If I spend too long hitting out of the sweet spot, I am likely to be sore or achy in a way that goes beyond normal fatigue.

This happens in life as well as sports; even if we are "hitting" fairly successfully, sometimes we feel the strain, stress, and resistance of being out of our sweet spot. As a young marketing manager, for example, I did my job well and was rewarded with "fun" projects and numerous promotions. But because working in marketing for a large corporation wasn't a good fit for me personally, I couldn't find and work from a sweet spot. I could get a hit, but there was no real ease: I always felt an element of strain, stress, and resistance that came from being in the wrong job.

A decade later I found myself hitting out of my sweet spot again, this time not necessarily because I was in the wrong field. I had work I loved, but the *structure* of my work was wrong. Once again, I was getting "hits"—a bestselling book, a prestigious job as the executive director of a revered research center at UC Berkeley—but hitting out of my sweet spot was exhausting, and eventually it took a toll on my health.

I hear similar stories from my doctor friends: They love healing people, but have a hard time working from their sweet spot under the constraints of the insurance companies.

Likewise, as a mom I have days where I miss the sweet spot altogether. It's not that I don't get through dinner and bedtime—the kids do end up fed and asleep. It's that when I miss my sweet spot as a mom, the dinner and bedtime routines utterly exhaust me; I feel the strain of traveling over a bumpy road rather than a smooth one.

When we are out of our sweet spot at work or at home, not only are we more likely to feel fatigued and overwhelmed, we aren't fulfilling our potential. We miss out on the feeling of "flow," when time stands still, and we no longer feel pressured or rushed, when life and work no longer feel so *hard*.

Athletes increase the odds that they'll hit the sweet spot when they learn to "groove their swing." When golfers groove their swing, for example, the sweet spot of the club strikes the ball cleanly and launches its flight. When we find our groove we increase the amount of time that we are operating from the strength and ease of our sweet spot. Being in our sweet spot is a felt sense; we know intuitively that everything is aligned.

Our sweet spot doesn't require conscious thought; our unconscious mind tells us that we are there through our bodies. Our unconscious knowledge is shockingly powerful—and far more extensive than our conscious knowledge. Consider that our conscious brain processes information at a rate of about fifty bits per second, while our unconscious, intuitive nervous system processes information at a rate of 11 million bits per second. Fifty versus 11 million. That's not a small differential, and it means that our unconscious minds are constantly cluing us in to our experience, both internal and external, through our bodies, if only we pay attention.

Try listening to the feedback that your body is giving you right now. Say something really untrue out loud, preferably to someone else. Try something like "I love it when my boss humiliates me in front of my team," or "I adore having the stomach flu." Then notice: How does your body react? The response will likely be ever so slight: a minuscule pulling back, or tensing of your jaw, or a tiny shoulder raise. When I say something that my unconscious mind hates, my body tries to tell me through a little heaviness in my stomach. If I spend too long out of my sweet spot and do something that feels wrong for me, I end up with a stomachache.

Now try saying something out loud that is true for you, and notice your body's reaction. Try something like "I love the ocean," or "I love the feel of my baby's head on my cheek." How does your body respond? When I say something that is very true for me, or when someone else says it to me, I get "chills of truth"—the hair literally stands up on my arms. And if I'm grappling with something hard, but the right answer comes up for me, I get "tears of truth." Tears that tell me that something is profoundly true feel qualitatively different from the tears that come from grief or hurt.

Buddha once said that "just as we can know the ocean because it always tastes of salt, we can recognize enlightenment because it always tastes of freedom." Our sweet spot always tastes of freedom and strength. And when we aren't living in our sweet spot, it always tastes of constraint and constriction. In life, as in sports, we feel the strain of not being in the sweet spot in our bodies: Our shoulders ache, our back hurts, or our stomach churns. We feel the friction and resistance inherent when we hit the frame of the racket or the part of the club head that meets the shaft. We might still land the shot—or the client or the promotion—but we feel the tension.

Just as we won't learn to groove our golf swing by working harder at the wrong technique, we won't find our sweet spot at work or at home by muscling through it. The tactics that most people use to cope with busyness—multi-tasking and using technology to cram more into each day—tend to backfire, as they did for me, making me sick and exhausted and far less productive, happy, and intelligent than I am now. We find our sweet spot by understanding the architecture of our minds and the biology of ease. We change our lives for the better when we use tactics that flow with our brain and physiology, not against them.

Living in the groove is, for many people, about bringing ease back into our lives. Ease—or having an "ease-ier" life—means different things to different people. Some people will come to this book because they need smoother sailing. They are headed in the right direction, but the waters are so choppy that they feel seasick. Some people need this book in order to dial up their creativity and their ability to sustain optimum performance in a highly competitive economy. Other people just want a more joyful and fulfilling life. Many are like I was, generally happy but also exhausted and overworked.

We can all locate the tremendous strength and power that comes from the sweet spot in order to become more productive and successful. Similarly, we need the sweet spot's ease and freedom in order to achieve happiness.

HOW I FOUND MY GROOVE

I knew in no uncertain terms that I would have to stop living in a constant state of fight or flight. I read, analyzed, tried out, refined, and tried out again all of the scientific research, empirically tested strategies, and experts' secrets. My goal was to create a "sweet spot equation"—a simple formula to taste both strength and ease more often. This book is the real-person application of that equation. It's not terribly complicated in the end:

Take Recess + Switch Autopilot On + Unshackle Yourself +
Cultivate Relationships + Tolerate Some Discomfort =
The Sweet Spot

Taking recess is actually a way to increase our brain power. It is about giving ourselves a break from overwork, but it is also about converting stress into productive and creative energy. When we use our brain's natural ability to run on autopilot, we let habits bear the burdens that we've been hoping willpower would shoulder. Unshackling ourselves from the things that tax us, like our smartphone's constant siren song, opens the door for more joy, and it is much simpler to do than you'd think. Connecting with others and cultivating our relationships may sound hokey (or hard), but there is solid science to back up what we gain when we nurture them.

Being able to tolerate a little discomfort is about three core life skills: (1) doing what it takes to develop mastery, which ultimately makes hard things easy; (2) having the courage to follow our passion and purpose instead of the crowd, which also makes hard things easy; and (3) being able to bounce back when the going gets rough.

To show you how quickly this equation can be to set into motion, at the end of each chapter I offer one absurdly simple way to access your sweet spot. This "Easiest Thing" section gives you one small, uber-simple way to instantly bring more ease into your life.

Each part of this equation, and each chapter in this book, is about generating more strength or ease or both. None of this is a dressed up way of saying "hey, just relax;" nothing makes me more tense than hearing that! Nor is this equation about having or doing or being less. It doesn't require leaning into work while leaning away from your family and personal life, or vice versa. I am living proof that we do not need to sacrifice success in order to be happier, and we don't have to compromise our happiness in order to be successful at work. Ease makes us better parents, friends, leaders, workers, healers, activists, artists, and colleagues. Finding our groove makes us more creative, intelligent, beloved, and productive across the board.

It's not that making the shifts that I recommend will always be super easy; sadly, I can't promise you Timothy Ferriss's *The 4-Hour Workweek*. But neither am I going to insist that you dramatically change your career or move to the woods without your smartphone. Our lives are like a set of interlocking gears of varying sizes. Often, we try to improve our lives by moving the large gears: by getting divorced, or married, or moving out of the city, or quitting our job. And sometimes it is very necessary to rotate these big gears. But these big ones are always difficult to move. *The Sweet Spot* is about shifting the small gears, the ones that rotate relatively easily. And because all the gears are interlocking, when we tweak a small gear, large gears start to move—effortlessly—as well.

Or think of it this way: The "minimum effective dose" (MED) is considered to be the lowest dose of a pharmaceutical product that spurs a clinically significant change in health or well-being. I had to find the MED in everything in my life: sleep, meditation, blogging frequency, checking my email, school volunteering, homework help, date nights, quality time with my kids, housework. I had to accept that more was not necessarily better and that our go-go-go culture was pushing me not only beyond my MED, but beyond the "maximum tolerated dose," the level at which an activity (or drug) becomes toxic and starts causing an adverse reaction.

My life has changed dramatically since the day I landed in the hospital with that brutal infection. Some of the changes lately have, incidentally, been shifts in big gears: I've changed my work structure and I've remarried; our fifteen-year-old diabetic dog passed away and we adopted a year-old puppy; my kids have embarked on middle school, and I became a stepmom to my husband's two kids. Yet the truly dramatic changes have not come from having a new job or a new husband or puppy or older kids or even becoming a stepmom. In fact, most of those structural changes in my life came well *after* I found my groove again.

And as you might imagine, the recent changes in my life at work and home have brought with them added stresses as well as joys. I now have four children instead of two, which results in additional chaos and the many challenges of being a stepparent in a blended family. Though I no longer have to worry about giving our diabetic dog shots, I have an energetic lab/border collie mix. And I've moved to a different county, which adds five more hours of driving to my weekly schedule.

So it wasn't these big changes that made my life better. For years previously I've been tweaking small gears and arming myself with small doses of strength and ease, and in so doing, I've re-wired my brain for happiness and sustained high performance—for profound joy, productivity, and intelligence. I've re-channeled the energy that stress was draining out of me into activities, habits, and behaviors that renew my vitality rather than waste it—that create my success, health, and happiness.

I'm far from perfect. It's just that I now have the ability to build more healthy habits without also building the stress that used to consume me. For example, I'm getting into the habit of keeping my kitchen clean all of the time instead of letting dishes pile up. It's not as simple as just intending to do it; I'm temperamentally more of a slob than a neatnik. There are a dozen dishes in the sink as I write. But the pileup is smaller than it ever used to be. I'm constantly building new skill sets and behaviors that run on autopilot, consciously re-engineering my life. You can engineer more strength and ease into your life, too, with a little know-how.

Ultimately, I re-created my life from knowing that there is enough—enough time, money, love—and that I am enough. Philanthropist Lynne Twist calls this mindset sufficiency:

[Sufficiency isn't] a quantity of anything. Sufficiency isn't two steps up from poverty or one step short of abundance. It isn't a measure of barely enough or more than enough. Sufficiency isn't an amount at all. It is an experience, a context we generate, a declaration, a knowing that there is enough, and that we are enough.

You, too, can live your life from a place of sufficiency. You can learn to live with an abundance of time and money and love and all of the things that you yearn for. In our materially rich but spiritually bereft culture, we often forget that how much we enjoy our lives really matters. How much meaning we find in this one lifetime actually counts. As Mary Oliver once wrote: "Doesn't everything die at last, and too soon? Tell me, what is it you plan to do with your one wild and precious life?"

Indeed, what is it that you will do with your one wild and precious life? I suggest you find your sweet spot: that place where you have both great strength *and* great ease.

PART ONE

take recess

The first part of the sweet spot formula is about learning how to increase our productivity at the same time we take more breaks and play a whole lot more. These first two chapters examine the biology of ease: Where is the tipping point between a stressful life and a flourishing one? How can we best turn exhaustion or anxiety into productive and creative energy?

CHAPTER 1

from working overtime to enjoying the seasons

We are all dying, some sooner, some later. The real exception is to truly live.

—Lee Lipsenthal, *Enjoy Every Sandwich*

A doctor friend of mine, Lee Lipsenthal, was dying from cancer, leaving children and a beloved wife behind. He came to our monthly Buddhism and neuroscience study group one last time to share what his impending death had taught him. Imagine you've just been told that you have less than six months to live, Lee said to us.

What do you need to do?

Whom do you need to talk to?

Where do you need to visit?

How will you spend your remaining time?

As I visualized my life with a terminal illness, on the precipice of my own death, I was profoundly struck by how totally out of whack my (real) life had become. In fact, my primary reaction to Lee's death meditation was that I would feel relieved to be dying.

This realization was shocking and, frankly, embarrassing. Lee understood, but imagine how insulting this sentiment could have been to him. He would have given anything to be as healthy as I was. It wasn't that I was unhappy with my life—far from it. But I was overwhelmed by it. My imagined impending death released me from the stresses of everyday life. It's obvious to me now that I needed a break—a figurative and literal recess during which I could recharge my proverbial batteries.

The trouble was (and is for so many) that I saw no way to take that break without giving something up. I did not see any ways to free up time for rest and reflection, nor did I see ways that I could simplify or reorganize my life for greater ease and less strain. But now I do.

The first part of the "sweet spot equation"—Take Recess—is about starting to breathe easier right away by giving yourself tiny moments to recharge throughout the day. I know, I know: You're really busy. Too busy to take any sort of break, much less "recess." Bear with me.

FULL PLATE, EMPTY LIFE

Everyone asks: How are you? And everyone answers: I am so busy.

"We say this to one another with no small degree of pride," writes Wayne Muller in his treatise on rest, "as if our exhaustion were a trophy, our ability to withstand stress a real mark of character. The busier we are, the more important we seem to ourselves and, we imagine, to others." Have you ever bought into this self-fulfilling prophecy? When we start to feel worthwhile because of our busyness, we start to believe the corollary: If I'm not busy, I'm not worthwhile.

> Executive coach, author, and minister Wayne Muller teaches that the Chinese symbol for busy is composed of two characters: heart and killing. In other words, busyness is devastating to our soul.

Most of our modern tasks are what researchers call "instrumental." They aren't fun; they are productive, stuff we "should" do, tasks to cross off of a list. The trouble comes when we eliminate the fun stuff in our lives, when play and rest get eliminated and we use a "get 'er done approach" to instrumental work. This trouble is best illuminated by a famous study by Mihaly Csikszentmihalyi (pronounced "CHEEK-sent-me-high"), the author of *Flow*.

Csikszentmihalyi unintentionally induced textbook cases of generalized anxiety disorder in people simply by instructing his subjects as follows: From the time you wake up until 9:00 p.m., he explained, "We would like you to act in a normal way, doing all the things you have to do, but not doing anything that is 'play' or 'non-instrumental.'"

Research subjects could make the beds and wash the dishes, drive the carpool, go to work, come home and make dinner, supervise homework and bedtime—any of this sounding familiar?—skipping those moments of enjoyment in the day that bring flow or rest. They avoided those things at work they found especially gratifying, skipped the lovely breather they'd take when the kids were off to school, refrained from juicy-but-not-productive sex.

Following these instructions for just forty-eight hours produced symptoms of serious anxiety in research subjects—restlessness, fatigue, difficulty concentrating, irritability, muscle tension—all by eliminating flow and play from their lives. In other words, we get anxious when we aren't having any fun. Management consultant and author Dan Pink writes about what happened to these particular research subjects:

The results were almost immediate. Even at the end of the first day, participants "noticed an increased sluggishness about their behavior." They began complaining of headaches. Most reported difficulty concentrating, with "thoughts [that] wander round in circles without getting anywhere." Some felt sleepy, while others were too agitated to sleep. As Csikszentmihalyi wrote, "After just two days of deprivation . . . the general deterioration in mood was so advanced that prolonging the experiment would have been unadvisable."

When we strip our lives of play and flow—as we so often do just to get everything done—our mood deteriorates. Here's the thing: A life made up of only "instrumental" tasks was an experimental anomaly for research subjects in the 1970s, when Csikszentmihalyi's study was run, but it has become the norm for many people today. Fun, rest, relaxation, and flow have been squeezed out of our lives in the pursuit of more. More sports and lessons for our kids (so that they can get into the best schools and get the best jobs when they graduate), and more work (so that we can keep our jobs, or we can earn more money so we can buy more stuff). We are poisoned by the hypnotic belief, writes Muller, that "good things come only through unceasing determination and tireless effort," and so "we can never truly rest."

Case in point: On May 14, 2013, a twenty-four-year-old "ad man" named Gabriel Li died of a sudden heart attack at his Ogilvy & Mather Beijing office. The official cause of death? Overwork. He'd been working overtime most days the month prior to his death, leaving the office at 11:00 p.m. He was at his desk when he died. Though the American advertising agency where he was employed denied that his death was linked to overwork, Li will be counted by the Chinese government among the estimated 600,000 people in China who die from work-related exhaustion each year.

Deaths like Li's are a global problem. The Japanese call sudden death due to cardiovascular and cerebrovascular disease *karoshi,* which means "death from overwork." Sudden cardiac arrest related to overwork happens in all industrialized nations. Stressed and exhausted employees are more likely to suffer from cardiovascular disease. Cortisol, a hormone that is released when we are stressed, is a chief culprit, as it causes the arteries to narrow.

THE ALTERNATIVE: PRODUCE—AND GROW—LIKE OLIVE TREES

My great-grandparents grew olives, and my brother runs the olive processing company they started, so I've learned a lot about olives over the years. Olives are an "alternate bearing crop," which means that they grow a lot of fruit one year, then mostly branches the following year, creating what is called a "short crop." They produce less fruit in year one in order to produce a large crop the next year. We can all learn from the olive tree. In addition to being a symbol of peace, olives are also a metaphor for how rest and rejuvenation are essential to productivity.

In today's hyper-busy world, most people don't rest or rejuvenate much. We don't allow ourselves the "non-instrumental" activities in life. Research does find that consistent and deliberate practice leads to elite performance (see Chapter 8 for more on that). But focused work is not the same as *unending* work. Even Olympic athletes must train and rest or they get hurt. Fruit trees forced to produce for more than one season, without being allowed to rest in the winter, lose their ability to bear fruit altogether.

In our fast-paced and technology-driven culture, we (and our employers) sometimes forget that we are humans, not computers. Like other animals, humans are governed by circadian and ultradian rhythms. Most people are familiar with the concept of our circadian rhythms. In the twenty-four-hour period when the sun rises and sets, we sleep and wake in predictable cycles. When we travel into different time zones, our circadian rhythms get out of whack, and as a consequence, our lives also can feel similarly discombobulated.

Our brains and bodies also cycle in "ultradian rhythms" throughout the day and night. An ultradian rhythm is a recurrent period or cycle that repeats throughout the twenty-four-hour circadian day, like breathing or our heartbeat.

Even in our sleep, we don't just exist in a singular, steady state. We cycle between dreaming and various types of non-dreaming sleep. There are five different stages of the sleep cycle, each stage identifiable by different brain-wave patterns. For example, Stage 1 sleep is characterized by slow theta waves, while Stage 4 sleep, which is deep and dreamless, is characterized by even slower delta waves.

Our brain-wave patterns also cycle when we are awake. About every hour and a half to two hours, we experience a significant "ultradian dip," when our energy drops and sleep becomes possible. When we work through these dips—relying on caffeine, adrenaline, and stress hormones to keep us alert instead of letting our bodies and brains rest—we become anxious and jittery, and our performance falters.

When we ignore our body's natural rhythms, we create a state of chronic jet lag for ourselves, which over time leads to clinical levels of depression and anxiety, stress-related diseases, and myriad substance-abuse problems (as we self-medicate to stay alert and to "rest"). As Wayne Muller writes in his book *A Life of Being, Having, and Doing Enough*:

When we are increasingly drained, pressed for time, and afraid . . . we are inclined to grasp for some substitute. We are more easily seduced by certain behaviors or possessions that promise to give us not precisely what we dreamed, but something that looks close enough. Most importantly, it is always the thing we can get easier, cheaper, and faster, in an increasingly busy life—in the bone-weary ache of our exhausted heart—and this kind of swift comfort can become irresistible.

Unfortunately, as our time and energy are spent more singularly on work, our plate gets too full to enjoy what is on it (or falling off of it).

FINDING THE "MINIMUM EFFECTIVE DOSE"

When we live our lives as though we are running one marathon after another, day after day, it is, frankly, impossible for life to feel anything but difficult. We know this about actual marathons; there is a whole protocol that runners go through when they finish a race so they can recover. They have medical and other support to begin repairing the damage to their bodies, and they know to rest for weeks or even months between races. Yet we don't have parallel support systems in place for our daily "marathons."

Instead of running one "marathon" after another with little recovery time between them, we can learn to honor the natural rhythms of our days and our lives. We can live more like olive trees, which produce olives for hundreds of years, than like our iPhones, which are built to last only a couple of years. We can take a *school day approach* to life, in which we work and learn and produce and create in predictable periods of time, and then we have equally predictable periods of play and rest and recovery. As in school, we take recess.

There's one more thing that we can learn from marathoners and olive trees: Our most productive pace is always the most consistent one. When we are producing and creating—when runners are in a race and when trees are growing fruit in the summer and when authors like me are writing a book—we are most successful when we are consistent in our efforts. Long-distance runners (and even sprinters) are more likely to win a race if they run each mile at a consistent pace. Expeditioners—people who walk across America—are more likely to succeed, and finish far more quickly, when they walk or trek the same distance day after day, rain or shine. This means they try to trek twenty miles on hard days when the weather is bad and the mileage is all uphill, and—this is the clincher—they stop after twenty miles on easy days, when the weather is mild and the terrain is downhill. Instead of cramming—working long hours and late nights before a big project is due—we human beings do best when we make consistent, predictable, daily progress.

These insights have translated in a few ways in my work. First, the type of work I do cycles like the seasons. Some seasons I focus on writing. Once a book or an article is written, I rest and explore new topics, turning my attention to less taxing work, and I take several weeks off and don't write at all. This is my cycle of creation and rest. In addition, when I'm in a production cycle, I write consistently, 650 to 1,000 words a day. I try to write this amount even on hard days, when I am traveling or have a lot of meetings or my kids are home from school. And on easy days—when I've blocked off six full hours of uninterrupted time to write—I stop once I hit the 1,000-word mark. For me, it is more difficult to stop writing on easy days than it is to churn out 650 words (basically just one rough page) on a hard day. But here's the thing: I've found that if I write more than 1,000 words a couple of days in a row, by the third day, the writing becomes rather joyless. Actually, it can be excruciating.

I feel like I'm trying to squeeze water from a dry sponge. If I finish my 1,000 words and still have time to write, I let myself edit, or I do research—both things that I find easy and joyful and that set me up for success the next day. And ultimately, I know I'm not slowing myself down—that I can complete a book in about six months (my spring and summer fruit production) at this consistent and very manageable pace.

When we take the approach of trees and successful runners and expeditioners, we find that we are able to live with both strength and ease. We free up time and energy to re-energize, to connect, and to find real and deep meaning.

Let me tell you, life seems pretty sweet to me these days, and not because I'm Oprah-rich and doted on by a support staff. I frequently have profound feelings that life is really, really good. I still feel astonished that even though I'm not working the long hours I used to, I'm more financially independent and secure. Consider that:

Every morning this week I rose from bed without feeling the need to press the snooze button. After a quick trip to the loo, I did a lovely meditation and then went for a short run or did a seven-minute strength-training circuit.

After showering and eating breakfast, I got my writing brain warmed up by reading several articles I'd clipped from various on-line sources—emails, academic journals, a couple of different blogs and online magazines.* I had more time than I needed to do this, so it felt luxurious to read and drink my coffee.

After getting the kids off to school, because I'd been pondering what I wanted to write in an unfocused way as I showered and ate breakfast, when I sat myself down in front of a huge blank pad, ideas poured out of me in an easy, non-linear way. I outlined this chapter in about ten minutes.

We overachievers sometimes feel guilty when things are as easy as my life often feels to me now. If it isn't hard, am I actually work-

---

* By the way, all these articles were organized in an Evernote notebook simply because I emailed them to myself with @READ in the subject line. No clipping or filing on my part.

ing? If I'm not working, am I worth anything? When I tell you that I outlined this chapter in ten minutes, do you discount its value, or can you begin to imagine that some of what we approach as the hardest things can indeed be the easiest?

These things—getting myself out of bed, meditating and exercising, starting my most important work first thing in the morning rather than checking my email first—used to be very difficult, if not impossible, for me. I used to press snooze two and even three times in the morning. I used to have to bribe and cajole myself to exercise, and I rarely meditated, even though I knew it was good for me and I had strong intentions to do it. And, distracted by email and seemingly urgent pings for my attention, I used to struggle to put "first things first"—to do the work that really mattered to me.

Moreover, I used to make these things much harder than they needed to be. This morning I ran for only nine minutes—while my children pressed snooze on their alarm clocks. For a former marathon runner, slowly jogging less than a mile a few days a week seems pathetically unambitious. But here's the thing: I'm now consistently running twenty miles more per month than before I drastically reduced my ambitions. This is because before I started doing just a little bit of exercise each weekday morning, I was spending a lot of time planning my exercise—choosing a half marathon to train for, choosing a twelve-week training plan—but very little time actually exercising. What working single mom can work out for an hour before getting her kids off to school? I know that some people do it, but I'd venture to guess that they aren't as well rested as I am now.

And guess what? I've found what doctors (and Tim Ferriss) call the "minimum effective dose" of exercise. I'm now stronger than I have ever been in my life. I'm the same dress size I was before I had my kids and when I was running marathons—but I'm also stronger because I've been doing one ridiculously unambitious strength-training circuit three days a week.

My body is also different because it doesn't hurt. I no longer have the hip and knee problems that plagued me in my twenties when I was running five or more hours a week but not stretching or strength training. And I no longer get sick all of the time, even though I've reached that age when people start complaining that their body is not what it used to be.

RE-LEARNING TO PLAY

When Lee took me through the death meditation, I realized that I was making my life much harder than it needed to be simply because I'd lost touch with the restful and playful parts of my life. I felt relief to be "dying" because it seemed the ultimate permission to prioritize the meaningful stuff of life, the things I really felt a desire to do. Which raised a really good question: What was it that I wanted to do in my last six months of life?

It turns out, I had no bucket list.

I could think of exciting things that I should want to do and, given a long life, would hope to do someday. But if I had only six months to live? I'd want to go back to the simple things that bring me joy, like cooking dinner for my family and taking the dog hiking with friends. I'd want to hang out with my kids reading young adult literature, and go to movies with my husband. I'd sit around and talk with my writer friends about their theories and books, and I'd read cooking magazines. I'd spend more time with my brother and his wife and their totally adorable baby. I'd want mundane things, like playdates for my kids, whose friends I love. I'd want to sit around and talk about weird spiritual things with my dad. I would hang out with my closest girlfriends and favorite couples all the time, preferably in a hot tub.

In short, these are things I already did sometimes, though much less than I would have liked. They are everyday things, not bucket-list things. It's not that I don't want to learn to track wild animals in Botswana—believe me, I did. But at that moment in which I envisioned having only six months to live, all I wanted was to enjoy my actual life more. I wanted a little more quality downtime.

I realized that I was living under the assumption that part of life is necessarily difficult. More than that, it's stressful. I thought life had to be hard—that's just the way it is. I was living in a constant state of fight or flight, created by a pernicious and unrelenting sense that I was not getting it all done. My system was reacting as though my life was being threatened when actually it wasn't. I was living in a continual state of alarm or exhaustion, and I didn't have to be.

Imagining dying jolted me in a way that Lee would later lay out in his wonderful book *Enjoy Every Sandwich*:

Some cures require a radical intervention of the soul: a change in our mindset and our way of being. These cures require us to stop racing through our busy lives, working, providing, and consuming. Some cures require that we stop and enjoy every sandwich.

So simple, and so obvious, and yet also so profoundly transformational for me. Sure, I'd been trying to enjoy every sandwich before. But with everything I had going on in my life, sometimes that was like trying to read in a very dimly lit room. Lee's magical presence helped me integrate into my life insights that I had been teaching for years. For me, Lee's life—and death—was nothing short of a "radical intervention of the soul."

We humans have dreams and values and priorities. We love and are loved by others. Our work and our companionship are important to the world and the beings in it. We make art and appreciate nature: a spectacular sunset or a sonata, a phenomenal meal or a particularly beautiful blackberry, a drawing from a child or a kiss from a dog. These "non-instrumental" things require our time and energy; in return, they bring us real joy and, ironically, they increase our productivity.

We humans need play. We need to laugh and delight in small things, like the smell of jasmine at dusk, or the summer sun streaming into the kitchen after breakfast. We need to play peekaboo with babies. We need to sing our favorite songs at the top of our lungs. We need to dance with our children and lovers and friends.

And because we humans are so wildly creative, we are constantly inventing amazing technologies, tools that save us time and effort. The key question remains, however: What will we choose to do

with all the found time and energy that we've invented for ourselves?

THE EASIEST THING:
TAKE RECESS

Today, take a good old-fashioned recess in the middle of the
day. Go ahead and do your hardest or most dreaded work—or
whatever you need to do—but after about sixty to ninety
minutes of focused attention, honor your ultradian rhythms
and take a break. Rest.

What do you find relaxing or rejuvenating? Is there an
article you've been wanting to read for fun? Does your most
vivid fantasy involve a nap? Do you want to spend a few
minutes looking at pictures of pretty living rooms on Pinter-
est? Perhaps you long to go outside into the great outdoors
(or the plaza across from your office) and let the sun shine
on your face. Just do it. The only rule is that what you do
during recess must be restful or playful; it can't be "instrumental" in any way. Anything that you have to do anyway
(shower, eat lunch) doesn't count, and neither does anything that exists on a to-do list anywhere.

Have fun!

CHAPTER 2

the stress/success
tipping point

The world obeys universal natural laws, and sometimes these laws are shockingly simple. Human psychology—complex as it is—may be no different . . . These laws . . . equip us to find our way to the more flowing, flexible, and dynamic life of flourishing.
—Barbara Fredrickson

We all know how dramatically emotions can affect us. We feel like we can't get out of bed in the morning when work is a nightmare, but we feel buoyant after a belly laugh with a friend. We can't remember anything when we are stressed-out, and we mix up our words when we are exhausted. We experience a warm, spreading feeling in our chest when a child's performance moves us; we are overcome by a sense of calm after a long walk in the forest. We eat a whole pan of brownies when a colleague makes us angry.

All our emotions, both positive and negative, can have a profound physiological effect on our bodies and our brains. We are most familiar with what happens in our bodies when we are stressed-out: that all-too-familiar fight-or-flight response. Something makes us feel threatened—or physically stressed, as when we deprive ourselves of sleep or catch a cold—and our body releases stress hormones, like cortisol and adrenaline.

Several things happen as a result. Our heart rate and blood pressure shoot up, and our breathing becomes more rapid. Blood retreats from our skin (which is why we sometimes feel clammy when we're stressed) and from our digestive system and is redirected to our large muscle groups and our lungs. Our spleen releases more blood cells, which allows all that increased blood flow to transport more oxygen to our muscles. Other fluids, like saliva, are diverted from nonessential sites, like our mouth (this is why we can get dry mouth right before public speaking). And the brain releases a small protein (neuropeptide S) that creates an anxious sense of urgency and an inability to fall asleep.

As if all that weren't enough, our fight-or-flight system also releases chemical messengers (neurotransmitters) that trigger the fear response and—here's the kicker—subdue brain activity in our prefrontal cortex. *That's the area of our brain that we need to think.* This front part of our brain helps us concentrate, inhibits the dumb or socially inappropriate things we are sometimes inclined to do or say, and produces rational thought.

This stress response would give us a shot at survival if we were being attacked by a great white shark in the Pacific Ocean and decided to try bopping the shark on the nose (something native Hawaiians recommend) or to making the long, necessarily fast, swim to shore because we would be able to react quickly, without being slowed down by pesky decision-making. However, this response is problematic in most of our lives today, because the stress we experience is rarely caused by a life-threatening event that warrants a fight-or-flight solution. If we're in a meeting with our boss's boss, for example, our ability to solve a problem, or even just respond with social grace, will be greatly blunted by our instinctual stress response.

And if we are trying to learn something while stressed-out, we're in even bigger trouble. While we will almost certainly learn to be afraid of future situations that are similar to the one we are in now, for the time being our short-term memory is shot. So don't count on being able to remember that new term or method that we heard earlier in the meeting.

THE REALITY OF MODERN *HUMAN* LIFE

If you were a zebra being chased by a lion, but then, luckily, the lion lost interest in having you for lunch, your system would return to normal. It would release calming chemical messengers fairly soon after the chase, and you would be back in a state of mindful bliss, calmly chewing grass as you gazed out across the serene African plain. You would not be reflecting on the surprise visit from a deadly predator, nor would you be worrying that the same lion is still lurking, waiting to kill you or your children. This is why, as the pioneering stress researcher Robert Sapolsky writes, zebras do not get ulcers.*

We humans, on the other hand, *do* get thousands of stress-related illnesses, for two reasons. First, because our environment is often loaded with hundreds, if not thousands, of cues that trigger that gnarly cascade of stress hormones, like the ding of an incoming text or seeing a child step off the sidewalk; getting cut off in traffic or dissed by a friend. Just the mere *thought* that someday soon you think you might have to do a presentation in front of a lot of people. It can be like living near a fire station that is in a frequent state of alarm.

This is not to say that we don't have legitimate worries or that we aren't dealing with profound stress. Most of us face terrible losses and illnesses at some point in our lives, and many have to contend with some awful dilemmas related to making ends meet. These stresses can be very real, and they can be very hard to cope with. But they don't actually necessitate the kind of physiological response that they trigger—the response that we would need if we were trying to fend off that great white shark or outrun a hungry lion.

Second, and even more significantly, we get sick because we be-

---

* A friend who works at the Centers for Disease Control and Prevention pointed out that Sapolsky isn't entirely correct, that ulcers are primarily caused by bacteria, not stress (http://www.cdc .gov/ulcer). Stress does play a major role in the way our bodies fight disease, however.

come sensitized to the experience of stress. Stress itself alters the way we are able to cope with future stress, and not in a good way. It changes patterns in our brain as though we are becoming more and more "allergic" to stressors. Our bodies tend to produce bigger and bigger responses to smaller and smaller triggers whether or not we realize that this is happening. (In fact, consciously we often become numb to our stress responses and simply stop noticing that our heart is hammering or our hands have gone clammy. But even when we aren't really aware of it, our body is still reacting.) So where the zebra has a full-blown stress response because it is being attacked by a lion, we humans can come to have them because our kid spilled the milk.

Unfortunately, this physiological stress response has huge consequences for our health and happiness. The neurotransmitters and hormones that are released affect virtually every system in our bodies. The stress response makes us unfocused, which hurts our productivity. It makes us less intelligent—socially, emotionally, and academically. And it makes us anxious, tired, and, after a while, depressed, in part because it alters the serotonin pathways in our brain.

Our physical stress response is very effective at protecting us in times of true life-threatening emergencies. But it is usually not appropriate for daily use; it is not designed to increase our health, strength, productivity, intelligence, ease, or happiness in the modern world.

THE "UNDOING EFFECT"

Because it doesn't work to will ourselves to just *relax,* we humans are constantly looking for ways to recover from the profound state of dis-ease that stress creates. We binge on comfort foods and smoke cigarettes and drink alcohol and take any manner of drugs to induce feelings of ease. All these things produce changes in our biochemistry and physiology that, at least in small ways, dampen the stress response, even if they create other problems in the process—like obesity, lung cancer, liver disease, isolation from others, or addiction.

The good news is that, consciously or unconsciously, we can counteract our stress response in healthy ways, too, and in the process create "physiologies of ease." When we crack a grin—a genuine eye crinkler that researchers call a "Duchenne smile"—our cardiovascular system calms. Striking a "power pose" for a couple of minutes by putting our hands on our hips like Wonder Woman reduces the amount of cortisol in our system, helping us think more clearly. Meditation lowers our heart rate and improves our focus; massage and other forms of nurturing physical touch release oxytocin—sometimes called the feel-good "love hormone"—into our systems, inducing feelings of profound well-being.

All these positive behaviors (and the positive emotional states they create) have unique biochemical and physiological effects in our brains and bodies. Laughing, for example, produces an extraordinary physical state of near total relaxation, in part because of the way that it forces us to exhale. Simply *exhaling* lowers our heart rate, counters the fight-or-flight response, and induces feelings of calm.

Anger, fear, and negative emotions increase activity in the part of our nervous system that increases our heart rate. Gratitude, compassion, awe, love, and other positive emotions, on the other hand, decrease our heart rate, among other healthy things. This is why Barbara Fredrickson, a positive psychology pioneer, has famously shown that positive emotions put the brakes on the part of our nervous system that creates the deleterious stress response—what she calls the "undoing effect" of positive emotions.

Consider this study where Fredrickson and her colleagues deliberately stressed-out their research subjects.

Applying considerable time pressure, we asked [the research volunteers] to prepare a speech on "Why you are a good friend." To build the psychological pressure even further, we told them that we'd videotape their speech and have it evaluated by their peers. As you can imagine, this surprise public-speaking assignment made people anxious. In-

deed, that was our goal—to make everyone who participated in this study anxious. And we thoroughly succeeded!

Understandably, everyone's blood pressure went way up. Fredrickson's team then could measure what might "undo" this stress response most quickly. After being told that they were actually going to watch a film clip instead of give the speech, the volunteers could begin to relax. Some subjects saw a video that evoked sadness by "showing a young boy crying at the death of someone he loved." Others got to watch clips that evoked serenity (by showing ocean waves) or mild amusement (by showing a puppy playing with a flower).

It was the volunteers in the last two groups—those who saw the ocean or the puppy videos—who recovered from the stressful event the most quickly from a cardiovascular standpoint. Their heart rate, blood pressure, and the constriction within their blood vessels returned to their baseline levels much faster than those who were primed with sadness rather than a mildly positive emotion.

The takeaway: When we've experienced stress, positive emotions return us to our natural state, unwinding the damage that stress does, and bring us back to ease.

BROADENING OUR PERCEPTION IN THE MOMENT

When we are happy, we are more creative and motivated, more productive and skilled socially because blood flows freely to our prefrontal cortex, allowing us to make better decisions than we would if we relied on the more primitive, instinctive regions of our brain that are activated when we are under stress. The prefrontal cortex is responsible for our executive function, and so we have more self-discipline and better self-control when we are happy than we do when we are stressed. We are more able to learn difficult things quickly and better retain what we learn over the long haul.

Our vision is also widened when we are in a state of ease. When we are stressed, our vision narrows, allowing us to focus only on the threat or approaching danger. But when we are happy, we can see the forest *and* the trees, so to speak. For example, in one study, researchers showed volunteers photos of faces and asked the research subjects to judge the gender of the person in the photo but ignore everything else. Behind the faces were photographs of houses or other places. Volunteers primed to be happy before this task were able to recall the houses in the photos, even though they were told to ignore them. People who were feeling unhappy or neutral didn't see the houses at all; they didn't pick up on the peripheral details. Although focus is undeniably good in most situations, when our perception narrows (due to a negative emotion like fear or disgust) we miss important content and contexts, our performance and our relationships suffer.

This means that when we are happy—or experiencing even a mild positive emotion—we are far more attuned to context. **This *broadened* perception opens up our sweet spot: that place where we experience the least stress, the greatest intellectual power, and the most sophisticated social skills.**

THE TIPPING POINT

Over time, our broadened vision and the other positive effects of happiness grow. There is, as doctors say, a dosage effect or, more accurately, a tipping point. All our accumulated moments of being able to see the forest and the trees—and of increased learning and creativity and connection with others—change who we are as people. Our better social skills over time build our relationships with others in ways that bring us new opportunities. Our increased motivation and self-discipline make us more productive, which can build greater mastery and success in our efforts. Fredrickson calls this the "broaden and build" effect of positive emotions. Happiness broadens our perception in the moment and builds our resources over time. It becomes an upward spiral of productivity and positivity.

This positive emotion tipping point is a psychological law just as the temperature tipping point at which ice melts into water is determined by a physical law. People whose ratios of positive to negative emotions are lower than 3:1 often "languish," as researchers call it. Their performance at work suffers, they are more likely to be depressed (and not recover), their marriages are more likely to fail—and they aren't happy. Their behavior becomes predictable to psychologists, and not in a good way. Languishing people become rigid. They tend to feel burdened by life.

Fortunately, something remarkable often happens when our ratio of positive to negative feelings hits or passes that 3:1 mark.* We flourish. Flourishing people, who make up only 17 percent of the American adult population, are happier and more resilient. They are high-functioning individuals who score well on things such as self-acceptance, purpose in life, environmental mastery, positive relationships with others, personal growth, creativity, and openness. Not only that, but they feel good and they *do* good. They are highly engaged with their friends, their work, their families, and their communities.

Everything we do in life changes our brain in some way. As neuropsychologist Rick Hanson puts it in his book *Hardwiring Happiness,* "Whatever we repeatedly sense and feel and want and think is slowly but surely sculpting neural structure." Day after day, our emotions shape our experiences and our brains.

This is why more than two hundred studies show that positive emotions precede success in virtually every arena that has been tested. Happiness is a tremendous advantage in a world that values performance and achievement. On average, happy people are more successful than unhappy people at both work and love. They get better performance reviews, have more prestigious jobs, and earn

---

* Although the math used by Marcial Losoda in 2005 to establish this tipping point was called into question by Brown, Sokal, and Friedman in 2013, we have lots of empirical evidence that our ratios of positive emotions matter a lot, and that a tipping point does, in fact, exist. Numerous studies suggest that the "broaden effect" of positive emotions doesn't show up until a person's ratio is above 2.9:1. In other words, many of the benefits of positive emotions are *inert* until the positive to negative emotion tipping point is reached. It may be that the 3:1 ratio is not a *universal* tipping point—I may need four positive emotions to each one negative, while you need only to average 2.8:1, for example. But ample evidence exists that, for most people, there is, indeed, a tipping point that hovers around 3:1.

is there such a thing as too much positivity?

Flourishing is not about feeling happy all the time or about trying to turn every thought and emotion into a positive one. Our human brains are differential systems; our perception of good depends, in part, on our experience of bad. Positive psychology pioneer Fredrickson compares this to sailing—flourishing people move through life using both sail and keel. Positive emotions put wind in our sails, propelling us forward, giving us direction. Negative emotions are like the weighty keel below the waterline. They balance our boat and help give us direction, too.

higher salaries. They are more likely to get married and, once married, they are more satisfied with their marriages. Happy people also tend to be healthier and live longer. And guess what? Our ratio of positive to negative emotions—whether or not we truly flourish—is largely within our control.

CHANGING OUR RATIO

To state the obvious, there are two ways to reach the positive emotion tipping point that we need to flourish. The first way is to increase the positive emotions in our lives. The second is to decrease negative emotions, or loosen the grip they have on our lives, which is the subject of the next chapter.

The rest of this chapter is about actually *creating the biology of ease* within ourselves through positive emotions. There are three essential ways to do this in a given day. First, we can take actions that will induce a specific positive emotion—like taking a moment to count our blessings in order to foster gratitude. Second, we can amplify the positive emotions and experiences that we are already experiencing, giving them more weight. Finally, we can use our body to stimulate the physiological effect of a positive emotion without first feeling the emotion itself.

a word of warning

Research indicates that faking happiness usually makes us feel worse. Consciously faking a smile, for example, or other pleasantries to cover our negative emotions (what researchers call "surface acting") without actually trying to change our underlying negative emotions will often *increase* our distress rather than foster a genuine positive emotion. This kind of toxic inauthenticity is known to be corrosive to our health (especially our cardiovascular system) and it damages our relationships with others.

By contrast, "deep acting" is when we genuinely work to foster more positive emotions in our lives. When we make this genuine effort to cultivate happiness, gratitude, hope, and other positive emotions, we usually end up increasing the ratio of positive to negative emotions in our lives. Below are a plethora of ways to foster a variety of positive emotions in your life—authentically.

(1) DELIBERATELY INDUCE SPECIFIC POSITIVE EMOTIONS

Positive emotions come in a lot of different flavors. When we seek to increase the quantity of the positive emotions and experiences we have in a given day, we need to think beyond happiness or pleasure. Think about contentment, bliss, engagement, mirth, frivolity, silliness—these are all positive emotions based in the present. We can also cultivate positive emotions about the past (like gratitude) and the future (like faith, hope, confidence, and optimism). A flourishing life is also fed by positive emotions that are global in nature, like awe and elevation and inspiration. Positive emotions that connect us to other people, like love and compassion, are our most powerful positive emotions, and they are the most important ones for creating a better world and a flourishing life—so much so that all of Part Four is dedicated to love, connection, and compassion.

DELIBERATELY PRACTICE GRATITUDE

One of the most powerful positive emotions we have is gratitude. Relative to many other positive emotions, we have reams of research indicating that gratitude is part of the happiness holy grail. Compared with those who don't practice gratitude, scientists have found that people who practice gratitude:

- Are considerably more enthusiastic, interested, and determined

- Feel 25 percent happier

- Are more likely to be both kind and helpful to others

And that's not all. Studies report long laundry lists of the benefits of gratitude. For example, people who jotted down something they were grateful for online every day for just two weeks (using an app created by the Greater Good Science Center) showed higher stress resilience and greater satisfaction with life and reported fewer headaches, less congestion, and a reduction in stomach pain, coughs, and sore throats.

Gratitude is a skill, like learning to speak German or swing a bat. It can be taught, and it needs to be practiced consciously and deliberately. Yet, unlike learning German, practicing gratitude can be blissfully simple. Just count the things in your life that you feel thankful for. Do it in a way that works for you; one size does not fit all with gratitude practices.

The key with routine gratitude practices is creativity and novelty. Think up a practice that you find fun and simple, and each time you practice, try to think of novel things that you are grateful for or new dimensions of those things and people you appreciate.

Here are some ideas to get started:

- *Contemplate death and destruction.* (Bet you didn't see that one coming!) When researchers have people visualize their own death in detail, their gratitude increases. This is a traditional Buddhist practice and essentially what my friend Lee Lipsenthal asked me to do (described in Chapter 1). Similarly, simply imagining *not* having something you love can make you feel more grateful for it. When researchers had volunteers envision the sudden disappearance of their romantic partners from their lives, they felt a lot more gratitude for them. We also feel more gratitude when we imagine that positive life events never happened—as when we imagine that we never landed a new job or moved closer to family.

- *Keep a gratitude journal.* This can be handwritten in a journal or kept online (there are loads of Web-based versions) or even just jotted down in your calendar. I'm not a big journaler, but I love the app Happier. Every day it reminds me to record something that makes me happy, something that I'm grateful for, either by typing it in or taking a photo. I can then share my gratitudes with my children—and I can see theirs. As an alternative, text your appreciation to people who have helped you out.

- *Give up—or change up—what you really love.* I know, depriving yourself doesn't seem fun, but entitlement and adaptation undermine appreciation. Gratitude actually arises naturally in conditions of scarcity—for example, when we are hungry, we are more grateful for food than when we are full. Not surprisingly, research shows that we enjoy things more when we give them up for a little while; for example, people who gave up chocolate for seven days enjoyed it more at the end of the week than people who indulged all week. More surprisingly, people report enjoying their favorite TV shows more when they are interrupted occasionally (even by commercials). This might be why Lent is a common religious practice!

- *Keep a group "gratitude list" or a collection of things that colleagues or family members feel thankful for.* Post a huge sheet of paper in a public place and ask everyone to contribute to it when the spirit moves them. Anything can go on the list, no matter how insignificant or important—people, places, stuff, events, nature. Variations on this theme are endless; try gratitude garlands, walls, trees—anything you can put a sticky note on or hang a tag on will work.

- *Start a tradition of writing "appreciations" on place cards at family dinners or on holidays.* Depending on your comfort level for group sharing, make folded place cards for each person present, and then ask people to write a few adjectives that describe what they appreciate about one another on the inside of the place cards. Don't ask people to write something about everyone present unless they want to—you don't want to force the exercise. But do make sure that everyone has at least one thing written inside their place card so that during the meal you can go around the table and share appreciations.

- *Write letters for "large" and "small" gratitudes.* Large: Write a thank-you letter to someone who is important to you but you haven't properly thanked for something non-material, and then deliver it in person and read it out loud. Small: Text a quick and unexpected thank-you note for kind words spoken, to someone who lent a helping hand or to say thanks for a fun day.

FIND INSPIRATION

Another positive emotion we can actively create in ourselves is inspiration. We often forget that inspiration, along with its cousins elevation and awe, are positive emotions that make us feel more content, joyful, and satisfied with our lives. Every Friday on my website, I post videos that inspire and move me. Most of them I watch repeatedly as a way to bring inspiration and elevation into my life. Similarly, the walls in my office, bedroom, and kitchen are covered in quotations and poems that inspire me. (Called "Thursday Thoughts," they, too, are posted on my blog.)

Awe comes with a wonderful bonus: It can make you feel less pressed for time and less impatient. Since time pressure and impatience can make your ratio of positive to negative emotions go in the wrong direction, it seems that there is always a two-for-one special running in the awe department.

> You can awe yourself with a grand landscape or by reading about a mind-expanding theory or by contemplating something that changes the way you think about the world. Researchers induce awe in volunteers fairly simply by showing them video clips of people facing awesome things like waterfalls and whales or by having them write about something that was vast and altered their perception of the world.

Once you find sources of inspiration and awe, connect to them regularly. Again, one size doesn't fit all. If it is your church, make sure you show up on Sunday. If it is your study group, stay involved. If it is nature, schedule regular hikes. If it is a guided meditation, listen daily. You get the point.

DREAM ABOUT THE FUTURE

Optimism, hope, faith, and confidence are all positive emotions about the future that can dramatically improve our ratios. Research has repeatedly shown that writing about our "best possible future self" makes us happier and more optimistic. Here's how to do it. Write for twenty minutes about your hopes and dreams for yourself in five or ten years. Where will you be living? Which friends and family will be in your life? What type of work will you be doing? How will you like to be spending your time?

The power of this exercise comes from having people (1) imagine and (2) articulate their dreams for themselves. Sonja Lyubomirsky argues in *The How of Happiness* that some of the power of this exercise comes from the writing process. In my experience, this exercise also works as a visualization. Just dreaming about your best future self can evoke positive emotions like hope and optimism. Loads of additional research has shown tangible benefits from visualization. People who use visualization techniques to see themselves doing well in their mind's eye tend to be more successful in their endeavors.

how to meditate

Sit in a comfortable position, spine straight and hands relaxed in your lap. Close your eyes and turn your attention to your breath. Breathe naturally, controlling your attention, not your breath. When your mind wanders—and it will—gently bring your attention back to noticing your breath. That's all there is to it!

If you are new to meditation, start with just a minute or so and build up to ten or twenty minutes. Or check out some of the free guided meditations on the resource page of my website; there are many different ways to meditate. I particularly like loving-kindness meditations; instructions for those are in Chapter 6.

Bonus points: Add an element of inspiration or faith to your meditation (both are positive emotions) by beginning or ending your meditation with a prayer (if you have a spiritual practice) or with a mantra that inspires you.

BLISS OUT

A terrific way to evoke feelings of peace and contentment is simple meditation. Scores of studies have shown the benefits of meditation to be broad and profound. Meditation lowers our stress and anxiety, helps us focus, and (somewhat ironically since it involves time dedicated to doing nothing) makes us more productive. Meditation even makes us healthier! After meditating daily for eight weeks, research subjects were 76 percent less likely than those in a non-meditating control group to miss work, and if they did get a cold or a flu, it lasted only five days on average, whereas control-group illness lasted an average of eight days.

DO SOMETHING REALLY INTERESTING

What are you curious about? What have you been meaning to look up? What is really interesting to you these days? *Go ahead, Google it!* Read that article of interest. Curiosity is a powerful positive emotion.

Fostering interest comes with a great bonus prize, too: It replenishes your energy. A series of studies shows that experiencing interest, or working on an interesting task (even if it is hard), energizes people for the current task and for whatever they work on next.

DANCE, LAUGH, OR MAKE A JOKE

Another one to file under "science of the blazingly obvious" is the now-proven fact that certain types of music and—here's a shocker—*comedy* induce positive moods. When I need the undoing effect of happiness after a particularly difficult day, sometimes all I really need to do is play some upbeat music or a video that makes me laugh.

In my early twenties, my friends and I would put on a few songs, always the same ones, and dance around when we got home from work. All that unself-conscious dancing and singing made us high-spirited even after the roughest day at our entry-level jobs. (And, come to think of it, we still do this when we all get together! Twenty years later, it is still one of my favorite happiness boosters.) Now neuroscientists have shown that while mentally fatiguing activities like thinking and creating induce physiological signs of stress, music reduces these signs (like the cortisol levels in our saliva).

The other well-studied effect of the dance party, as we call them in my household, comes from getting a little exercise. Physical activity is even better at inducing good moods than happy music, and it is crucial to the way we think and feel. Exercise prepares our brains to learn, improves our mood and attention, and lowers stress and anxiety. When we've been really angry or had a fight-or-flight response, physical activity helps clear the adrenaline out of our system. Happiness researcher Sonja Lyubomirsky says that exercise may just be the best short-term happiness booster there is. So if a dance party isn't in the cards for you, take a walk.

Another obvious one to have in your bag of tricks is to bookmark several videos, TV shows, or websites that consistently make you chuckle (*The Onion* and *Modern Family* are my favorites). Mirth is not a waste of time or a luxury. Laughter lowers stress hormones (even the expectation of laughter can do this) and elevates the levels of feel-good beta-endorphins and the human growth hormone.

(2) AMPLIFY THE POSITIVE EMOTIONS YOU *ALREADY* FEEL

Sometimes good things happen, but we don't actually register the positivity in a way that we'll benefit from. Fred Bryant is a social psychologist and author of *Savoring: A New Model of Positive Experience*. He researches the benefits of being really aware of your feelings when something is going right. Bryant and his collaborators have found that savoring can strengthen your relationships, improve mental and physical health, and help you find more creative solutions to problems. In other words, savoring creates the physiology of ease, along with all the benefits.

Boost your happiness with this savoring technique. Take a mental photograph. Pause, and "swish the experience around in your mind," as Bryant instructs, making yourself more aware of your positive feelings and what you want to remember, such as the sound of your children giggling or the sight of a beautiful vista.

Celebrating good news is also a form of savoring, as is repetitively replaying and reveling in happy moments—like a graduation, a fantastic soccer game, or a vacation. A more extreme form of savoring is Rick Hanson's method of "taking in the good." Hanson, who writes about how we humans are hardwired to mostly remember bad things while forgetting the good, puts it this way. Our mind acts "like Teflon for positive" memories and "Velcro for negative ones." This is not good for our emotion ratios: If most of the memories we store are negative, we come to perceive the world as depressing, even threatening.

Fortunately, Hanson gives us a method for making our positive feelings and events more "sticky." Here's how to "take in the good."

First, practice actively looking for the positive. Those flowers we planted in the fall are blooming; our neighbor was so nice to help us with a difficult project; work was particularly fun today. The key to actively looking for the positive, according to Hanson, is to "turn positive facts into positive *experiences*." In other words, we take a moment to really *experience* something good from our day.

Next, draw out—really savor—those positive experiences. The idea is not just to hold something positive in our awareness for as long as possible, but also to remember the positive *emotions* that go along with it. Think of something good that happened today (for example, the head of my high school just called to talk about an idea he is working on, and it was a really fun conversation for me), and then think how *good it felt* (the intellectual exchange was refreshing, fun, and energizing for me). This evokes what was rewarding about a positive event and helps use our brain chemistry to strengthen connections associated with the memory.

Finally, let it all sink in. Take this image—"sinking in"—as if it were literal. Take the example of a precious conversation with your spouse or child or a mentor at work. Hanson invites us to recall the conversation later and feel that experience "entering deeply into your mind and body, like the sun's warmth into a T-shirt, water into a sponge, or a jewel placed in a treasure chest in your heart."

(3) SKIP THE EMOTION AND GO STRAIGHT TO THE PHYSIOLOGY

Here's an amazing fact: Facial expressions and body postures alone can actually make us feel. Tighten your jaw and narrow your eyes as if you are really angry. Your body will usually release adrenaline and your heart rate will speed up as if you are *actually* angry. The same thing is true for positive emotions. This means that sometimes we can feel happier just by smiling.

ACTIVATE YOUR SMILE MUSCLES

Facial expression alone, without first feeling the corresponding emotion, is enough to create discernible changes in your nervous system. Move your facial muscles so that you are technically smiling (remember that this won't work if you are pretending to be happy and you aren't). When you lift the corners of your lips and crinkle your eyes, your body will release all kinds of feel-good brain chemicals into your system after a couple of minutes. If you simulate a smile by holding a pencil horizontally between your teeth or mimic that act, you will likely slow your heart rate and start to feel calmer and happier. The same study shows that you'll also find things funnier for a while. (Warning: I've found that the pencil clenching trick works, but it makes me drool.)

Again, I'm not advocating that we force ourselves to smile, or feel happy when we're in the thick of bad feelings. As I stated before, we'll just make ourselves feel worse, and we'll probably make the people around us feel worse, too. Why? We aren't actually very good at hiding how we are feeling. We exhibit microexpressions that the people we are with might not know they are registering but that trigger mirror neurons—so a little part of *their* brain thinks that *they* are feeling *our negative feelings*. So trying to suppress negative emotions when we are talking with someone about something upsetting—like when we don't want to trouble someone else with our own distress—actually increases stress levels of both people more than if we had shared our distress in the first place. (It also reduces rapport and inhibits the connection between two people.) All this is to say: Process your negative feelings before you start actively fostering positive ones; see Chapter 10 for instructions about how to do that. This means that we use the smile trick when we are ready to *move on* from negative emotions or as a pick-me-up when we have the blahs, but not when we are trying to suppress or deny difficult emotions.

STAND LIKE WONDER WOMAN

Starting in sixth grade—about the time when I became painfully self-conscious and really didn't want my mother's advice—my mom started to nag me incessantly about sitting and standing up straight. She got my pediatrician to talk to me about it. She even created a code word (I can't remember why, but it was "green") for us that meant, "For God's sake, improve your posture!" so she could remind me in public, theoretically to avoid embarrassment.

Oh, how I wish I'd listened to my mother. It turns out that I probably would have been happier and more confident in middle school if I had tried harder to sit up straight. Research shows that in adults, a straight spine increases confidence, while "a slumped posture leads to more helpless behaviors," writes Emma Seppala from the Center for Compassion and Altruism Research and Education (CCARE) at Stanford. Hunching or slouching makes research subjects feel more stressed and makes them more likely to give up in the face of challenge.

For an even more dramatic result than simply standing up straight, adopt a "power pose." Amy Cuddy's research on body language at the Harvard Business School shows that when we position our body in an open "power pose," we change our body chemistry in measurable ways. (To picture a power pose, think of the victory V we make with our arms when we're triumphant, or the confident guy leaning back in a chair with his arms behind his head and feet on his desk, or Wonder Woman's classic hands-on-hips stance.) Cuddy's research team had people take a power pose for just two minutes (they didn't know what they were doing or why, so they weren't taking the pose because they already felt confident). Amazing things happened. Their testosterone levels went up 20 percent; testosterone increases our risk tolerance and our dominance in a social group. And here's another great two-for-the-price-of-one: Their cortisol levels *fell* sharply (cortisol is the stress hormone related to our fight-or-flight response).

Here's the really astonishing thing: When volunteers took power poses for two minutes before a stressful mock job interview, no matter how they answered the questions posed to them, they tended to be rated by the interviewers more favorably and were more likely to be selected for hire than those who took closed, low-power poses. The "power pose" volunteers' body language alone impressed itself on the interviewer's unconscious mind.

So if you see me before a speaking engagement in the bathroom standing like Wonder Woman, now you'll know what I'm doing.

THE EASIEST THING: NUDGE YOUR RATIO UPWARD

Feeling overwhelmed by the multitude of ways you can bring more positive emotions into your life? There's no need for that! Just doing one new thing that fosters positive emotions could put you over the 3:1 tipping point. Plenty of research has shown that people improve

their feelings of well-being markedly just by counting their blessings once a week. Think about taking one small step rather than
remodeling your whole life.

Here's how to do that: First, take a deep breath. There—you've
induced a little ease and started improving your ratio already.

Now, think about what the easiest activity from this chapter
would be for you. Is it easy to watch a few YouTube videos that
make you laugh? Go for an awe-inspiring walk in the woods? Practice thinking optimistically by visualizing your best possible future
self?

Do whatever appeals to you, whatever seems fun and easy. If
after you've done that you are still feeling overwhelmed, not to
worry. Part Three is all about decreasing overwhelm and other negative emotions in our lives!

PART TWO

switch autopilot on

When we use our brain's natural ability to run on autopilot, we let our unconscious brain do work that we'd otherwise get done through the sheer force of our ironclad will (or not get done, due to lack of self-discipline and focus). Many people think that habits are hard to create, and they can be, especially when you don't know the basic brain mechanics behind habit formation. Here's the good news: Habit creation is a skill like any other, and once I teach you the basics and you practice a little, you'll be able to re-engineer your daily routines so that you're in the groove.

CHAPTER 3

doing without trying

We are what we repeatedly do. Excellence, then, is not an act, but a habit.

—Aristotle

It is one thing to *know* what to do to live from our sweet spot, to be happy and intelligent and successful and productive, but quite another thing to actually be able to *do* those things on a daily basis. Before you even picked up this book, you probably knew that you *should* exercise and sleep more and maybe eat kale every day, for example. Sometimes we are able to do these things—but other times we don't even come close, despite our knowledge of what is healthy and despite our best intentions.

That is, unless we've made these beneficial activities into habits. Then we'll probably do them come hell or high water. This is because habits are the way to best bridge what we know we *should* do and what we *actually* do.

Habits take the effort out of our daily tasks: they are the ultimate form of ease. We do what needs to be done without having to *will* ourselves to do it. This goes for easy stuff we do every day, like brushing our teeth; for physical skills, like being able to swing a tennis racket well without having to think about which muscles to move; and for high-level intellectual tasks, like when a doctor intuitively employs learned techniques that lead to a "eureka!" moment. When we make something habitual we free up the power-center of our brain to fully focus on the game strategy, a solution to a problem, getting our most important work done.

THE BIOLOGY OF HABITS

Biologically, our routines and habits access a part of our brain that
runs on relatively little gas compared to the newer (in evolutionary
terms) part of our brain—our smarty-pants prefrontal cortex, the
area needed for disciplined thinking. Unfortunately, there is a little
design flaw in the prefrontal cortex. The more you use it to direct
your behavior throughout a day, the less reliable it becomes. Low
blood sugar? Our decision-making will falter, whether we realize it
or not. This means that when we are too tired to think—as we often
are—we default to our habits. Which means that our habits are
critical cornerstones for generating ease in our lives.

Habits live in an older part of our brain called the basal ganglia,
a relatively primitive knob of tissue deep in our noggin that acts as
our own personal autopilot. It controls breathing and swallowing,
and that weird way that we sometimes drive to work feeling sort of
unconscious.

Once our habit center is programmed, it requires relatively little
conscious effort to accomplish truly amazing feats. In his book *The
Power of Habit,* Charles Duhigg gives a detailed account of the way
Olympic swimmer Michael Phelps won world records by honing his
habits. Everything he did during a race, from his pre-race stretches
to his post-dive glide, was directed by his basal ganglia and not his
conscious or deliberate thought. By making his races habitual, he
freed up his prefrontal cortex to focus his attention on each milli-
second of the race, adjusting and observing to winning effect.

THE ELEPHANT VERSUS THE RIDER

For starters, it is important to realize that 95 percent of all our brain
activity isn't actually conscious. Our unconscious brain controls a
lot of things we *think* we are in conscious control of, like what we
eat and whether or not we check our email compulsively during a
meeting. Sometimes we do have conscious control of these things,
but often we do not; this is where habits come into the picture.

Often our habits are choices we make initially (like deciding to start flossing) but eventually don't have to think about anymore. Our good old basal ganglia just does it. A lot of our actions today won't be things we actively decide to do; they are things that *our habits* directed and therefore "decided" that we would do. When a habit kicks in, we act out a familiar behavior or feel a particular emotion reflexively, without any conscious thought. Sometimes that's a good thing (flossing) and sometimes it's not particularly productive (biting our nails). The point is that we *can* manipulate them both into being.

As Jonathan Haidt artfully describes in *The Happiness Hypothesis,* these brain functions fall into two categories: automatic and controlled processes. *Automatic* processes (like our habits) are ruled by the same parts of our brain that lend animals their sophisticated automatic abilities, like birds that navigate by star positions and ants that cooperate to run fungus farms. Automatic processes allow us to drive a car while chatting with a passenger, react to a threat with a fight-or-flight response, or laugh at a joke without first thinking through why it is funny. By contrast, *controlled* processes require language and conscious thought and are pretty much unique to humans.

Haidt uses the metaphor of an elephant (the automatic processor—these are our habits) with a tiny rider atop (the controlled processor—our willpower). As much as we might want the rider to direct the elephant, the rider is merely the elephant's closest adviser and, at best, a guide. The elephant is in charge and pretty much goes where it is used to going, stopping for things that pack a reward (food, love) and running from things that signal danger. The rider can provide direction, but only when the elephant doesn't have conflicting desires of its own. "An emotionally intelligent person," writes Haidt, "has a skilled rider who knows how to distract and coax the elephant without having to engage in a direct contest of the wills." And even when the rider is able to change the elephant's behavior, it requires a big investment of energy.

All of this is to say: If we want to live with great ease and power, we need to use our effort to train the elephant, not convince the rider.

Does this mean that in the name of ease, we are giving over the best parts of our self by focusing on unconscious habits? Am I suggesting you should swap out your conscious, rational thought for a less intelligent, unconscious, lumbering beast? No. Your rider can do incredibly complicated, beautiful, sensitive things that habit can never replicate. But that rider is easily tired and fuel inefficient; it might be much smarter than the elephant, but it isn't as strong and doesn't have the stamina to keep making decisions all day long. Moreover, our rider—conscious thought—is slow, processing only an average of fifty bits of information per second. In contrast, our elephant—our unconscious brain—processes about 11 *million* bits per second.

I don't know about you, but I'm now choosing to go with faster, easier unconscious processes whenever possible.

ANATOMY OF A HABIT

Your brain, unlike my mother, doesn't distinguish between good habits and bad habits. Once we form a habit, the neural pathway that controls that habit—like the software code that runs our favorite app—exists in our brain forever. This is why we tend to have such a difficult time quitting habits, even those we know are bad for us. But it is also why when we form a good habit like walking to work in the morning, it's locked in, and we can get out the door without even thinking about it.

Even though it is nearly impossible to eliminate the neural pathway of an existing habit altogether, we *can* transform an existing bad habit into a good habit. My clients look at me like I'm nuts when I say this, until I tell them about some poor lab mice.

Researchers trained these particular mice to habitually press a lever when they saw a light. In exchange, they got a food reward. Then they tried to "break" the mice of their habitual behaviors by poisoning the food so it made them violently ill, or by electrifying the floor the mice would need to cross to press the lever so they received a painful shock if they stepped on it.

The mice learned that the food was poisonous and the floor was dangerous. When they were offered the poisonous food or when they saw the electrified floor, they smartly steered clear, except when the researchers showed them the light. The light trigger seemed to have a magical pull over the poor creatures, leading them to habitually press those levers and suffer the consequences. Once the habit was triggered, mice would walk across an electrified floor, or eat the poisoned pellets, even after they'd been shocked or vomited.

Because the mouse doesn't have much of a rider, it is unable to stop this habitual act even when it knows that the food is poisonous or the floor is electrified.

Your rider is definitely more intelligent and has more willpower than those ill-fated mice, of course, but—in important respects—not much more. This is why we often find ourselves "absentmindedly" eating the French fries put down in front of us even though we know they are going to raise our cholesterol or add calories we're trying to avoid. The rider says "only one more," but the elephant munches on! The rider can, with great effort, push the basket away, but when the rider gets distracted, the elephant reaches out its trunk and draws the basket closer.

THE TRIGGER

The mice experiments demonstrate the three essential components of a habit: a trigger, the routine (what we usually think of as the habit itself), and the reward. The mice were shown a light, which triggered their routine (pressing the lever) to dispense the reward (the food).

The *trigger* is what tells your brain to go into automatic mode and which habit to use when it does so. It sets the elephant off down a particular path.

Triggers can be emotions (feeling left out might trigger checking Facebook or calling an old flame), things in your environment (for example, seeing a water bottle triggers taking a drink), specific times of day (seeing that it is 10:30 p.m. might get you moving to the bathroom to brush your teeth), certain sounds (hearing a child cry can cause a parent to get out of bed in the dead of night without thinking), and certain smells (the aroma of fresh cinnamon rolls in an airport famously leads people unconsciously to purchase them).

THE ROUTINE: THE GROOVE—OR THE RUT

The actual habit part of the habit—the behavior or the routine—is the path that the elephant walks down. Walk down the path the first time and the rider will have to guide the elephant. Walk down it a dozen times and the elephant will start to wear a path. Walk down it every day for a month or so, and you'll have a clear road, with no rider needed for guidance.

This is exactly what is happening in your brain. When you establish a habit, neural connections—pathways—are formed, and each time you enact a routine, the neural path grows stronger, more permanent. We can think of habits either as grooves (good and even hard behaviors that are easy because they are habitual) or ruts (bad habits, or routines that make you feel stuck, block growth, or make your life harder or less healthy).

You might have a great bedtime groove going on. The moment you pick up your toothbrush, you trigger a whole chain of activities that you then do in the same order without thinking and without effort. You put toothpaste on the brush and brush your teeth; you tie your hair back and wash your face; you take your vitamins; you put on pajamas; you close the bedroom door and turn out the light and crawl into bed.

Each of us has hundreds of these little routines—grooves or ruts for our elephant—that carry us through the day. A routine can be a single behavior or a feeling, or it can be a series of behaviors and emotions that we do in the same order every time. Simply hearing your alarm go off in the morning can be a powerful trigger for a morning groove that brings great ease into your life as you start the day—or a morning rut that creates anxiety. (I'm thinking of the people who press snooze until they won't be able to comfortably get to work on time, and then check their email on the phone before they are even out of bed, increasing the pressure to get to work while losing even more time to do so. You know who you are.) Either way, we have much more control over our habits than we tend to realize. Although our brain unconsciously forms habits when we do things the same way again and again, we *can* consciously choose and cultivate routines that work better for us, like a calming, easy morning routine rather than a stress-inducing one.

Routines can be physical behaviors, of course, like putting your napkin on your lap when you sit down to eat, but they can also be habitual mental and emotional patterns. For example, coming home to an empty house might trigger the routine thought "I am always alone and I don't want to be," which in turn generates the routine emotion, "I feel lonely and sad." Or you may get into traffic on the way to work, which triggers your routine pattern of feeling stress or rage. Or hearing the garage door open may trigger positive thoughts and feelings about seeing your family at the end of the day.

THE REWARD

New habits are formed by training the elephant with important chemical messengers in the pleasure system of our brain. When we receive a reward or engage in certain desirable activities (eating, shopping, having sex, accomplishing something, taking certain drugs), feel-good neurotransmitters (the chemical messengers) create feelings of enjoyment *and an accompanied desire to repeat the activity.* Animals, kids, grown-ups—we all learn to repeat behaviors that lead to rewards.

The great thing about the reward center in our brain is that it is mostly associated with our motivation to do something rather than the activity itself. So my kids don't actually have to enjoy emptying the dishwasher, they just need to feel a sense of accomplishment (that's an intrinsic reward) *immediately* after they finish doing it. Similarly, I don't actually have to enjoy waking up at the same time every day, but there needs to be something intrinsically rewarding about doing it, or I'll have a darn hard time repeating the behavior.

Rewards help your brain figure out if a particular routine is worth remembering or repeating in the future. The rewards need to be good enough that they create or satisfy a craving in our brain, but they need not be complicated or external, like money or food. In our materialistic culture, we tend to bribe ourselves (and our children and employees) with external rewards: allowance, dessert, a lunch with the boss, a shopping spree, a paid day off. But material rewards are difficult to tie directly to a particular behavior in a neurological sense because often the timing is off.

Say you promise yourself a new pair of shoes if you get to work on time for a month. You diligently set your alarm thirty minutes earlier than normal so you have enough time to get out the door. You even move your alarm across the room so you can't press snooze, and you turn it up extra loud so you can't ignore it. All this works like a charm the first day because when your alarm wakes you up, you think about the cute shoes that you are desperate to call your own. But the second day you're tired, and you forget to think of the shoes. Your brain unconsciously notes the inherent pain, not the reward, in getting up so early. That night, you accidentally forget to set the alarm, and by day three you're late to work again. Your inner elephant has figured out that there is no reward baked into setting your alarm and getting up early.

So even though nonmaterial or intrinsic rewards seem so much less dramatic—so much less *rewarding*—they work better than an external reward because of their *immediacy.* For example, when we exercise a lot, we start to crave the endorphins that exercise provides. Or maybe the reward we crave is a sense of accomplishment or triumph. Rewards are often simply good feelings rather than negative ones—compassion rather than rage toward a fellow driver, a state of calm in the morning rather than the anxiety and stress of rushing, a feeling of contribution, connection, and accomplishment when a young child empties the dishwasher or when we finish a big project with our team.

When we repeat something a few times that is inherently rewarding, our brain starts expecting and craving a reward, and so the trigger cues not just the routine but also the *craving for the reward.* I watched this happen somewhat unintentionally with my own bedtime routine. One day, instead of collapsing into bed before I'd taken a few minutes to pick up the house and hang up my clothes, I put on my headset and called a friend. While I was talking to her I cleaned up, and by the time I got off the phone, I retired in a pleasurably neatened house. The next day it wasn't practical to call a friend while I was cleaning up (there were too many people around), so instead I let myself listen to an audiobook. The day after that, I talked to my dad on the phone for twenty minutes. Before long, I began to crave the entertainment of my audiobook or the social interaction of a phone call at the end of the day, as well as the visual reward of an organized house. Now, when I have the feeling that the day is over and I'm ready for bed (that's my trigger), I feel a twin desire for a neat environment and connecting with one of my friends or listening to a book. So I put on my headset and do a little twenty-minute household cleanup. (And if the book or the conversation is particularly good, I've been known to clean out a drawer or two!)

WHEN YOU ARE READY

Fair warning: The next chapter is a habit-crafting intensive. If you aren't ready to invest more time and effort into learning how to get yourself into new habits, that's okay! Maybe try out The Easiest Thing, below, and then skip ahead, without guilt, to Chapter 5. Learning about doing something and actually doing it are two different activities and two different mindsets. If you aren't ready to make a new resolution right now, you'll risk putting down this entire book, possibly forever. And we don't want that.

THE EASIEST THING: ESTABLISH A TINY HABIT

You probably have hundreds of habits you're now thinking you'd like to establish, but my best advice right now is to choose just one ridiculously easy habit. Start now with what Stanford habit researcher

BJ Fogg calls a "tiny habit." The reason I want you to think small is that deliberate habit formation is a skill. Starting with a tiny habit is like learning to dog paddle before you learn the breaststroke.

So choose something small, like taking a daily vitamin or flossing around just one tooth (that's BJ Fogg's suggested starter habit)—anything that takes *less than thirty seconds* and requires little physical effort and little money (if that is a concern for you), and doesn't require that you go against a social norm (like flossing at work in the public bathroom). It should take very little time but not require that you time yourself (for example, "floss my teeth for thirty seconds") because timing yourself is a hassle. This tiny habit needs to be something that you do at least once a day—*no exceptions*. Here are some of Fogg's suggestions for tiny habits:

> "**After** I pour my morning coffee, **I will text my mom.**"

> "**After** I start the dishwasher, **I will read one sentence from a book.**"

> "**After** I walk in my door from work, **I will get out my workout clothes.**"

> "**After** I sit down on the train, **I will open my sketch notebook.**"

> "**After** I hear any phone ring, **I will exhale and relax for two seconds.**"

> "**After** I put my head on the pillow, **I will think of one good thing from my day.**"

> "**After** I arrive home, **I will hang up my keys by the door.**"*

* This list is from BJ Fogg's excellent online tiny habit program, which you can sign up for here: http://tinyhabits.com. And you can get more examples here: http://bit.ly/tiny-examples.

Once you have a habit, write it out in Fogg's format, above. A tiny habit should take very little willpower. The main thing is to focus on your reward—how can you make this tiny habit intrinsically rewarding? (If you need suggestions, skip to Tip 7 on page 62 in the next chapter.)

I know, I know: Tiny habits seem so *tiny*. By necessity, they need to be ridiculously easy, and this makes them feel trivial and unimportant. Remember, tiny habits are about skill building and about inching your way toward lifelong routines and ease.

CHAPTER 4

cracking the habit code

A journey of a thousand miles begins with a single step.
—Lao Tzu

Ready to make a change in your life? What new habit would you like to create for yourself? You can change up the routine in a bad habit, transforming it into a good one, or you can start from scratch.

We human beings are more successful making changes with the support of other people, so take a moment to join our online community before you start. Go to christinecarter.com and click the "Cracking the Habit Code" button. Once you've registered (free if you purchased this book), we'll send you one of the tips below each day, along with a work sheet. You'll also be able to ask me questions online and give and receive support from others.

Not sure yet what habit you'd like to create first? Here's an example from my own life. Getting myself into the habit of exercising in the morning is something I'd wanted to do for ages. At the time I started doing this, I was consuming a huge amount of energy trying to get myself to exercise. I'd plan elaborate workouts for myself, but alas, I'd always find an excuse to skip them. Since exercise is one of those things that I know brings great ease and power into my life—contributing dramatically to my physical, emotional, and intellectual strength—I decided that I needed to train my elephant to just do it. I learned from my research that if I got my trigger, routine, and rewards in place, I could establish the habit.

Does this mean that I exercise every single morning now? Of course not. I'm still human, not an automaton. If I have a cold or

I'm on vacation—anytime my normal trigger is absent—my habitual routine doesn't run. But most days, my alarm goes off and I get up and go through my now well-established exercise routine.

21 tips for 21 days

How long does it take to get into a new habit? Conventional wisdom tells us that if we can repeat something every day for three weeks, a habit will be formed.

I have good news and bad news about this. First, the bad news: It is nothing but a myth that habit formation takes twenty-one days. (The earliest references to this notion that I can find are from a plastic surgeon who noted that it took his patients about three weeks before they got used to their new look after having a nose job. Twenty-one days to stop doing a double take in the mirror is not exactly a scientific finding.) Actual science shows, not surprisingly, that there is a wide time range for simple habit formation. The easier the behavior, the less time it takes to form a habit. On average, it takes sixty-six days to form a habit. Hard things, like routinely exercising in the morning, typically take much longer than this.

The good news is that the simpler a habit, the less time it takes; automatically drinking a glass of water at breakfast, for example, takes an average of only twenty days. And neurologically, we know that the brain starts to wire itself for greater automaticity the first time we repeat a behavior. This means that even if a behavior isn't totally automatic after repeating it every day for a week, we are still making huge strides toward forming our habits in just a day or so.

So why have I outlined a twenty-one-day plan for you below? Because breaking habit creation into small, digestible chunks makes it less daunting—and that increases our odds of success.

Read through all the tips, and capitalize on your desire to start immediately by beginning with "The Easiest Thing" (at the end of this chapter). Then, each day put one of the tips below into practice.

TIP #1: SKETCH A *DRAFT* OF
YOUR WHOLE ROUTINE

The first step in getting into a good habit is to spend some time actually designing the habit or routine that you'd like to get into. So instead of just saying to myself, "I *must* exercise every day," I needed to actually create a "flight plan" for myself that would include *exactly* what the elephant does once it's on autopilot.

The key is to figure out where the routine actually *starts*. Most morning routines actually originate for me the previous evening because what happens the night before can dramatically influence how tired I am in the morning, and therefore whether or not I'm able to get up early and jog.

So here's my "flight plan," or the blueprint for my whole morning routine, which includes exercise (and begins the night before).

> **9:15 p.m.:** Turn off all screens: TV, computer, phone, iPad (to prevent getting a second wind at night, which keeps me up too late).

> **Before bed:** Put exercise clothes on chair next to bed, including shoes, heart rate monitor, headphones, and the armband that holds my phone.

> **About 10:00 p.m.** (school nights): Lights out! Perhaps because this is now a habit, I generally fall right asleep.

> **Eight hours later:** My alarm goes off—this is the trigger for my whole morning routine. After a quick trip to the loo, I'll throw my exercise clothes on and then meditate for seven to twenty minutes. Although I know I'd get more out of this with a different and longer meditative practice, I'm more intrinsically motivated to listen to a guided meditation or to use the Headspace app. I like Deepak Chopra's recordings because they are inspiring, which embeds a reward (inspiration is a positive emotion, which tells my

brain that the practice is something that would be good to repeat). It might not have the same payoff, but it is certainly easier for me to get the elephant to do this than to do the Transcendental Meditation I've paid good money to learn how to do.

6:20ish: I let Buster out (if I'm home), and drink a full glass of water.

Usually around 6:30 a.m.: I begin my "better than nothing" exercise circuit. This started as a set of fifteen push-ups, thirty sit-ups, and twenty-five squats, all of which takes me only a minute or so. If all I have is a few minutes, that's all I do. Really! These days I usually use the iPhone app Seven, starting my daily exercise with a seven-minute circuit of twelve different high-intensity exercises. On Mondays, Wednesdays, and Fridays, I follow this seven-minute circuit with a ten-minute run, and then a three-minute walk/cooldown, and another couple of minutes of stretching. On Tuesdays and Thursdays, I do one or two more seven-minute circuits. On Saturdays, I sometimes go for a slightly longer run, and on Sundays, I go for a three-mile hike with a friend.

This might not seem like a very ambitious exercise plan to you—some weeks I truly do only the "better than nothing circuit" and *nothing more*. But those weeks I'm still doing 75 push-ups, 150 crunches, and 125 squats! And after a year of habitually doing at least some exercise every morning, I woke up one day to realize that I was in the best shape of my life! Clearly I've never been all that athletic—not a single varsity sport in my high school career—but these days I can definitely keep up with my CrossFit-obsessed husband when we hike, surf, and ski.

The reward embedded in my exercise routine? I listen to books on tape. *Really easy* and gripping fiction—the stuff my teenage daughters read, like *Divergent, Harry*

Potter, and the *Hunger Games* books. This is for entertainment only; no actual effort can be involved or it doesn't motivate me to exercise. (I read a lot of other things, too, at other times of the day—books that make me think big thoughts and feel big feelings—but there is a time and a place for everything. For me, Chaucer is not for exercising. Not that I actually ever read Chaucer. But you get the point.)

When possible, I also exercise outside because I love being outdoors. If it is raining or too cold or I'm in a new city and afraid I'm going to get lost, I take to the treadmill, which would normally be boring were it not for . . . *Downton Abbey! Modern Family!* All my favorite TV shows! That's right, folks: I sometimes indulge myself with TV first thing in the morning.* I used to feel guilty about it, but I've come to realize that it enables and reinforces my health and happiness.

7:00ish: Hit the shower, get dressed, et cetera. This is when my kids are usually up and in their own shower themselves, and I know that I'm at most risk of getting distracted. This is another mini-routine, but it's one that I didn't really have to work to automate because I found that I was already doing everything pretty much in the same order.† (Except, funnily enough, putting on deodorant—sometimes I'd do it right out of the shower, other times after I got dressed. Which means that I would often forget this critical part of my morning routine! Here's the thing about this mini-routine: Because there was no inherently embedded reward, it was hard to get through it in a timely way. I was prone to doing much

---

* I got a very basic treadmill on Craigslist for free, and I watch TV shows via Netflix, Apple TV, or Hulu on a first-generation iPad that my dad no longer was using.
† Here is the mini-routine: brush teeth; shower; brush hair; dry off and put on lotion and sunscreen; get dressed (in my personal "uniform," cued by the calendar and weather, which is another routine); put on deodorant; put on makeup (another mini-routine); make the bed, unless my husband gets up after me (last one up makes the bed in our house).

more rewarding things, like lingering in the hot shower or checking my email on my phone in the bathroom or cuddling in bed with one of my sleepy children. All these things are so much more inherently rewarding—and so much more derailing—than running a brush through my tangled curly hair.)

So I started timing myself. I *challenge* myself to ever-greater efficiency, to a faster and faster morning routine. This is fun enough for me; I particularly like seeing how short I can make my shower here in drought-ridden California. But it did add an element of complication—I had to get into the habit of noting the time before I started, and watching the clock. I learned (the hard way) that I couldn't use my iPhone to time myself, because I'm prone to getting sucked into whatever texts and calls came in after it went into silent mode the night before. So I just moved a clock to the bathroom, and I keep an eye on that.

7:30 a.m. (school days): Make and eat breakfast. Another mini-routine, this one is always triggered by the clock. I help my kids prep their breakfast and finish off their lunches, and then I make my breakfast (unless I'm in someone else's kitchen or a hotel), pretty much always a variation on the theme of eggs with vegetables, prepped over the weekend, or a high-protein smoothie. Breakfast takes me exactly five minutes to make. (My kids usually have a banana and peanut butter smoothie and toast with avocado on top.) The reward is getting to actually sit down with my family with a healthy and delicious breakfast.

7:55 a.m. (school days): Clean the kitchen (kids do their own dishes, so this is an easy job) and take the kids to school. The reward is—you can make fun of me if you want—the satisfaction of an empty and fully clean kitchen sink. If we are all in the car on time, without rushing, we do a celebratory dance (imagine us "raising the roof" of the car) and listen to an audiobook in the car. Lest you think that all the trains *always* run on time in my house, I'd say this occurs about three times per week. That is very good for us; if you have kids, you understand why.

I know that I can get through this whole routine in an hour and a half by shortening my shower routine to a little less than twenty minutes and breakfast to about ten minutes. On a slow morning, or one where I have more time to meditate and exercise, it will take three hours.

Although this may seem like an excruciating level of detail, here's why it's so totally worth it. I'm not making *any* decisions in the morning. I do everything the same way every morning, in the same order, on autopilot. Sure, sometimes the flow is interrupted, but due to all the repetition, my inner elephant now rarely strays from the comfort of this well-worn path.

Most people don't take the time to deliberately construct a routine, so they interrupt themselves constantly (maybe by deciding to make the coffee before showering one day but making it after showering the next day). In so doing, they alter their routine just enough that it takes self-control to get back on track. I don't know about you, but I'm like most human beings: I don't have a lot of self-control at six in the morning. I need to rely on autopilot instead.

TIP #2: IDENTIFY THE MINI-HABITS WITHIN YOUR LARGER ROUTINE

Once you have a draft of your full, idealized routine, identify all the mini-habits within it. My larger morning routine actually consists of at least seven mini-habits: waking up, meditating, getting dressed, exercising, showering, eating breakfast, and cleaning the kitchen. And within those mini-routines, there are several even tinier micro-habits—the way I brush my teeth and put on my makeup, and how I take my vitamins while the blender is running for the kids' breakfast smoothies, for example. Each of these things has a trigger, a set of automatic behavior patterns, and some sort of inherent reward. What are your existing micro-habits? What mini-habits do you need to establish?

TIP #3: NOW, THROW AMBITION OUT THE WINDOW

The most important thing that we can do when we are creating a new habit is ditch our ambition. You read that right. *Ditch your ambition to do everything impressively.* If you are anything like me, this will be the hardest part. When I decide to do something, I tend to go big. For example, every time I used to start a new exercise plan, I was overly ambitious, planning to train for a half marathon instead of a 5K, planning to meet with a trainer three times a week when I had time for only one meeting a month, planning to stretch and strength train for thirty minutes a day instead of the ten minutes that is really necessary. We ambitious people are programmed to think and behave like Aesop's hare. We want our success instantly. We want our natural ability and speed to carry the day. But in truth, we will succeed only if we think and behave like Aesop's *tortoise*.

If we want our habits to stick, we need to start really, really small. It is hard for us humans to make lots of behavior changes all at once. Creating a new habit or routine can take a great deal of energy and focus, and we have only so much self-control in a given day to work with.

Here's the thing: It's much better to succeed at just one small thing at a time than it is to fail at bigger things or many things at once. Almost all of us can pull off a brilliant couple of days, or even weeks, when we eat perfectly or do the full exercise routine or meditate diligently in lotus position for forty minutes twice daily.

But unless we have a really big catalyst for our change, like a very scary health diagnosis or other crisis-level event that provides us with immutable motivation, we'll usually crash and burn soon after takeoff. We'll have a couple of good days, but then we'll have a bad day and skip our exercise class or order grilled cheese with fries instead of kale salad for lunch. The next day we'll decide that the whole routine is too hard and we'll skip it again, resolving to make revisions tomorrow. The day after that we'll hardly think of it at all. We're back at square one.

The alternative to being super-ambitious when we create new goals is to build slowly. When I first started meditating in the morning, my goal was just to go and sit on the meditation cushion for thirty seconds every morning. (Yes, I really did this. Usually I sat a little longer, but not always.) Maybe your goal is to just sit down at your desk and *open* the document you are writing your novel in, or take thirty steps on the treadmill, or clean five things off your desk.

Here's how unambitious I want you to be. Make sure that your first "routine" is not a routine at all but a simple behavior or thought that takes less than thirty seconds to do or think. Do this knowing that you are starting to carve a neural pathway in your brain that will eventually become an unshakable habit. The first few steps can be hard, though, so you need to do something *really, really, really easy*—something that requires so little effort that your brain doesn't put up any resistance when you start it, and you can feel successful for completing it. You want to create a habit that doesn't depend on effort or willpower, so this first extraordinarily unambitious habit is about *initiating the neural pathway—starting to form the groove*—and nothing else.

TIP #4: LOOK FOR "KEYSTONE" MINI-HABITS

Sometimes there are mini-habits, like the ones I listed above in my morning routine, that are embedded within our larger plan and act as "keystone habits"—habits that have the power to shift or dislodge our routines and create a chain reaction. For example, a keystone mini-habit to ensure that I perform my morning exercise is to turn off all screens at 9:15 p.m. the night before. I turn my computer all the way off. I set my iPhone to go into "do not disturb" mode automatically so that I don't get any texts, calls, or alerts. I don't let myself turn on the TV, which I find too stimulating at night. This keystone habit dislodged a whole series of bad habits that I'd gotten into, both at night and in the morning.

My rule of no screen time after 9:15 p.m. opened up time for me to meditate in the evening, spend more time with Mark and Macie (my other children are asleep or reading in bed by then), and read. All these things contribute to feelings of ease and happiness in my life. It also meant that I naturally started going to bed earlier, when I was tired (imagine that!). These things are all very rewarding and therefore motivating to me. Going to bed earlier in turn made it easier to get out of bed in the morning, which made it possible for me to re-engineer my morning routine to be more relaxing. See how a small habit can create big change?

Lest you think that I have some sort of superhuman discipline around technology, please know that I'm not exerting a lot of will-power to do this. My computer is set to automatically go off at 9:15 p.m. My iPhone automatically goes into silent mode. My colleagues at work and my friends and family know that not only will I probably not read and respond to email at night, but they are encouraged to make fun of me if they notice that I'm breaking my own rules. So it's not that I don't ever check my email or send a text after 9:15 p.m. Lord knows I sometimes do. It's just that I've set myself up to follow my rule more often than not, especially when I need to get up early in the morning.

Another example: I noticed when I was getting into the habit of exercising in the morning, a key factor for my success was simply setting an alarm. This might sound really obvious, but before I engineered this habit, I would often wake up *without* an alarm and get through my morning fine. But changing my wake-up time every day required more energy and undermined the solidity of my key trigger. Waking up just fifteen minutes late would derail my whole morning. So I learned (the hard way) that a keystone habit was simply setting an alarm the night before.

TIP #5: PLAY OFFENSE

It is extremely important whenever we are establishing a new habit to really think through all the seemingly minor details. We need to decide what the key factors are for our success and how, specifically, we can set ourselves up to overcome any obstacles that we may face.

So take a minute to think about what tools you need to embark on your new habit. What obstacles will you likely face? People who plan for how they're going to react to different obstacles tend to be able to meet their goals more successfully. For example, research shows that recovery from hip-replacement surgery depends in large part on having patients think through obstacles to their recovery and then *make a specific plan* for how they will deal with those obstacles.

It's very painful to get up and move around after hip surgery, but recovery is generally much more successful if a patient actually gets up and walks around a lot. In this particular study, patients who had just undergone surgery were instructed to think about getting up and walking around afterward and then plan for the pain they would feel. So if their goal was to walk to the mailbox and back every day, they had the participants actually think, *Okay, I'm going to get about halfway there and it's going to hurt like heck and I'll want to turn around.* And this is the key part: Patients wrote down what they were going to do when they got halfway there and it hurt like heck. These patients recovered faster—they started walking twice as fast and could get in and out of a chair by themselves three times faster than people who didn't make a specific plan to deal with the pain.

> A large meta-analysis of eighty-five studies found that when people make a specific plan for what they'd like to do or change, anticipating obstacles if possible, they do better than 74 percent of people who don't make a specific plan for the same task. In other words, making a specific action plan *dramatically* increases the odds that you'll follow through.

What obstacles can you predict and plan for? Don't forget to include the people in your life who (often unintentionally) throw up roadblocks. For example, my husband was not a fan of my morning exercise routine when he noticed how early I was going to bed, and I was successful only when I planned out how I'd respond to his attempts to convince me to stay up later with him. I had to firmly explain to him that he was hindering my success and I needed him to be a supporter, not a detractor, of my morning routine. I let him voice all his "better ideas." He thought I should be able to work out mid-morning like he does (that doesn't work for me since the morning is my best writing time when I'm home, and when I'm traveling there is no consistent trigger) or in the afternoon when my energy is flagging (nope, I'm either picking up the kids from school, or I'm at work—again, no consistent trigger). Eventually he stopped trying to convince me that *his* routine would work for me, and executing *my* routine got easier.

TIP #6: IDENTIFY YOUR TRIGGER

Consciously designate the trigger for your habit: something that is the same *every time you want your habitual routine to be enacted*. My morning routine is triggered by my alarm going off at about the same time every day. (So the alarm is a trigger, and so is the time of day.)

> If you've got a habit that you don't want to do every day, choose a trigger that occurs only when you want to do the habit. For example, "Do a thirty-minute yoga video twice a week" isn't a habit. It's a to-do item for your task list because there's no clear trigger and therefore no clear automaticity. But if you work only three days a week, you can use work as your trigger: "Do a thirty-minute yoga video every non-work weekday as soon as I walk in the door from dropping the kids off at school."

If you are changing a bad habit into a good one, you'll need to work with your existing trigger. Perhaps you are in a habit of going out to get a venti (20-ounce) caramel macchiato at 11:00 a.m. every day, but you want to save yourself the $5.50 you're spending on this habit and drop the pounds you've put on by consuming so much sugar every morning. You may have several triggers here: time of day, low blood sugar, boredom at work, the need for a break or social interaction. You'll have to work with all the triggers that are relevant for you. This is not as easy as simply making a list of your existing triggers. You'll need to be *aware* of them before you can actually work with them. So if you aren't sure what triggers a habit you are trying to change, take several days to simply notice and write down everything that happens—thoughts, feelings, patterns in your environment, behaviors you notice *before* your habitual behavior.

Even if you aren't changing a bad habit to a good one, you'll be more likely to stick with your new habit if you use an existing trigger. So vow to exercise (or meditate or clean up or whatever it is you want to get into the habit of doing) every day when you get home from work, or right after you brush your teeth at night, or while you wait for the water for your tea to boil. In the venti caramel-macchiato example, your trigger might be the urge to get up from your desk at 11:00 a.m.

After much experimentation, I found that the only trigger for exercise that worked for me was waking up in the morning, something I obviously had to do every single day. Because I work from home and travel a lot, finishing up work in the afternoon didn't serve as a good trigger because there was no cue that was the same every day, like walking in the door from work or changing out of my work clothes. Lunchtime was also too unpredictable. If I didn't have a lunch meeting, then I found that I was always too hungry or too full to go for a run.

TIP #7: DESIGNATE INTRINSIC REWARDS

We human beings may say that we are pursuing happiness, but really what we tend to pursue is *reward*. Anything that we might desire counts: a cashmere sweater, a pretty little cupcake, attention from a mentor, a sense of accomplishment, a positive feeling. When our brains identify a potential reward, they release dopamine, a feel-good chemical messenger. That dopamine rush motivates us toward the reward, creating a real sense of craving, wanting, or desire for the carrot that is being dangled in front of us.

Fortunately, we can make dopamine work *for* us rather than against us as we build our habits. To get into a good habit, you'll need a really rewarding reward. Rewards need to be immediate or, even better, built into the routine when possible.

We can do this by making the activities themselves more rewarding—more fun. This is what I did when I switched my silent, sitting meditation (a very serious, long vipassana—like eating kale for the mind) to meditating along with a Deepak Chopra recording (short, inspiring, and easy—like an iceberg wedge salad with bacon and blue cheese). I was getting a lot out of the longer vipassana meditations when I did them, but I wasn't meditating regularly. Just as any salad is better than none, I decided that at this stage in the game, any meditation is better than none. It might not be a sure road to enlightenment, but it's closer than hitting snooze in the morning.

I'm also a huge fan of the "Yay me!" reward. Even something as small as a short mental victory dance can trigger a little hit of dopamine, enough to tell your brain to repeat whatever you just did. So when I hear my alarm and sit up in bed, I congratulate myself. I do this for all the important mini-habits built into the overall routine: turning off electronics at night, setting my alarm before sleep, turning off the light before 10:00 p.m., putting on my workout clothes before I do anything else in the morning. If you heard my running internal commentary, you'd think I was utterly crazy, what with the "Yay me! I did it again!" constantly throughout the evening and early morning. But it works!

TIP #8: MEASURE YOUR PROGRESS

Another important aspect of successfully getting into a habit is measurement. What we measure, we improve. (Or "What gets measured gets done.") For example, we know that when people weigh themselves every single day, they lose more weight than if they weigh themselves just once a week. This is because measurement drives *awareness* of behavior. For example, if you record everything you eat in a food journal, you'll be much more aware of what you eat than if you weren't diligently noticing and recording your food intake. So much of what we do is unconscious. Measurement is about making ourselves conscious of our bad habits while we train ourselves to unconsciously act out good habits.

In this day and age, tracking or measuring our progress is easy. (It's so easy that we can sometimes get caught up in the measurement of things by spending more time playing with our recording devices than we do establishing our habits. Google the terms "quantified self" or "Health 2.0" or "body-hacking" and you'll find a huge amount of information about how people measure their every move.) I like the app Way of Life to track new habits and minihabits, and I measure my runs using an app called MapMyRun. My children have elaborate "habit trackers" that they post online for their father and me to monitor (they are usually working on little habits like keeping their dirty socks out of smelling distance from my office). One of my friends diligently records her weight every morning using a scale that sends the data to an app on her iPhone.

TIP #9: FIGHT SELF-SABOTAGE

A potential land mine to avoid: As you track your behavior, don't let yourself feel so good about the progress you are making that you unleash what researchers call the "licensing effect." The licensing effect occurs when we behave virtuously and then "cancel out" our good deeds by doing something naughty. When we behave in line with our goals and values—whether it's as large as exercising every day for a month or as small as not taking a plastic bag at the grocery store—we ironically risk backsliding. (It's as if the elephant says, "I've been good! Just let me lie down here, or at least have a snack!")

Consciously or unconsciously, we tend to feel that healthy or virtuous activities entitle us to partake in less-good activities. Smokers will smoke more, for example, when they believe they've just taken a vitamin C tablet. Similarly, philanthropists tend to give away less money after they've been reminded of their humanitarian attributes. One study even found that sometimes when certain people buy eco-friendly products, they become more likely to cheat and steal!

Avoid the licensing effect by reflecting on your goals and values rather than your accomplishment. Why did you ride your bike instead of drive? What larger mission are you trying to fulfill? How will you or others benefit from the habit you are working on? Questions like these can help us avoid self-sabotage.

Another way to avoid the licensing effect, also called "moral licensing," is to avoid using moral terms to define our progress. Perhaps you are working on staying calm rather than yelling when your kids are bickering. Measure your progress by tracking the number of deep breaths you consciously took when triggered by their bickering rather than patting yourself on the back for being such a nice, calm parent. Becoming a "better parent" is a moral term, while taking deep breaths is more neutral. Avoiding moral judgment can help you avoid "moral licensing."

TIP #10: BUILD YOUR WILLPOWER MUSCLE

The rider—our willpower or self-control—is like a muscle in that it fatigues. The more we use our self-control throughout a given day, the more fatigued it gets until our rider is basically asleep, slumped atop the big beast. The elephant can now do whatever it wants.

This is not good news in our astonishingly complex world because the rich environments that we live in are constantly depleting our willpower—sending our riders to sleep while we still need them. Use of willpower in one realm depletes it for all other realms. So if we're trying to stick to a budget, making any calculation about money will tax our willpower. Simply having a bowl of candy (or anything that you are trying not to eat) in view can be a real willpower depleter. For many men, turning away from the incessant media images of seductive women expends energy needed to be present at home with their wife and kids. Anytime you are trying to impress somebody—at a job interview or on a date—you'll deplete your willpower. Trying to fit into a social group or office culture that doesn't really fit your values takes willpower, and therefore will deplete it. The same is true if you have to control your irritation with a bad team player, or if you have to control your desire to compete with people on your team at work. Constantly shielding our attention from a steady onslaught of emails, texts, calendar alerts, Facebook notifications, and tweets takes willpower.

But there's some good news, too. Our rider is also like muscle in that it gets stronger with use. The weirdest thing about the research on willpower is the phenomena that when we start consciously working on one thing that takes self-discipline, we also tend to start improving our lives in other areas as well. For example, when researchers asked college students to pay attention to one area of their lives—trying to improve their posture throughout the day, or to attend to their finances for a few weeks—they frequently do other things that might end up on a New Year's resolution list, too, like watching less TV, working out more, and improving their eating habits.

The important thing is to *focus only on one small thing,* but know that benefits are accruing. Even though you may be working on only one mini-habit, you're building up the willpower you'll need to take on more.

TIP #11: PRE-DECIDE AS MUCH AS POSSIBLE

When our limited store of willpower is depleted, we are likely to do what is familiar or easy rather than practice a new behavior. We can outsmart this brain booby trap three ways. First, **pre-decide as much as you possibly can** (where you will go, how you will get there, what you'll bring with you). So instead of deciding whether to drive or walk to work in the morning right before you leave, commit *the night before* to the decision to walk in the morning.

Second, and *this is the critical part,* **structure your environment to support your decision.** Put your work shoes deep in your backpack and your walking shoes by the door. Knowing that you are going to be tempted to drive, put your car keys in an inconvenient place that you won't want to venture into in the morning. (Have access to a dusty attic? That'd be perfect.)

Finally, **make a specific plan for what you will do when challenges arise,** because they will. If you wake up to find it raining, pre-decide that you'll wear your blue rain jacket and take that huge golf umbrella your dad left in the closet. If you wake up late, pre-decide that you'll ride your bike instead of drive.

TIP #12: COMFORT YOURSELF

To boost follow-through on our good intentions, we need to feel safe and secure. When we are stressed, our brain tries to rescue us by activating our dopamine systems. A dopamine rush makes temptations *more* tempting. Think of this as your brain pushing you toward a comfort item . . . like the snooze button instead of the morning jog, onion rings instead of mixed greens, or that easy taxi to work rather than the less-than-comfortable urban bike ride.

As Kelly McGonigal, author of *The Willpower Instinct,* writes, "Stress points us in the wrong direction, away from clear-headed wisdom toward our least-helpful instincts." When we're relaxed, we'll choose the locally grown organic apple, the earlier bedtime, the stairs instead of the elevator. And when we're stressed? Personally, I have a weakness for tortilla chips and spicy queso.

When my friend Dan Mulhern gets nervous before a presentation, he forgets essential stuff (like the power cord for his computer, his remote control, all copies of anything he printed last minute, his business cards). The way he tells it, he doesn't show up with anything he didn't pack the night before. *However,* he never forgets to bring a Diet Coke: That's the elephant for you.

The takeaway: Sometimes the best thing that we can do in pursuit of our new habit is to preemptively comfort ourselves in healthy ways before the elephant takes matters into its own hands. What makes you feel safe and secure—and doesn't sabotage your goals? Perhaps you need to seek out a hug or watch a funny YouTube video. (As we saw in Chapter 2, positive emotions act as powerful brakes on our stress response.)

TIP #13: TAKE A NAP

We can shore up our willpower with sleep for two simple reasons. First, even mild sleep deprivation makes our brain's alarm system overreact to stress. As noted above, more stress equals more enticing temptations and less willpower. Second, sleep deprivation impairs how our body and brain use glucose (our primary fuel), which in turn impairs the metabolic process by which cells absorb glucose so they can use it for energy. We all know from experience that self-control takes a lot of energy, and low energy equals low willpower. Getting seven to nine hours of sleep each night can help us muster the self-control we need to get into a new habit.

can't get more sleep?

I know, I know, you don't have time to sleep. You're very busy and important. Or you think you are the exception to the rule—that you are a part of the 2.5 percent of people who feel rested with less than the seven-plus hours of sleep that doctors and sleep experts prescribe. Maybe you *wish* you could get more sleep, but you just can't find a way to put sleep above your other priorities.

Ask yourself what your other priorities are. Your health? Your happiness? Productivity and success at work? Raising happy and healthy children? Here's the truth: You will not fulfill your potential in any of these realms unless you get the sleep your body, brain, and spirit need. A mountain of research supports this claim.

If you aren't getting at least seven hours of sleep a night, make this the first new habit you take on. If it feels totally impossible to you to get to bed earlier, try increasing your sleep by four to five minutes a night until you've adjusted your schedule enough that you are getting eight hours of shut-eye. For example, it might feel totally impossible to get to bed before midnight. But *surely* you can hit the hay by 11:56 p.m. Add a few minutes every day for two weeks and you'll gain an hour (and all the increased productivity, creativity, and happiness that come with it). Stick to it until you're going to bed early enough to get eight hours of sleep.

My friend Jennifer Granholm, who was the governor of Michigan during the economic downturn, doesn't really like to sleep, and she insists that she doesn't need more than six hours a night. Many people tell me that, like Jennifer, they do fine on less than seven hours of sleep. It *is* true that 2.5 percent of people are able to flourish with less sleep than the rest of us. Jennifer is an exception in so many ways that I just might concede that one of her many gifts may be that she needs less sleep. Are you a Jennifer Granholm? Here's how to tell. Let yourself get seven to nine hours of sleep for a week or two—perhaps while you are on vacation. Does your mood improve? Your productivity increase? Your self-control become formidable? You be the judge.

TIP #14: TAKE TEATIME

Although I wasn't an English major at Dartmouth, I hung out in the English department, where every day at 3:00 p.m. tea and cookies (ten cents each) magically appeared in the library. Turns out that the daily treat helped me and many others study. Self-control takes a lot of brainpower—it burns a lot of energy. That energy is fueled by glucose, or what we commonly think of as "blood sugar." So exercising willpower can take a big toll on our blood-sugar level. (Researchers have figured this out by measuring people's blood-sugar levels before and after they perform tasks that require self-control.)

We all know that it can be hard to focus or resist temptation if we are hungry. (This experience is behind the common advice to not shop for groceries when you're famished.) The curious thing is that it isn't really about our absolute blood-sugar levels or how much fuel we have in the tank as much as it is about whether or not our blood sugar is rising or falling.

A series of famous studies has established that people who are given lemonade, or anything that boosts blood sugar, perform much better on tests of self-control. It's as though our brain is budgeting our blood sugar: If glucose is dropping, the brain switches into conservation mode and doesn't activate the areas needed for good self-control. But if glucose is increasing, the brain thinks, "Well okay. I'm going to have enough fuel to get through this difficult task, so I'll boost the willpower center." Heaven help us if we are trying to resist the temptation of a sweet food—which our brain sees as both a dopamine-stimulating reward *and* a blood-sugar assist—while we are hungry.

A similar effect on our attention and self-control is seen when we start to get even mildly dehydrated. Research participants who are only 2 percent dehydrated—not enough to feel thirsty—start to have trouble focusing their attention. Drinking water corrects their brief attention deficit disorder. Researchers aren't sure why, but they theorize that it is the brain's way of getting us to pay attention to our basic survival needs rather than our big thoughts or ambitions.

TIP #15: NEVER SAY NEVER

When temptation is right in front of you, it's hard to turn down. But when we tell ourselves "no," we often increase the urgency of a temptation by making it forbidden fruit. Instead of telling yourself that you can't have that cookie or you can't watch TV, tell yourself you'll have the cookie in a few hours if you are still interested, or you'll record the show and watch it after you've gone for a walk. And then go distract yourself!

TIP #16: GATHER YOUR "CABINET"

As the saying goes, no man (or woman) is an island, and when we are establishing new habits, it is best not to go it alone. You don't have to be the president to need a cabinet of close advisers for advice and inspiration, so surround yourself with people who understand what you are up to and support you. I can't underscore enough how critical this is for success.

The first and most obvious reason that we need a support team is that our cabinet can help hold us accountable, acting as a bit of external willpower when our self-control falters. Most of us care what other people think of us, and when we make our intentions public in some way—even if our public is just an inner circle of close friends—our intentions have more power. Beyond that, other people can keep us on track when we are so depleted that we no longer care what other people think. When I was trying to wean myself from my diet based on sourdough bread, my husband was a huge help. When I'd ask him to order me a tuna sandwich on a sourdough roll for lunch, he'd come back with a plain tuna salad for me (and then run for cover). Similiarly, whenever I need help getting back into my morning routines after a vacation, my good friend Kendra Perry, a life coach, holds me accountable by texting me daily.

Second, there is a plethora of empirical evidence that we are herd animals, and we typically do what our peers do. (Please don't think you are the exception to this rule. While I don't doubt that you are in many ways a maverick, odds are that you also look and act a lot like your peers in many other ways.) Compelling research demonstrates that our behavior is influenced not just by our friends but by our friends' friends' friends. This is the elephant at work. He or she is more likely to follow the *herd* than the rider on its back, especially if the rider wants it to take an unfamiliar path. Because the behavior of others is highly contagious, we do well when we hang out with people who are already in the types of habits that we are trying to establish. This means finding a meditation or running group if you want to meditate or run habitually, or simply hanging out more with people you admire (which is fun anyway).

Behavior change experts Chip and Dan Heath build on Haidt's elephant and rider metaphor by writing about how we can "shape the path" for the elephant. Choosing the herd that we want to follow is a great way to do this. We can also decide which herd we *don't* want our inner elephant to follow. If you are trying to eat more healthfully, by all means don't start dating a junk-food devotee. Or if you are trying to drink less alcohol, surround yourself with friends who are more likely to invite you out for a hike than a drink, so that you don't feel isolated because of your new habit.

TIP #17: EXPAND (REALLY, REALLY) SLOWLY

Once you feel the pull of your unambitious habit—you feel yourself automatically going to sit in your meditation chair or heading to the treadmill or ordering a side salad at lunch—take another tortoise step. Meditate for an additional minute or walk for an additional thirty steps or think about replacing your after-lunch double caramel macchiato with a lower-in-sugar latte. And then once this feels easy-peasy, add a little tiny something else to your routine.

Remember that if you resist the urge to be more ambitious or do more, you'll increase your odds of being successful over the long haul. And while it might feel a bit frustrating to think that after ten weeks of exercising every morning, increasing by only one minute a week, you'll be exercising for only ten minutes a day—not enough to lose that extra ten pounds you've been meaning to get rid of— consider that you've gained three uber-important things.

First, you've gotten yourself in the habit of exercising! This is everything your doctor ever wanted for you. Second, you're getting ten more minutes of exercise every day (over an hour a week) than you were getting eleven weeks ago; this is something that your body

something is better than nothing!

Even once you've expanded to your full-length routine, designate a routine that may not be ideal but is better than nothing—a routine that you can always come back to. I have my little two-minute three-exercise routine that I affectionately call the "better than nothing circuit." If I'm traveling or I oversleep or am just not feeling all that well, I can do this simple circuit of three exercises in my pajamas. And because it takes only a few minutes, I just do it—there isn't any internal resistance to doing it. Here's the key: I do this *every single weekday* because I want the groove of this habit to be *deep*, and because I've chosen to anchor my exercise to something I do every weekday: wake up to an alarm and then meditate. For the rest of my life, as long as I wake up to an alarm, I'm going to wake up, go to the bathroom, get dressed, meditate, and then exercise (even if I only do a two-minute routine).

If I'm really not feeling well, I make myself go through the entire routine *in my head*, visualizing myself doing each of the exercises. This may sound crazy, but what I'm doing is preserving and deepening the neural pathways in my brain that lead to the habit.

loves you for. It is enough to give you a little more energy, help you sleep better, and give you a little hit of human growth hormone—all things that will make you feel younger, smarter, and more alive. All these things are going to help you get into your groove, making your life easier. So YAY YOU! And third, you've shown yourself that you *can* get into a habit and stick with it. The sky is the limit now!

TIP #18: EXPECT (AT LEAST MINOR, SOMETIMES MAJOR) FAILURE

Unless you are some sort of superhero, you will not be able to get into this new habit perfectly the first time. You'll trip and fall and royally screw up. Research indicates that 88 percent of people have failed to keep a new resolution. In my experience as a human being and a coach, 100 percent of people starting a new habit lapse in their attempt. Faltering is a normal part of the process, but it's important that we distinguish between a *lapse* and a *relapse*.

If you imagine yourself climbing a hill, a lapse is a little trip, or maybe a trip and a fall. It might hurt, and you might *want* to stop climbing. A lapse becomes a relapse when we actually *do stop climbing*. A lapse might be a bad day; a relapse is a week so bad that you give up altogether. It is critical that we distinguish between our lapses and a full-blown relapse, and that we respond appropriately to each lapse. To restate this: It doesn't matter *if* you have a lapse, or even a relapse, but *how* you respond does matter. The next few tips will guide you through these inevitable lapses and relapses.

TIP #19: BEWARE THE "WHAT THE HELL" EFFECT

Say you've sworn off sugar, but one morning you eat a piece of pie for breakfast. You're now at risk for what researchers formally call the Abstinence Violation Effect (AVE) and jokingly call the "what the hell effect." If you've already blown your diet today, why not go hog wild? What the hell—you can begin again tomorrow, right? Wrong. The more damage you do during your binge, the more likely you are to slip again the next day, and the less confidence you'll have

in yourself that you can change. As soon as you notice a slip, try the
following to avoid getting into that "what the hell" moment:

- Don't get too emotional about your slip or succumb to
  self-criticism. Instead, **forgive yourself.** Remind yourself that lapses are part of the process, and that feeling
  guilty or bad about your behavior will not increase your
  future success.

- **Rededicate yourself** to your resolution (now, in this instant, not tomorrow). Why do you want to make the
  changes that you do? How will you benefit? Do a little
  deep breathing and calm contemplation of your goals.

- Make a **plan for the next time** that you will face a similar challenge. What will you do differently? What have
  you learned from your slip? What temptation did you face
  that you can remove? Is there a keystone mini-habit that
  you need to tweak? Were you stressed or tired or hungry—
  and if so, how can you prevent that the next time?

- **Reach out to your cabinet ASAP.** Ask them to support you in getting back on track.

TIP #20: REGROUP, REVISE, AND DOUBLE DOWN

This may be blazingly obvious, but in order to do better tomorrow,
you'll need to know what caused your trip-up. So again, what obstacle did you fail to see or plan for? How does your routine need
tweaking? Is your trigger consistent? Does your reward need bol-
stering? Did you take on too much too soon? Figure it out, and
make a specific plan for what to do if you find yourself in a similar
situation again.

When I was first trying to squeeze a workout into my morning
routine, I felt like I was failing more mornings than I was succeed-
ing. Every day brought a new tweak to the routine. For example, at
first I thought that I could get away with seven hours of sleep at

night. But after three or four mornings of pushing the snooze button I realized I was too tired and had to turn the lights out earlier. Then I thought that I could read before bed on my iPad; that was a no-go, too, as the light from the screen kept me from falling asleep quickly. In the morning, my built-in reward wasn't rewarding enough until I let go of the "need" to listen to something "smart" (literature or the news or TED talks) while I jogged and let myself listen to something "fun" (funny memoirs and Dan Brown novels). I also needed to make it logistically easier, so I got an armband to hold my iPhone so that I could listen not just while running but also while I did push-ups.

For several days in a row, I didn't foresee minor obstacles that proved challenging, like not having the right workout clothes with me, or feeling really hungry mid-workout. But after I'd encountered each obstacle once, I could make a plan for what to do the next time. It took about six weeks before I settled into my routine. This habit is now fully grooved. The neural pathway has been formed in my brain, and I've kept at it for a couple of years now. (It is still constantly evolving in tiny tweaks, depending on my workout and training needs or to make it work with my ever-changing work, travel, and family schedules.)

Getting in a major habit like this one has not only paid off in terms of more energy and strength, better sleep, and greater patience with my kids, but it has also become foundational experiential evidence of the power of habits—even though I had to make so many tweaks in the beginning.

TIP #21: SEE RELAPSE AS AN OPPORTUNITY TO BEGIN AGAIN, STRONGER

I'd venture that all of us start this process of forming a new habit from the context of having failed before, often many times. So what do we do if we've tried this before, or if we spend twenty-one days forming the perfect habit, only to go on vacation—or something else that disrupts our normal routine—and come back feeling like all is lost?

All Is Not Lost. Anytime we get into a habit, or even start to get into a habit, we start to train the elephant, to carve a path that we can retrace again later. So think of each time you start a habit cycle as an upward spiral that has circled back to where it began but is now one level higher. It may feel like you are back at square one, but neurologically you aren't. You're actually in a better place than you were before (maybe only slightly, if it is a perennial New Year's resolution that lasts only a couple of weeks, or maybe you're in a *much* better place if you actually got into the habit for a while). So if you relapse, simply begin again with step one, keeping in mind that you are now armed with lots of new knowledge about what worked and what didn't.

In sum: Instead of seeing a lapse or a relapse as an indication that you aren't good enough to establish a habit, see it as a clue that will help you *better create a good habit* that will stick with you for the rest of your life—and help you become a good habit *creator* who can do this again and again.

THE EASIEST THING:
START WITH THE
HAPPIEST HABIT

Are you ready to create your new habit? I know you probably have big plans for yourself to do something really hard or unfun. The easiest thing to do, however, is also the best thing to do, in this case: Start with the easiest possible habit for you to get into.

What's something that would make you really happy if you did it every day? What habit would have the biggest built-in reward? Maybe you really love walking outside at dusk, as I do. Make a daily walk as the sun goes down the first habit you establish. Or perhaps there was something in Chapter 2 that would really bring you joy that you'd like to make a habit, like keeping a gratitude journal? Start there.

PART THREE

unshackle yourself

We all have lots of clutter—mental, emotional, and physical—in our lives that constrains us and weighs us down. How much would you like to be free from unending pings from your smartphone? From the junk drawer you can never find anything in, anyway? From the tasks on your to-do list you dread? From the stuff you feel you should do, but really aren't your idea of a good time? From the nagging thought that you didn't do something well enough? Help begins on the next page.

CHAPTER 5

easing "the overwhelm"

Before you allow yourself to question your entire life and any decision you have ever made, check: hormones, sleep deprivation level, messiness of house, whining level of children, ridiculousness of colleagues. If none of these is the guilty party responsible for your unhappiness, then you may indeed have bigger problems.

—Kristin van Ogtrop, *Just Let Me Lie Down*

Although it's often less fun and more effort in the short run than fostering positive emotions, we can also increase our happiness and stress resilience by ridding ourselves of unnecessary *negative* emotions.

I say *unnecessary* because all negative emotions are not to be negated. It is necessary for us to grieve our losses, to feel afraid when we are in danger, to feel fury when we are wronged. But sometimes our negative feelings *aren't* like the keel of our ship. They aren't helping us navigate or stay balanced, and they are more like the anchor dragging us down. Three negative circumstances in particular are big anchors for many people: overwhelm, dread, and rumination.

DEALING WITH "THE OVERWHELM"

The most anchor-like negative emotions for me are feelings of exhaustion and being overwhelmed: the sense that I can't possibly get everything done. Brigid Schulte, in her important and practical book *Overwhelmed: Work, Love, and Play When No One Has the Time,* documents dozens of scientific research threads indicating that most well-educated people in the United States—indeed, in the industrialized world—feel caught in the snare of overwork and exhaustion at work and at home. Two-thirds of us working folks regularly feel like we don't have enough time to get our work done, and 94 percent have felt overwhelmed "to the point of incapacitation."

There are two somewhat counterintuitive facts about "The Overwhelm," as Shulte calls it, that are important to recognize if we are going to reduce or even eliminate the negative feelings that come from being overwhelmed and exhausted.

First, feeling overwhelmed prevents us from working and living from our sweet spot. In fact, it makes us dumber than if we were stoned or deprived of an entire night's sleep! It also makes us irritable, irrational, anxious, and impulsive. Neuroscientists call the state of feeling overwhelmed "cognitive overload." It impairs our ability to think creatively, plan, organize, innovate, solve problems, make decisions, resist temptations, learn new things easily, speak fluently, remember important social information (like the name of our boss's daughter), and control our emotions. In other words, it impairs basically everything we need to do in a given day.

Second, although we experience The Overwhelm individually, it is also a *social and cultural phenomenon*. Sociologists and time-study scholars have been documenting the rise of our modern busyness culture—the perception that those who are busy are important and powerful while those who are idle (or even those who make time for leisure) are underemployed, lazy slackers whose lives lack meaning and relevance. It is hard to overstate just how pervasive and pernicious this cultural climate is. How much we've got going on has become an indication of our social status. Like the herd animals we are, we conform to this misperception.

We humans are hardwired to remain with the herd even when we *know*, on some level, that the herd is leading us in the wrong direction. Say a researcher shows us two lines on a piece of paper, and one line is clearly shorter than the other. Then she asks us which line is longer. Alone, we will, of course, point to the obviously longer line: It's not a difficult question or a visual trick. But, if we are in a group of people who have already indicated to us that the *shorter line is longer,* three-quarters of us will not only *say* that the shorter line is longer but actually *believe* that the wrong answer is right. Really. That experiment has actually been done!

Here's the thing: When it comes to our cultural beliefs that busy people are high status, the herd is leading us in the wrong direction, off a cliff. Busyness is *not* a marker of intelligence, importance, or success. Taken to an extreme, it is more likely a marker of conformity or powerlessness or fear. We often work long hours in part because we are *afraid* that we will lose our job or we won't have enough money to have all the latest stuff. We schedule our kids in every enrichment activity possible because we are *afraid* that they won't develop the mastery, intelligence, and athletic prowess they need to get into the right schools or land the right jobs. We "helicopter parent" in our new time-and-energy-intensive ways because we are *afraid* that our children will fall down or be average or simply feel discomfort, boredom, or disappointment.

All this is to say that easing the overwhelm in your life may mean straying from your herd, which can be a terrifying experience. Whenever I notice that I need to stray from the herd—to defy a cultural norm—I need to muster extra courage (more on how to do that in Chapter 9) and fully acknowledge that it can be pretty frightening to do things in ways that will likely be perceived by others as threatening, dangerous, or just plain stupid. We are often dealing with two types of fears. One is conscious, like a fear that our kids aren't going to get into college; the other is more subliminal, rooted in our herd mentality, our desire not to be different or left behind. When I recognize that I'm dealing with both types of fears, I somehow feel more able to do the right thing.

Without further ado, here are my favorite strategies for systematically eliminating the things in life that overwhelm you.

DECIDE ON YOUR FIVE TOP PRIORITIES AND SAY "NO" TO EVERYTHING ELSE

"Saying 'no' has more creative power than ideas, insights and talent combined. 'No' guards time, the thread from which we weave our creations," Kevin Ashton wrote in a *Medium* post called "Creative People Say No."

"We are not taught to say 'no.' We are taught *not* to say 'no.' 'No' is rude. 'No' is a rebuff, a rebuttal, a minor act of verbal violence. 'No' is for drugs and strangers with candy."

And yet we can't do everything, so we must sometimes say "no." But in order to even be able to say "no," we need to have an effective filter for all the invitations that come our way: Invitations to attend and contribute, requests for help, opportunities to join or to do—even for those things that we think we *should* do that don't come from any outside source but rather from a place inside ourselves. Before we can muster the strength to say "no," we need to be totally clear about what to say "no" to.

Perhaps you think it would be a good idea to get a master's degree at night, or maybe you're wondering if you should sign your kid up for basketball, or you're debating about your desire to keep going to the book club you've been part of for a decade. These types of questions aren't about how best to manage our time, or about whether or not there is enough time. They are about our priorities. Because we *can't* do everything, we need to make choices. Which means that to the extent that we can, we need to say "no" to all the things that don't reflect our values and highest priorities.

Which begs the questions: What do we most value in life? What are our tippy-top priorities? How can we spend our time in a way that best reflects our ideals?

Knowing the answers to those questions is often not so simple. My friend Michelle Gale, an outstanding executive coach and former Twitter executive, knows a thing or two about managing The Overwhelm. She encouraged me to do what she does: Sit down every year and write a simple intention (or personal mission statement) to use as a litmus test or filter for all new tasks, projects, and activities. Hers is "I'm committed to raising consciousness in myself and the world through my practice, my community, and my work." This is a lofty statement, but having talked with her about it, I know that she is clear about what "raising my consciousness" really means to her, so it guides her well. Before she puts anything on her to-do list or commits to anything, she runs it through this filter (which she has committed to memory, by the way). She asks herself if the activity, task, or project will help her raise consciousness in herself or her world. If it won't, Gale says "no," swiftly and without guilt.

I know, I know. Writing an intention like that, or a personal mission statement, sounds hard. And you know what? It can be. It can be hard to know what our life's purpose is, what guiding principles we should use to manage our time. (If you are struggling with this, I'd encourage you to work with a life coach, or join a group that explores this at your church or community center. This sort of self-exploration is richly rewarding.)

I don't have a personal mission statement like Gale; clearly I'm a wordier (and less evolved) kind of gal. To be honest, I wasn't able to even articulate my most important priorities until nothing seemed to be working in my life. This point came several years ago when I was sick all the time and totally exhausted, a financially strapped single mother trying to bootstrap a new career and family together. I realized then, at an all-time low, that I needed to identify my priorities and start scheduling my time accordingly.

I once saw time-management guru Peter Bregman, author of *18 Minutes: Find Your Focus, Master Distraction, and Get the Right Things Done,* advise people on Fox Business News to pick their top five priorities and then spend 95 percent of their time doing *only* those activities, saying "no" to virtually everything else. This idea made a lasting impression on me because I—working single mom that I was—was convinced that there was *no way* I could spend 95 percent of my time doing things that fell into my top priorities. I was too busy just making sure the trains ran on time!

But it turns out that now I do (and I'll share how I managed that below). To give you an idea of how this worked for me, here are my five main priorities this year, in order of importance:

(1) Maintain my own health and happiness. Because this is my top priority, I first schedule the things that most affect my happiness. I make time for sleep, exercise, and my friends and family, and I say "no" to those activities—fun as they might be—that interfere with my sleep, exercise, and time with my closest friends. When I skip exercise or shortchange myself on sleep, I might cross more off my task list or answer more emails, but that puts my first priority—staying healthy and happy—at risk. And if I get sick or so stressed-out that my energy is drained? Well, that puts my other priorities at risk, too. So I always remind myself: It takes less time to exercise in the morning than it does to recover from the flu, should I get run down. (This doesn't mean that I'll never catch another cold, but it does mean that I'm less likely to!)

(2) Nurture others. My children and husband first, extended family next, friends and community after that. This is about raising amazing human beings who are healthy and happy, and about cultivating a deep sense that I am part of something larger than myself. In order to honor this priority, I need to schedule a fair amount of family time on my calendar. Because I actually have this *scheduled,* I can more easily say "no" to other things that come up. I simply say that I have a scheduling conflict.

(3) Write this book. I love writing, but because it often lacks the urgency that, say, a sick child or a website outage commands, it can get shunted to the bottom of my to-do list. To prevent this, I blocked out fifteen three-day "at-home writing retreats," six hours per day, during which I scheduled *nothing else:* no meetings, calls, trips to the chiropractor or vet or grocery store. You get the picture.

(4) Work toward being a truly great speaker— someone who is profoundly inspiring, hugely dynamic, and very well paid. I've learned that I can handle about twenty speaking engagements a year; more than that and I start to get burned out and I stop improving.

(5) Maintain my website, newsletters, and online classes as a profitable microbusiness that supports my books and speaking engagements. This means that I need to spend some time on marketing, PR, and administrative work.

As I mentioned, when I first started thinking about my top priorities, I wasn't even coming close to spending 95 percent of my time on them. In addition to my top five priorities, I had a coaching practice as well as a half-time position at the Greater Good Science Center. Spending 95 percent of my time on my top five priorities leaves only about five hours a week for other things. Something often has to give; for me, it was my health. Like many working mothers, I had put my own well-being on the back burner, never exercising and rarely getting enough sleep. I was sick all the time.

Guess what? Now I spend closer to 98 percent of my time doing something that falls into one of those five buckets. The only things on my to-do list this week that aren't in a top-priority category are:

- Rent a car for an upcoming trip to Ojai, for a board meeting

- Attend a Greater Good Science Center meeting

- Return a call about a fund-raising effort I'm involved in

(When I look at this list, I realize that I could delegate the first item to my assistant or intern. More about that below.)

How we schedule our priorities doesn't have to be entirely proportional. We might value family most in life, but spend the biggest chunk of our time working. The key is alignment with our values. Does work support the life you have with your family? Or do you expect family to support your work life?

To truly align our time (and the activities we fill it with), we need to give up the three big "scarcity lies" that our culture teaches. As outlined by Lynne Twist in *The Soul of Money*, the lies are:

- *"There isn't enough"*

- *"More is better"*

- *"It just is the way it is and I don't have the power to change it"*

First, we need to give up the idea that *there isn't enough time* for the things that matter most in life. That belief (or, more accurately, that resignation) is a quick ticket to joylessness.

To truly align our time with our values, we need to lay claim to a place of time sufficiency, even if we have to will it into existence. We need to understand that *we have enough time* to be successful at work, to find happiness and meaning, to have rich and rewarding relationships with our friends and family members. There actually *is* enough time in the day—when we act on our priorities, with discipline, and when we accept that an authentic "good enough" is often better than a false "great at everything."

We also need to give up the deep-seated conviction that *more is better*: more work, more enrichment activities for the kids, more vacation time, and more stuff—even things like more "quality time" with our kids, more friendships, and more social functions. Parents spend more time today with their kids than they ever have, even when we compare mothers today to stay-at-home mothers in the 1950s. Yet we feel that even more time together would be better.

When we realize that more is not always better, we can recognize when we already have *enough*.

Equally important, we need to question our belief that *"this is just the way things are"*—that there isn't any time for friendship, that we really are okay with the nanny or day care doing all the fun stuff with the kids, that we'll go on vacation with our family *next* year or the year after. We are not powerless to the market forces and consumer culture that create pressure to prioritize work and money, but when we believe and act as though we are, we cannot make our time reflect our values. The most important thing? Remembering that *we get to decide,* for the most part, how we spend our time.

Once we are scheduling our time from a place of sufficiency, we can add back time for our highest priorities. I'm not saying that time is an unlimited resource and we can waste it or that we will never have to say "no." Rather, I'm saying that there *is enough* time when we manage our priorities carefully.

STOP MULTI-TASKING

Unless you're a professional juggler—a clown or performance artist who must toss multiple balls in the air and pay attention to them simultaneously—multi-tasking talent is nothing to brag about. When we focus on just one task at a time, we're actually more productive in the long run and less exhausted at the end of the day. This is because multi-tasking exhausts more energy and time than single-tasking does. Take it from productivity experts Tony Schwartz and Catherine McCarthy:

Distractions are costly: A temporary shift in attention from one task to another—stopping to answer an email or take a phone call, for instance—increased the amount of time necessary to finish the primary task by as much as 25 percent, a phenomenon known as "switching time."

Despite the cold, hard facts, I often find it harder to single-task than to multi-task. For example, I have to totally remove all distractions to single-task. I do my best writing at a desk I've set up in a large closet that doesn't get good phone reception. I group my daily tasks into two categories: "Think Work" and "Action Items." Then I block off time on my calendar for both things. I do my Think Work at the closet desk totally uninterrupted, setting a timer so that I take a break every sixty to ninety minutes.

My Action Items take less focus, but I still tackle them one at a time in sequence—not parallel. Unless I'm working my way through my email, my email application is closed. I answer the phone only for scheduled calls. I leave my iPhone in do-not-disturb mode (so that I can see if my kids' school is calling, but that's about it), and I reply to texts when I'm taking a break. Having these rules for myself has dramatically increased my productivity and decreased the panicky feelings that I don't have enough time to get it all done.

Sound neurotically organized and focused? Believe me, it didn't come easily. I work from home most of the time, so the pull of all the things that I could be doing instead of writing is usually more powerful than any intention I have to *just focus*. (Some of the things that tempted me this morning were the laundry, the breakfast dishes that didn't fit in the dishwasher, chatting with my neighbor, retrieving the dog's ball from behind the sofa so he stopped barking at it, email, texts, a quick thank-you note, bills, yesterday's mail, and chatting with my husband on the phone. I'm naturally *very* distractible and messy—a "big-picture thinker, but not so much a detail person," as my father would often euphemize when I was younger. So I had to carefully construct a work *structure* for myself that would support focus rather than allow me to hop from one easy but not important task to another.)

Outsmarting overwhelm in this way—by forcing myself to stop multi-tasking—was a process. I had to create a formal ritual to get myself into the zone. As I'm brewing myself a second cup of coffee or tea, I take a quick peek at my calendar and email on my phone. Is there anything urgent? The idea isn't to respond to emails; it's a check that keeps me from worrying while I write that I *should* have checked my email, and keeps me from wondering if there is anything on my calendar that I should be preparing for. Then I head up to my closet office, with my coffee and a full glass of water. (I've also had a snack and used the restroom. I'm like a toddler going on a car trip.) I do a quick cleanup, removing yesterday's coffee cup from my desk, closing books left open, putting pens back in their place. I put all visual clutter in deceivingly neat piles. I put my phone in do-not-disturb mode, and close any unnecessary applications or windows that are open on my computer. I launch Pandora and choose the "listen while writing" radio station I've created (mostly classical piano because it doesn't distract me like music with lyrics does). I tell Buster, my trusty canine colleague, to go to his "place"—a bed right next to me where he's trained to stay while I work.

I write at a standing desk that has a small treadmill under it. When I'm ready to start writing, I start the treadmill. Walking slowly while I work has a lot of positive outcomes; one of them is that it more or less chains me to my desk. Finally, I launch the app 30/30, which times my Think Work and break time.

At first, I actually felt guilty for carving out such dedicated time to focus on my "most important" work. Perhaps that sounds ridiculous to you—it's *most important,* after all! But honestly, I felt like I *should* be more responsive to my colleagues' emails throughout the day, and I *shouldn't* be creating the scheduling nightmares that blocking off dedicated work time does because it's basically at the same time every day. So it's very hard to schedule a meeting with me in the morning, when I do my best Think Work, or in the afternoon, when I pick up my children from school. This means that it's pretty hard to get me to go to a meeting.

So how did I ultimately let go of the guilt? I switched herds. Instead of trying to conform to the norms of the ideal office worker (which made me feel a little terrified anytime I was straying from that path), I started to see myself as an artist. I read everything I could about other writers' and artists' work habits, and talked to a half dozen successful writers about how they get things done. Guess what? They have writing rituals just like the one that I set up. They had already carved the path. Following my *new* herd made the whole thing easier for my inner elephant. Even if you aren't self-employed like me, I welcome you to join my herd.

---

are you traveling with the right herd?

Even if you aren't a writer or an artist or working from home, you may need to switch herds, too. Who in your office seems to be in a groove? Who is clearly producing great work through great focus? How can you lead your existing herd in this new direction? Know that when you stray from your herd—when you defy social norms—it will be threatening to many people. Presenting the science around performance and productivity can help.

My extensive pre-work ritual is what it takes for me to be able to establish the focus I need to hit my stride at work, to get into what Mihaly Csikszentmihalyi calls flow.

[A] *person in flow is completely focused . . . Self-consciousness disappears, yet one feels stronger than usual. When a person's entire being is stretched in the full functioning of body and mind, whatever one does becomes worth doing for its own sake; living becomes its own justification.*

When I go through my pre-work ritual, I can get into a flow state fairly automatically. Although the neuroscience on this is embryonic, I do believe that my pre-work focusing ritual helps my brain produce the type of brain wave (gamma) that puts me squarely in my working sweet spot. Gamma waves produce the most brain power with the least strain. This is similar to how my bedtime ritual helps me slip easily into a deep sleep (when my brain produces delta waves).

when multi-tasking works

Even though I preach the evils of multi-tasking at work, I actually double-task all the time. For starters, I walk on the treadmill while I work. I also sweep dog hair off the floor while I talk on the phone. I fold laundry while I watch TV. I listen to audiobooks while I drive. I return work calls while I walk the dog. I do mindless food prep (washing and chopping vegetables—anything I can do on autopilot) while helping the kids with their homework. I chat with my friends on the phone while washing dishes or tidying the house. I brush the dog while going over the weekly schedule with the sitter. I doodle in meetings. I'm sometimes less accurate while multi-tasking in this way, but errors in these types of activities are not all that important. Notice that my multi-tasking combines one intellectual endeavor with some kind of mindless or physical effort. In my experience, we get into trouble only when we try to do two "thought things" at once.

ELIMINATE "JUNK STIMULI"

Another way to eliminate feelings of overwhelm in our lives is to get rid of a lot of the "junk stimuli" that comes our way throughout the day. We are bombarded, day and night, with loads of crap: TV ads (or even news!) we aren't interested in that we watch anyway. A mailbox full of advertising and other "dead tree marketing." Emails upon emails mingling with Facebook posts and tweets and texts.

Left unchecked, all this junk stimuli will bleed us dry. It's exhausting even as it is often entertaining. Do a quick audit of all the clutter in your life. Start with your environment. Where is there junk stimuli—stuff that makes you feel tired when you see, hear, or otherwise experience it? Consider visual clutter, like that over-stuffed kitchen drawer you open every day looking for a paper clip. Ponder auditory clutter, like whiny kids who make you tense or the neighbor who really does need to fix his car alarm. Think about on-line and media distractions. (You might enjoy them, but for mental health and personal energy conservation, consider indulging in them only occasionally, as a treat.) Then follow this three-part plan to eliminate junk stimuli.

FIRST, RID YOUR ENVIRONMENT OF PHYSICAL CLUTTER

- Clean out one drawer or shelf every day religiously until everything in your home has a place—and everyone in your household knows where that place is. Commit to five minutes a day, every day, until the job is done.

- Find a large box for donations or other giveaways, and put it somewhere accessible until you are finished with this process. Donate or recycle anything that hasn't been used for a year. This goes for clothes, dishes, books, furniture (yes, furniture), games, toys, shelf-stable foods and spices, the super-awesome tortilla maker you've really wanted to try out since you picked it up in the 1980s, and that tent you haven't pitched for three years. Remember that the stuff you keep is for today, not some imagined future. Be ruthless. You will thank me later every time you open a tidy, nearly empty drawer or cupboard. (Okay, okay: I do acknowledge that some folks have a stronger hoarder instinct than others. It's true, you never really know when you will want to read that book or pitch that tent. But there is a cost involved to keeping those possi-bilities alive. Remember that these things contribute to The Overwhelm, and overwhelm makes us dumb, irrita-ble, and impulsive.)

NOW, LIMIT THE AMOUNT OF STUFF YOU LET BACK INTO YOUR HOUSE

- Cancel all nonessential snail mail. Sign up to get your bills online. Cancel all catalogs and junk mail. (I like the free app PaperKarma: You take a picture of catalogs, mailers, credit-card offers, phone books—and it gets you off the mailing lists.) You can get everything you need online or in a digital version, including ticket information from your local theater, updates from nonprofits you love, and concert schedules. Without PaperKarma, you may have to call the sources of the snail mail to ask them to remove you from their lists; I've had to plead and beg in the past (despite what I think are federal laws). Again, be ruthless when you ask to be removed from these lists. All that direct mail is clutter.

- Put a recycling bin right by the door that you walk through with the mail, and don't open junk mail. Photograph it for PaperKarma, then rip it up and recycle it.

- Before you go shopping, take time to make a list of what you need. I've found that having a list can drastically decrease the number of items I buy on impulse that I don't really need. (I also have a better chance of moving through the store efficiently when I have a plan, thereby making up the time I spent making a list.)

FINALLY, GET RID OF ALL UNNEEDED MEDIA AND AUDIBLE STIMULI

- Turn off the ringer on your landline, if you've still got one and you still get junk calls (even though you are on the Do Not Call registry).* Have friends call your cell

---

* http://www.donotcall.gov.

phone, and use your landline only to check messages or
dial out.

- Turn off your TV unless you specifically intend to watch
  something. Don't expose yourself to advertising; it is junk
  stimulus in and of itself. Record your shows and fast-
  forward through the ads.

- Identify sources of irritation or unwanted stimulation in
  your household, like whining, too-loud music, background television, or a pet hamster that runs endlessly on
  a squeaky wheel (and smells bad, to boot). Make a concrete plan for how you will eliminate these junk stimuli
  over the next few weeks. I'm not suggesting that you get
  rid of the hamster; just put it in a place where it won't
  bother you. (And do grease that annoying wheel!) And
  I'm not saying to get rid of the whining kid. Instead, make
  a plan to eliminate the whining. Some of these things will
  not be easy. See my other book, *Raising Happiness*, to
  help deal with whining kids.

- If your home or work space is noisy, play soothing music
  or play white noise in the background. Ironically, it will
  help filter out distracting noise. This is also a proven way
  to sleep better! (I like the app White Noise.)

PREVENT RECURRING
LOW-LEVEL STRESSORS

Despite the many optimists (defeatists?) out there proclaiming that
"some stress is good," I just don't buy it. While it is true that stress
can be motivating—its evolutionary function, of course, is to propel
us out of the path of a charging lion—personally I feel better when
I'm motivated by emotions other than fear.

Longtime stress researcher Robert Epstein conducted a study

Reduce Mental Clutter by Making a Plan

Lingering to-do items tend to be low-level stressors for me. I'd be rich if I had a dollar for every time I've woken up at 5:00 a.m. worrying about an unfinished project, an email I forgot to send, an appointment I didn't have a chance to make, or something I meant to do, but didn't.

Researchers used to think that this low-level worrying about unfinished tasks was our unconscious mind trying to help us get things done by reminding us of what we still needed to do, and that the reminders—or distracting thoughts and worries—would persist until the task was complete. This in itself is a worrying theory for those of us who have never-ending task lists.

But now research shows that simply *making a plan* to deal with an unfinished task makes a huge difference in our ability to focus on other things without being constantly reminded by our unconscious mind about what else we need to do. It's not so much about deciding *what* to do—by making a list or something—as it is about deciding *when* to do it. When we don't know *when* we plan to do the things that are on our task lists, our thoughts will typically wander from whatever it is we are doing to our undone tasks. As it turns out, our unconscious isn't nagging us to *do* the task at hand, but rather to *make a plan* for when we will get it done.

So before you leave work or hit the hay this evening, take a look at your task list and make a plan for completing unfinished tasks. Knowing what the next step is for undone items, and when you will do them, can make you a whole lot happier.

that makes this totally clear. The people who are the least stressed-out are very good at preventing stress rather than just knowing how to cope with it (though coping skills don't hurt, either). So we need to spend a little time identifying the things that make us stressed in our day-to-day lives. Really listen to your body for this one. When do you feel nervous? When is your breathing shallow? Your shoulders tensed and aching? When are you likely to snap at your kids or lose your patience?

Before taking stock like this, I was already very aware of how work pressures were stressing me out. But when I spent some time jotting down the other times when I felt anxious, I realized that I am frequently most tense when I'm running late. And I was always running late. Sources of stress vary for each of us; for example, my friend Aaron usually feels stressed when he gets home from work and realizes he doesn't have enough food in the house for dinner and doesn't have the energy to go out.

embracing the better-than-nothing plan

Sometimes planning—preventing stress from occurring—becomes just one more thing that we need to do, which contributes to The Overwhelm. Remember that you don't need to plan everything perfectly to make things easier. Aaron tries to plan a few meals a week, and he shops on the weekend for those that he can imagine. This means that, most nights, he feels prepared for dinner or knows that he has to stop at the store for, say, only the guacamole he forgot. He's given himself a head start, which makes dinnertime less daunting.

So take some time to re-engineer your routine and recurring stressors. Epstein's study suggests that *planning*—preventing stress from even occurring—is the most effective way to manage stress. For school-day mornings to be calm in my house, for example, I've learned I need to wake up a full forty-five minutes earlier than I wish was necessary (why can't the kids just get dressed when I do?) and get backpacks packed the night before, even though the kids and I *never want to do* these things at the end of the day. (Not wanting to do something is very different from feeling stressed-out and rushing to do it in the morning.)

In order to avoid the routine stress of always running late, I need to plan to arrive where I need to be ten minutes early rather than quickly checking one more thing off my list before I leave. Aaron needs to plan his meals and grocery shop over the weekend. This doesn't mean he has to eat everything he shopped for in the order he planned; he is still free to change his mind and/or remix ingredients. Planning ahead doesn't have to make us rigid. But avoiding preventable stressors like these not only makes life feel easier, but it leaves us with more energy for the things we need to accomplish.

SILENCE THE SMARTPHONE SIREN SONG

Do you check your email, texts, voicemails, Facebook, Instagram account, or Twitter feed within an hour of waking up or going to sleep? While you're in line at the store? During dinner with your family? Would you check it at a church while waiting for a funeral to start?

If so, ya ain't alone. Harvard Business School professor and author of *Sleeping with Your Smartphone,* Leslie Perlow, did an amazing study with the Boston Consulting Group. She found that before her intervention, 70 percent of BCG executives checked their phone within an hour of waking up; 56 percent checked their phone within an hour of going to bed. (No doubt many use their phones as their alarm clock and checked before they even got out of bed in the morning.) Half checked their phones continuously throughout their vacation and on weekends.

There is something gratifying about constantly checking our email and our social-media feeds. The distraction is pleasurable because it gives us what researchers call "variable ratio reinforcement." In other words, we are drawn to our smartphones in the way we are drawn to slot machines. We never know when we'll get a satisfying message on Facebook or an email with good news, so we just keep checking.

Even though our brain tends to seek that variable ratio reinforcement, which suggests pleasure, usually we aren't consciously checking our email for fun or recreation. We check constantly to abate our anxiety that we are missing something. Are we supposed to be responding to something urgent at work? What if someone called about something really important? Constant device checking looks a lot like an addiction (or obsessive-compulsive disorder). One study found that many people respond to "phantom phone vibrations"—they think they feel their phone vibrating even when it isn't.

do you check your email before you get out of bed?

If you are using your smartphone as an alarm clock, odds are that you are tempted to check your email before you even get out of bed. Is this *really* the best way to start your day? Maybe it is. Perhaps checking your email is your highest priority, and you have time for it before breakfast.

If that isn't you, however, you aren't alone. Most people do much better when they put off checking their email until they are actually at work. Here's an easy solution: Bury your email application on your phone in a folder on a back page. That way, when you turn off your alarm, you won't see your email icon, and you won't see how many unread emails you have. This is akin to hiding Halloween candy from your children so they don't start begging you for a piece first thing in the morning, when they see it. If that email strategy doesn't work (because you are, um, *addicted*), remove your email from your phone altogether for a few months, or use an old-fashioned alarm clock until you've kicked the habit.

And even if you aren't *addicted* or don't check your emails and messages and feeds *compulsively,* often your mental health is still, in fact, at stake. Certainly your productivity and satisfaction with your life are. Perlow's intervention with the Boston Consulting Group executives was nothing short of transformative. She required that participants establish "Predictable Time Off" (PTO)—time when they would not check their email or work remotely from, say, the family dinner table.

Work satisfaction and, ironically, *productivity* shot up for the BCG executives, and dramatically. Before establishing PTO, only 27 percent were excited to start work in the morning. After PTO, 51 percent were. Before, less than half were satisfied with their job, but after, nearly three-quarters were. Satisfaction with work-life balance went from 38 percent to 54 percent. And people found their work to be more collaborative, efficient, and effective; for example, just establishing PTO made 91 percent of the consultants rate their team as collaborative, up from 76 percent when they were checking their email at all hours of the day and night. Perlow explains:

[B]usy managers and professionals tend to amplify—through their own actions and interactions—the inevitable pressures of their jobs, making their own and their colleagues' lives more intense, more overwhelming, more demanding, and less fulfilling than they need to be. The result of this vicious cycle is that the work process ends up being less effective and efficient than it could be. The power of PTO is that it breaks this cycle, mitigating the pressure, freeing individuals to spend time in ways that are more desirable for themselves personally and for the work process.

What all this means is that unless we want to feel overwhelmed and exhausted, we need to unplug. A lot. Specifically, we need to carve out times and spaces that are insulated from checking behaviors. This can be very, very hard when it doesn't come as a company mandate, as it did at the Boston Consulting Group, because it can require that we stop traveling with the herd a few times a day. But even though it might be difficult, and require some courage, I promise, it's worth doing. Here's how.

Step 1: Disable Push features, alerts, and notifications on your mobile devices and desktop and laptop computers. This is the hardest step for many people. You don't have to turn off your phone altogether, but do turn off distracting dings and vibrations (junk stimuli) when you are working or focusing on something besides the incoming emails and texts. Most people do not have the self-discipline or mental fortitude it takes to ignore an incoming text or email. But when you interrupt yourself to check what just came in, you lose time, focus, and productivity (see Stop Multi-tasking [page 87]). Give yourself the gift of being fully present with your attention wherever you are, feeling whatever you are feeling, even if that feeling is boredom (at first). Allow yourself to truly connect with the people who are in your presence, even if it is a checker at the grocery and you don't know him or her. In the next chapter, I'll reveal why this will make you more productive, intelligent, and happy.

Step 2: Designate the spaces in your life in which you will not use devices and computers. Just because we can take a laptop into the bathroom does not mean that this is a sensible thing to do. (Fecal matter can be found on one in six cell phones. Do we need to outlaw pooping and texting at the same time?) Similarly, your bed is for sleeping, not for checking Facebook, even though you can. Neither is it safe to text in the car, while driving yourself, nor is it polite if you're a passenger in a car and the driver is a friend or someone expecting conversation. Tempted to check your email at a red light? Turn your attention to your breath and just breathe: You will gain more in productivity and well-being from the one-minute relaxation. Remember, boredom is not a health hazard, but technology overuse is.

Step 3: Decide on the *times* during which you will not use a device. For example, here are some times in my life when I try hard not to text, be on the phone, email, or check my Facebook feed:

- During meals. There is nothing so important that it can't wait twenty minutes, and I don't want to lose this important downtime (if I'm alone) or time to connect with my friends and family.

starting small works

Feeling panicky at the prospect of unplugging? Start with very small chunks of time, or very limited spaces. Commit to unplug for just twenty minutes—at dinner, for example—or to just leave your device out of your children's rooms, or do not check email before you are actually out of bed one morning per week. Often, we need to give our nervous system time to adjust; we need to have the experience that our heart does not actually stop beating—or that a crisis has not erupted at work—in the few minutes that we've turned off our phone. (In fact, we enjoyed it! We were more efficient and less stressed!) The idea is to build internal fortitude through positive experience *slowly* rather than trying to massively make over our lives in one fell swoop.

- While someone else is helping me with something, like a clerk in a store.

- While I'm working, unless I'm working on answering and writing emails.

- After 9:15 p.m. In the evening, all my devices automatically switch over to their "do not disturb" setting and are turned off entirely thirty minutes before I go to bed. Why thirty minutes? Because the low-energy blue light emitted by our tablets and smartphones stimulates chemical messengers in our brains that make us more alert, and it suppresses others (like melatonin) that help us fall asleep.

- Before breakfast. I've found that if I start checking my email first thing in the morning, I derail my carefully constructed morning routine. (See Chapter 3.)

LIMIT YOUR CHOICES

Barry Schwartz, the psychologist who wrote *The Paradox of Choice,* has done interesting research on the consequences of living in a culture that assumes that more choices are better than fewer. The gist of what Schwartz's research famously shows is that having a lot of choices is a curse on our happiness.

Schwartz divides the world into people who, in the face of their many choices, maximize and those who "satisfice," or accept the first available option that meets their criteria. Maximizing is a form of perfectionism; we maximize by searching out all the best possible options when making a decision, hoping to make the "perfect" choice. We satisfice when we choose something based on preset criteria and move on. Satisficing doesn't mean settling for something less than we really want; it is just a different way to go about making a decision.

Happy people have different decision-making processes than do unhappy people: Happy people tend to satisfice. Maximizing is very tempting for perfectionists, and it is associated with unhappiness and discontent.

This may be hard to believe, especially if you are a perfectionist, because it seems like maximizers would have higher standards and so could be expected to make better decisions that make them happier down the road. Not necessarily. Maximizers actually tend to be less happy with the decisions they make (when they finally make them). Why?

Consider this example from my own life: My mother wanted to reupholster the cushions on my kitchen banquette for me. I was thrilled with this generous offer. The kitchen was white, with nothing else going on, so she could do anything. She spent a day looking at possible fabrics and came home with a trunk full of samples. Not having a lot of time, and not wanting to overwhelm myself, I took one look at her car trunk and said, "Let's just consider the blue and orange fabrics that are washable."

Dismayed, my mom went along with this initial weeding out of 90 percent of what she had chosen. There were now only seven fabrics for me to look at. I chose two immediately that went to-gether well, and was thrilled. My mom, on the other hand, could see all the choices I *didn't* make, and felt loss and doubt about the choice I'd made. She wanted me to "think about it for a while," which I didn't, knowing that I wasn't going to have time to revisit the decision or see the samples again. My mom, on the other hand, drove around with the samples in her trunk for a week considering them, wondering if we made the right choice. I'm happy that the cushions match my kitchen nicely, and I can sponge them off when one of the kids (or I!) inevitably spill something.

how to satisfice instead of maximize

(1) **Outline your criteria for success.** What are the objective signs that a project is finished or an option good enough? If you are choosing toothpaste or a new car, what are the things you just can't live without? No need to set your sights low; just set your sights on something.

(2) **Choose the first option that meets your criteria, or stop working the moment the pre-decided "finished" signs appear.** If you are looking for a toothpaste that whitens without a specific chemical, for example, but you aren't all that concerned with price since they are all priced similarly, choose the first whitening toothpaste you find that doesn't have the substance you want to avoid. If you are buying a car, go ahead and do your research to find the one that meets your criteria, but *stop researching* when you've unearthed your options. Don't suddenly start considering cars out of your price range, for example, just to see what you are missing. People with decision paralysis or perfectionists who have a hard time calling it quits might also want to set time limits—say, two minutes—to decide, or no more than a half hour a day browsing car websites.

(3) Once the decision is made or the job done, **focus on the positive aspects of the choice or accomplishment.** Focusing on what might have been is not a happiness habit. Enjoy the fruit of your work.

Even if you don't have a project or a big decision to make, limit your choices. In my experience, this is a very effective way to reduce the overwhelm that comes from living in a place where I am confronted with so many choices all the time. The bonus is that I end up feeling happier with the choices I've made. For example:

- I buy the same brands again and again, from the same retailers, no matter if it is toothpaste, breakfast sausage, carrots, soy milk, cereal, or gas. I even stick to the same variety and color of apple. Once something meets my criteria, I don't make decisions about which brands or varieties to buy again or where to shop. I get variety in my life in arenas other than the grocery store. If this sounds horrible to you—perhaps you take great joy in trying lots of apple varieties —see where you find relief in constraining your choices. Perhaps you decide to shop only at one store, or choose only one new brand or variety per shopping trip.

- I have only three or four "uniforms" that I wear day in and day out. If I'm exercising, I like a particular style of Athleta pants, a T-shirt, and a zip-up fleece. Speaking engagement? A J.Crew suit dress and blazer. (I have three of each in different colors. Bet you didn't know happiness experts could be so dang boring.) Casual workday? Lucky brand jeans and a T-shirt, and a turtleneck sweater if it's cold. I keep a Patagonia jacket—the down kind that can be stuffed into its own pocket—in my purse. I get variety in my shoes and jewelry, which is quite enough variety for me.

- I eat pretty much the same thing for breakfast and lunch every single day, and our family dinners follow a formula, too. Want to know what it is? Monday Meatballs (usually some variation on an Italian spaghetti and meatballs), Taco Tuesday, Wildcard Wednesday (usually some sort of

one more piece of daily decision-making advice

Whatever you do, don't waffle. Embrace the choices you make. This advice is derived from what Dan Gilbert, Harvard psychologist and author of *Stumbling on Happiness,* calls "the unanticipated joy of being totally stuck." His research has found that people naturally prefer what they perceive themselves to be stuck with. Consider this experiment: Gilbert and his colleagues had college students rank their favorite Monet prints, and then he gave them the choice to take one home that they ranked three or four (out of six). Fifteen days later, he asked the students to re-rank the prints, and they (of course!) ranked the print they chose to take home much higher this time, and the one that they *didn't* choose much lower. This works even when the research subjects have a serious amnesia disorder and literally can't remember which print they chose to own.

These data get even more interesting when we look at what happened in a different experiment, when Gilbert and his collaborators let photography students take home one of their two favorite photographs but had them give up the other to the class instructors. Students in one group made their choice and then immediately had to give up the photo they didn't choose. Students in another group were allowed to change their minds about the choice they made and had several days to reverse their decision about which photo to keep. The students who had to make their choice without the possibility of change tended to be far happier with the photograph they chose when asked about it later. The other students, however, who were allowed to waffle about their decision, and even change their mind if they wanted to, ended up being far less happy with the choice they made. Go figure.

The lesson here is that the brain naturally justifies its choices and actually creates positive sentiment about them—but only when it perceives that a choice is complete and can't be reversed. This is what Gilbert calls our psychological immune system. So make your decisions and be done with them.

chicken dish, like paprikash made in the slow cooker
while I work), Thursday Thaw (something from the
freezer I cooked the previous weekend), and Friday Fast
Food (not literally—usually homemade pizza or burgers).

Maybe this seems boring—and honestly, it can be—but it is also
easy. Of course I take into account when I'm out of town or we
might have a social engagement. I don't plan those meals, but by
cooking variations on the same themes, I save a lot of energy that I'd
otherwise be expending trying to decide what to eat (and what to
buy). I make the same quantity of food regardless of who shows up
at the table: enough for eight people. Although there are usually
only six of us, I want the kids to feel free to invite friends to dinner
whenever they want. And the leftovers are always packed for school
lunches (which solves *that* problem). I eat more for pleasure and
variety on the weekends, and when I go out to eat.

We all have a limited capacity for decision-making in any given
day. Eventually this capacity fades, and with it the quality of the
decisions we make, and our self-discipline in general. In other words,
making a lot of decisions, even small ones, tires us out. Knowing this
makes me feel better about restricting my choices. And I no longer
think of myself as settling when I make a decision without exploring
all the options. I'm practicing satisficing, and I'm happier than I
would be in the long run if I were to maximize. I also have more
energy and clarity when big decision-making moments come along.

WHAT TO DO ABOUT ALL THE STUFF
YOU CAN'T SAY "NO" TO

Now that you've gotten rid of all the junk and clutter in your life that
is overwhelming you, it's time to deal with the stuff in life that you
dread doing—to prune that never-ending task list and neutralize the
toxic situations in your life. This section is for dealing with what
can't be considered junk clutter, which you can just trash and move
on. This section is for things that aren't so easily discarded: a toxic

relationship; a long, stressful commute to a job you actually love; a daily task you feel you *have* to do but you always dread doing. It's for the things that don't fall into your top five priorities but that you can't seem to say "no" to. It's even for the things that *do* fall into a top priority but you still really, really, really don't want to do. Listen to your body and your unconscious for these items. What people give you an unpleasant feeling in the pit of your stomach? What do you consistently procrastinate doing? What would you celebrate raucously if you never had to do it again? Consider that these things are a steady source of negative emotion for you. For these things, I use Martha Beck's three B's method: Bag it, Barter it, or Better it.

DO YOU DREAD IT? THEN BAG IT IF YOU CAN

If you feel hassled by a long task list, weed that puppy down with gusto until it is a realistic representation of what you actually can accomplish given your current status as a human being (and not a supercomputer).

Start by automating as many of the routine tasks on your list as you can. Set up auto-pay for your bills. Create a standing grocery order (I use planetorganics.com; it chooses seasonal fruits and vegetables for me). Switch to a dry cleaner that picks up and delivers your laundry on a set schedule. Word of warning: Don't automate anything that brings you joy.

For most people, email is a to-do item that never quits and contributes to daily feelings of stress. Rein it in. Which emails do you *really* have to read? Which *must* you respond to? Consider boldly deleting everything that you don't absolutely need. I love Gmail's tabs because they allow me to batch-delete emails that I don't have time to read before I get sucked in and read them anyway. And I use a "bypass the inbox" filter for a lot of emails; they go straight to a file, where they wait for me until I have time for them. Feel free to respond to email on your terms; there is no law in the universe that says you must sacrifice your sleep, feelings of well-being, or other priorities so you can get through your email.

Further prune your to-do list of more major items with this question: If it turns out that my life is a lot shorter than I hope it will be, which of the things on my list right now will I wish I hadn't wasted time on? Pay particular attention to anything you do just for prestige or praise or to feel superior to others, anything that makes you tense or anxious but doesn't contribute to your growth over the long haul, and anything that involves toxic people or situations.

Also take a little time to identify arenas in which you are "shoulding" on yourself. What things are you doing not because they are good for you or because they bring you joy or because they are a top priority, but just because you feel you *should* do them? Do you dread volunteering in your kids' classrooms but do it because you want people to think you are a good parent? Why not find a way to contribute in a way that you love?

Finally, remember your reason for being, and your reason for saying "no," and then bag things *before* they end up on your calendar by cultivating well-practiced ways to say "no." Mine is, "Oh I'd love to do that, but I can't this time. Let me help you think of someone else who can help you." Or the vague and strangely effective, "That isn't going to work out for me this time, but thank you for asking."

CAN'T ELIMINATE IT? BARTER OR BETTER IT

There are lots of things in life I dread doing that I can't simply bag. I hate doing dishes and emptying the dishwasher, so I've entered into a barter with my kids. They do these things (with my husband's help), and I plan the meals and lead the cooking. I hate scheduling travel, but I don't mind proofreading, and so I've bartered these non-household tasks with my husband. He schedules our vacations and travel, making reservations and such, and I proofread the marketing pieces he sends out for his business. When I was newly divorced and trying to get my career off the ground, I had an extra room but no money to hire help. One of the best things I ever did was arrange for a graduate student to live with us rent-free. In exchange, she helped me keep my house from imploding on itself; she kept up with the breakfast dishes and helped me with the kids and the laundry in a very significant way.

That said, sometimes bartering is better when it is just delegating or hiring out help, if you can. I could never have survived as a single working mother without my longtime house cleaner, Marly. As a liberal sociologist, I've long felt guilty about letting someone else clean my toilets, but after many discussions with Marly about it, I've come to understand that she loves her job, and she loves our house, and she loves me and my family. Just because I hate cleaning doesn't mean that she also hates it, and while I still can't imagine that she enjoys cleaning toilets, I do see that—for her—being a housekeeper is a calling, not a job. (More about this in the Conclusion.)

Another example: I hate taking the garbage cans to the curb each week. It involves a tricky gate, a flight of stairs with a heavy garbage can, and stinky compost. Since this is a task that must be done, and because my husband hates doing this, too, we pay our across-the-street neighbor, a teenage boy, a few dollars a week to do it. And my father, who lives nearby, often puts the cans back once they've been emptied. He enjoys the simple pleasure of helping us out. More in the next chapter on why this actually is a valuable barter for him (because clearly I get something, but he gets something valuable, too).

A word of caution about hiring help, however: I do think it is possible to hire out too much. The important research of Arlie Hochschild, a sociologist and author of *The Time Bind, The Second Shift,* and *The Commercialization of Intimate Life,* makes it very clear that although, with enough money, it is certainly *possible* to hire people to do pretty much whatever we might dread doing ourselves, it's not *advisable* to hire someone to live your life for you. (Not to mention that managing all that help is a job unto itself!) I could pick up relatively healthy and inexpensive prepared meals from Trader Joe's for dinner every night (believe me, I sometimes do, and I'm not judging those who do!). But I don't always do this because I love the connection that the kids and I have when we cook together, even if we don't have time to be particularly creative. Freeing up the time it takes us to cook would lead me to fill my time with something I love less (driving the kids around to their various activities, perhaps) or with something I already have enough of (work).

Similarly, there are some things that we might not enjoy because they bring up painful but *necessary* negative emotions (remember, this section is about eliminating *un*necessary negative emotions). These difficult things are still important for us to do. I don't love planning birthday parties (my father was right, I'm not a details person), but it is important *to my children* that I don't distance myself from these meaningful annual events. Or you might not want to plan your grandmother's memorial service—too painful, the grief is too hard, you don't have the time—but plan it yourself you must. The takeaway: Barter, delegate, or hire out help for routine things that are toxic to you or you truly just don't like doing **to make time for more meaningful activities.**

What if we can't bag a dreaded task or situation and we can't barter or delegate it? Perhaps you have a poor relationship with your sister, but you can't delegate interactions with her to your spouse, and your relationship with her isn't bad enough that you just want to bag it altogether. First, bag or barter as much of it as you can. Perhaps you love her relationship with your children but you dread dropping them off at her house and picking them up because of the way she criticizes you at every turn. Barter or hire the dropping off and picking up part, and *better* the other times when you need to interact with her. Maybe she's particularly mean at family dinners after she's had a drink. So don't serve alcohol, and get her engaged in a game with the kids before she starts spoiling for a fight. Some dreaded relationships can benefit from therapy, too—though not all. I'm a firm believer that life is too short to try to change toxic people, and some toxic people or situations are better avoided than improved.

My favorite way to better a dreaded situation is to make it entertaining. Perhaps you hate your commute, but for the time being you can't eliminate it. What can you do to better it? Commute with friends and turn it into a party? Use the time to listen to audiobooks? Watch movies on public transportation? I clock about ten hours a week of predictable drive time, and I've come to love my time in the car because I use it to listen to fiction. (And there is an added bonus: Research shows that literary fiction helps us develop social and emotional intelligence, which the next chapter will reveal to be at the heart of our happiness and success.)

FINALLY, STOP OVERTHINKING THINGS

Say you're a gazelle on the African savanna and a leopard tries to make you his dinner. He catches, instead, a nearby baby giraffe and rips it to shreds. You get yourself to safety, and because you are a gazelle and not a human, your heart settles back down and you treat yourself to some grass for dinner.

But imagine now that this happened to you—a human being. You've escaped the leopard today, but for crying out loud, what about tomorrow? What about the children? Your brain keeps thinking terrifying thoughts about how you almost died and about the baby giraffe and the injustice of it all. And every time you think about the leopard, your fight-or-flight response is activated again, and your body surges with fear and worry about something that is actually no longer happening.

This happens to us all the time. Something bad happens, and because of our evolutionary ability to plan and predict the future, we imaginatively (and then emotionally) keep making it happen again and again. Sometimes this is useful: It helps us avoid leopards in the future.

But we also create a lot of unnecessary negative emotions by ruminating on negative events. This is like the reverse of savoring positive emotions; rumination amplifies and prolongs negative emotions. I'm all for feeling deeply, even if the emotions are difficult or negative, but we also need to move on once we've felt what we need to feel.

When people hear that I encourage my coaching clients to move on from unpleasant feelings, many worry: "Well, make sure you aren't denying their negative emotions," they tell me, worrying that I'm "sending the message that bad feelings are bad and should be avoided."

Rest assured, I do believe that all feelings, good or bad, are okay. I see emotions like sadness, frustration, anxiety, and jealousy as windows into our worlds, as part of the keel that balances and steers us. I am not encouraging anyone to just buck up, or stuff down bad feelings.

But sometimes enough is enough, and we need to move on from bad feelings. The truth is that rumination is bad for us. As psychologist Sonja Lyubomirsky explains in *The How of Happiness*:

Overthinking ushers in a host of adverse consequences: It sustains or worsens sadness, fosters negatively biased thinking, impairs a person's ability to solve problems, saps motivation, and interferes with concentration and initiative. Moreover, although people have a strong sense that they are gaining insight into themselves and their problems during their ruminations, this is rarely the case. What they do gain is a distorted, pessimistic perspective on their lives.

Or as renowned compassion and mindfulness researcher Paul Gilbert has famously said, "Attention is like a spotlight—whatever it shines on becomes brighter in the mind." So instead of continuing to shine a spotlight on negative events—mistakenly thinking that we are solving our problems by doing so—we need to turn our attention to positive distractions. Instead of thinking a negative thought, and then feeling a negative feeling, and then thinking the negative thought again and again and again, we need to picture a stop sign in our heads (really, I do this; I visualize a stop sign), and choose a strategy from Chapter 2 for fostering positive emotions.

Or we can employ my favorite Jedi mind trick for dealing with pain. It's mindfulness. We can simply observe and become familiar with the tricks that our minds are playing on us. Watch your thoughts and emotions, and label them. "Oh look, I'm thinking that thought about my husband not being a good listener again." Ask yourself how much you've bought into the thought, and if you are ready to let it go. "I'm really hooked by the idea that he isn't compassionate, but that thought is making me feel despair. It isn't getting me anywhere to keep looking for evidence that he isn't compassionate. I'm ready to stop ruminating on this." And then imagine that the thought that hooked you is now in a bubble or cloud, and let it float away.

what is mindfulness, exactly?

Jon Kabat-Zinn, the medical researcher who first "translated" Buddhist mindfulness practices into a secular program called Mindfulness-Based Stress Reduction (MBSR), defines mindfulness as the "awareness that emerges through paying attention on purpose, in the present moment, and non-judgmentally, to the unfolding of experiences moment by moment." Scientific research on mindfulness—pioneered by Kabat-Zinn and encouraged by His Holiness the Dalai Lama—gives us ample evidence that mindfulness is really good for us. Practicing mindfulness boosts our immune systems, increases our happiness, and decreases stress and depression. It literally changes our brains, improving our ability to learn, focus, remember, regulate our emotions, and be more empathetic. And if that isn't enough, mindfulness can strengthen our relationships when we are upset, helping us feel closer to our partners and making us more satisfied with our spouses.

THE EASIEST THING: DO NOTHING (LITERALLY!)

I realize that it is somewhat ironic that a chapter dedicated in part to reducing exhaustion has probably overwhelmed you with ideas for how to eliminate overwhelm. Feeling exhausted before you begin? Here's what you can do:

Nothing.

Well, not nothing: Keep breathing. Even if you are dying to get to the next chapter, don't turn the page yet. Take twenty minutes to unplug entirely: turn off computers and phones and anything that might alert you to an incoming communication. (The world will not stop spinning if you disconnect for twenty minutes, but your head might.) Sit in a comfortable position, or lie down. Now: Do nothing. Stare into space. If you start feeling bored or antsy, that's normal. Just notice what you are feeling. If you start feeling sleepy, that's okay; just notice if you are starting to fall asleep. Don't judge yourself.

The good news is that by letting yourself get a little bored each day, or taking a breather to just *be,* without also *doing* anything, you open space for creativity and all the positive emotions discussed in the previous chapter.

Here's some more good news: We haven't even begun to touch on the most powerful positive emotions of all—love, empathy, and compassion. If you suspect that you could best increase your happiness by creating stronger and more positive connections with others, the next chapter is your ticket.

PART FOUR

cultivate relationships

Want to know what the key to happiness is? The Beatles certainly sang it: All you need is love. In addition to making us feel more satisfied with our lives, our relationships can also make us healthier and more successful. To improve our relationships, we need only do two things: First, foster positive feelings toward the people around us—Chapter 6 will give you several fun strategies for that. Second, we need to cope with the ways that people are annoying and disappointing and even hurtful in a manner that doesn't further damage our relationships. Chapter 7 outlines common relationship sticking points—and strategies for getting unstuck.

CHAPTER 6

how to die happy, giving, and beloved

But who could have foreseen . . . that he would die a happy, giving, and beloved man? Only those who understand that happiness is only the cart; love is the horse.

—George E. Vaillant, *Triumphs of Experience*

If we look back at the past two centuries of research in sociology and psychology, the single strongest finding about our well-being is that our health, happiness, and longevity are best predicted by the breadth and the depth of our positive social connections—our friendships, relationships with family members, closeness to neighbors, and perhaps whether or not we know our grocery checker's name. People with many social connections are less likely to experience sadness, loneliness, low self-esteem, and problems with eating and sleeping, and are more likely to experience life positively.

This means that building stronger connections with people we already know, and building new and positive relationships with people we don't know at all, can lead to a happier, healthier, more successful, and ease-ier life. Social connections help us live and work from our sweet spots by bringing us both strength *and* ease.

Why? As it turns out, all positive emotions were not created equally. Love and the similar emotions that we experience when we feel connected socially—like affection, warmth, care, fondness, and compassion—are more powerful than the others. In Barbara Fredrickson's words:

Love is our supreme emotion: its presence or absence in our lives influences everything we feel, think, do, and become. It's that recurrent state that ties you in—your body and brain alike—to the social fabric, to the bodies and brains of those in your midst. When you experience love . . . you not only become better able to see the larger tapestry of life and better able to breathe life into the connections that matter to you, but you set yourself on a pathway that leads to more health, happiness, and wisdom.

The longest running study of human development, The Harvard Grant Study, has charted the physical and emotional health of more than two hundred Harvard alumni since 1938 (which means that many of the study's participants are pushing a hundred years—or pushing up daisies). The Grant Study makes it clear that "the most important influence, by far, on a flourishing life is love," as one of the researchers behind the study, George Vaillant, put it in *Triumphs of Experience.*

It isn't just that people who are more connected are the happiest people. They are also the most successful at work and at school. When college students feel a sense of belonging, their grades go up. In one study, African American college students were asked to read a short testimonial from older students about how they had been worried about fitting in but that things had turned out well. They then had to make a short video testimonial about their own experience of fitting in. This one simple intervention "led to an enduring improvement in GPA in nearly every semester of about 0.2 GPA units (for example, a GPA of 3.6 instead of 3.4)," writes UCLA neuroscientist Matthew Lieberman.

Beyond feeling a sense of belonging, an "ability to build relationships" predicts how well people do at work. This relationship capacity proved to be more highly rated than their "a focus on results" in determining whether or not a manager is rated among the top 10 percent of leaders in a given company. Similarly, a person's social skills (which are strongly related to the breadth and the depth of their social connections) are twice as important as intelligence for predicting whether or not they will emerge as a leader when they are assigned to a random team project.

And a deep well of research shows that positive social connections protect our health. Again, according to Fredrickson:

[A lack of connection] is, in fact, more damaging to your health than smoking cigarettes, drinking alcohol excessively, or being obese. Specifically, these studies tell us that people who experience more warm and caring connections with others have fewer colds, lower blood pressure, and less often succumb to heart disease and stroke, diabetes, Alzheimer's disease, and some cancers.

As Matthew Lieberman, author of *Social: Why Our Brains Are Wired to Connect,* puts it: "Increasing the social connections in our lives is probably the single easiest way to enhance our well-being." This is because what makes us human is our *sociality*—our desire for and focus on social connections, loving relationships, and warm interactions with others.

Many, many economic studies have sought to put a dollar value on our social lives, estimating how much more money we need in order to increase our sense of well-being. Giving our time, for example, is associated with greater feelings of well-being equivalent to the increase that someone making $20,000 a year in the United States would experience if suddenly he or she were earning $75,000 a year. Giving money to worthy causes is like doubling our salary in terms of our happiness. But here's the real commodity that's worth a wheelbarrow full of cash: Having a close friend or relative whom you get to see on most days has the same impact on your well-being as making an extra $100,000 a year; being married is also "worth" an extra $100,000 annually on average.

(Surprised that such hard-to-measure things can be quantified? Economists use enormous databases and sophisticated statistical methods to figure out these things. The process involves taking a random sample of individuals, recording their happiness levels at different points in time, and then running regression equations to work out the implied "shadow price" of different behaviors, emotions, and relationships.)

We Americans spend a lot of time working, hoping to increase our feelings of well-being by making more money. But we'd do better to cultivate our close connections to other people because when our relationships flourish, so do we. This is because love sets into motion the same physiology of ease that other positive emotions do, but often more powerfully.

One reason that social emotions are so powerful is that the system in our brain responsible for our social thinking, the dorsomedial prefrontal cortex, turns on *whenever we are not actively engaged in a cognitive or non-social task*. The dorsomedial prefrontal cortex is the part of our brain that enables us to make educated guesses about what another person is thinking or feeling, and helps us connect with others and harmonize our actions with theirs. It's turned on so much in most people that neuroscientists named this brain system the "default network" (before they knew its function). They saw that it was always active when their research subjects weren't solving a problem, and they realized that it was the human brain's default mode. Social thinking is our brain's preferred state.

Perhaps for this reason, when we learn with our social connections in mind—as when we learn something with the intention to teach it to someone else—our brain retains the information far better than when we just try to memorize something. Researchers call this the "social encoding advantage." For example, my children learn difficult concepts better and more easily when they know that we are going to ask them to teach the whole family what they learned at dinnertime. We humans are hardwired to stay connected to our clan and are richly rewarded with greater success, happiness, and health when we do.

THE POSITIVE EMOTION AMPLIFIER

The advent of social media connections has introduced a lot of confusion when it comes to the strength of our social fabric and our ties to one another. Are we more connected now than ever before? Or is "connectivity" through electronics different from real, face-to-face, or even voice-to-voice connection?

Our suspicion that our online connections are qualitatively different from our face-to-face interactions—that time spent communicating with our friends and family via text, email, and social media is different from time spent talking in person—is correct. We understand intuitively that something different happens within us when we communicate with someone in person.

That difference is something that Barbara Fredrickson calls "positivity resonance," and it is nothing short of a positive emotion amplified into something bigger than it would be if we were alone. Positivity resonance happens in a fleeting micro-moment of emotion as a trio of tightly woven events:

> We share one or more positive emotions with another person.

> Our biochemistry and body language synchronize with the other's.

> We care about each other and show a willingness to invest in each other's well-being.

If I smile warmly at you, you can share in my positive emotion with me. A part of your brain will light up as though you've just smiled warmly yourself. In an instant, our brains synch up. Similarly, if I'm telling you a story and you are listening attentively, your brain activity will mirror mine strikingly. Much fuss has been made about mirror neurons, but new research shows that there is much more at work here than a few isolated mirror neurons firing in a single area of the brain. In fact, *all* your brain activity will be nearly the same as mine—something neuroscientists call "neural coupling." (Those of you who are in touch with your inner adolescent can stop snickering now.)

Note: Neural coupling occurs between all sorts of people, not just couple types. It's not just about lovers or people in established relationships.

We understand the emotions of those we are with through this synchronicity. When I smile at you or laugh, you understand what my smile or my laugh means because *your* facial muscles fire in imperceptibly tiny ways, mimicking my expression, stimulating the emotion in your own brain. So if I laugh derisively, you "intuitively" know my laugh is mean because you actually experience the emotion yourself, right then. If instead my laugh is an expression of genuine mirth, or my smile an expression of authentic joy, you feel this as well. Understanding other people's emotions "is not just abstract and conceptual," Fredrickson explains; "it's embodied and physical."

Our shared emotion leads to a shared physiology. Our heart rates and breathing will slow together and start to synchronize. This internal activity leads to external behavior changes. People who are experiencing a positive connection—positivity resonance—start to unconsciously mimic each other in their body language. And studies show that positive emotions literally open our hearts; they expand the part of our rib cage that houses our heart, lifting and expanding our chest cavity. This unconscious gesture makes us more inviting to others and more open for connection, explains Fredrickson, and signals to others that they, too, can relax.

While any positive emotion can expand your heart cavity in this way, positivity resonance speaks with its own unique body language. When you and I are really connecting, observers can see four unique nonverbal cues:

- We frequently smile at each other (in that authentic, eye-crinkling manner researchers call the Duchenne smile)

- We use open and friendly hand gestures in reference to each other (like outstretched palms)

- We lean toward each other (literally bringing our hearts together)

- We frequently nod our heads, signaling that we affirm and accept each other

People experiencing "positivity resonance" are actually doing a synchronized dance. They are one unit rather than two separate individuals. This positivity resonance is different from the love or affection or compassion we feel when we are alone, or even when we receive a sweet text from a friend or a lover. When positive emotion resonates back and forth between two or more people, it is *amplified*. It grows bigger than it would if we were alone.

As an affectionate extrovert, I probably have always been a bit predisposed to creating micro-moments of positive connection with others. But learning that making connections with others can actu-

should we talk to strangers?

A half dozen new studies demonstrate the power that positivity resonance *with strangers* has to make us happier. In one study, researchers randomly assigned volunteers to talk to the strangers who sat down next to them on the train during their morning commutes. Pretty much no one thought they were going to enjoy giving up their morning solitude to make small talk with someone they didn't know and would probably never see again. But guess what? The volunteers enjoyed their commutes more than the people in the study who got to read their books and finish their crossword puzzles in silence. What's more, not a single study participant was snubbed. Other research indicates that the strangers being chatted up in public spaces similarly *think* they won't want to talk, but then end up enjoying themselves.

In another study, researchers measured how much people enjoyed interacting with people they barely knew, and how much they enjoyed connecting with loved ones. Turns out that interacting with both types of people made both introverts and extroverts happier—and the more social interactions they had, the happier people were.

Finally, research shows that even just *acknowledging* someone else's presence by making eye contact and smiling at them helps people feel more connected. So yes: Talking to strangers strangely makes us happy.

ally help me have an easier day made me want to make an effort to connect with people around me even more often by simply saying hello and smiling at folks I'd normally just pass by. Knowing how critical eye contact can be for connection, I now try harder to look everyone in the eye. Knowing that we best communicate warmth and connection through touch, I'm likely to touch your arm while we are talking, or to rest my hand on your shoulder just before we part. Before I read all this research, I would actually resist hugging people when I thought it more socially expected to simply shake their hands—now I usually embrace my huggy-nature and just go for it. (No pun intended.)

What science teaches us, and what I've learned through experience, is that the positivity resonance between me and a stranger is surprisingly similar to that within our most intimate relationships. Biologically, we have basically the same reaction, and we reap similar physiological benefits when we connect with a stranger as when we connect with our best friend. The big difference is the frequency and speed with which we have micro-moments of "positivity resonance." With a spouse, family member, or good friend, we have these moments more quickly and more often than with an acquaintance.

Another big takeaway for me is that our most committed relationships—our marriage, and relationships with our closest family members and best friends—are *continually created and reinforced in real time* by repeated micro-moments of love and care. We sometimes forget that marriage is not created by the wedding and that the ceremony when we make a lifelong commitment is, in some ways, nothing more than a couple of hours of amplified love. As such, that positivity resonance, however intensely felt in the moment, will fade until those moments are re-created.

All this is to remind us what we already know (but sometimes wish wasn't true): Relationships need cultivating and tending. As Brené Brown writes:

Love requires tenacity and grit. It's work. It's the most difficult thing I've ever done. So when people say, "Love shouldn't be this hard," I think, Why not? *We get so much from our most important relation-ships—it makes sense that we have to invest a lot of time, effort, and some serious self-reflection into them.*

Whether or not we experience the things we do to cultivate our relationships as work or as play probably depends on our personality and on the particular relationship. The point is that the particular behaviors and actions we take—consciously or unconsciously—enable our relationships to flourish.

Some of the work we need to do is to recognize and cultivate the right environment for our relationships. The amplification of posi-tive emotions has a few particular preconditions. Positivity reso-nance can arise only when we *feel safe;* that is the first precondition. If our system is alarmed, if the person we are with (even if it is a "loved one") is threatening in any way or is triggering a fight-or-flight response in us, we will not experience a synchronicity of positive emotions or the benefits of love amplified.

The second precondition for positivity resonance is a *physical connection.* Our bodies and brains synch up by witnessing the non-verbal cues that come with a positive emotional connection, through eye contact, through unconscious mimicry of facial expressions, through our vocal tones, and through touch. So while we may feel a profound swell of love when we receive a love note from our spouse, our love is singular. It does not resonate between us; it isn't ampli-fied.

And there is a third thing: We need to create connections all the time. These micro-moments of positive connection are like all emo-tions: *fleeting.* Connection between us and another is evoked, it arises, and it fades. When we think of love, we usually think of the *bonds* that are created through positivity resonance. But as the Bud-dhists say, the finger that points to the moon is not the moon; our marriages and commitments and genuine bonds of love are *not* the emotion of love itself.

Micro-moments of positivity resonance are tremendous and powerful resources that can, in fact, affect our future with our be-loveds. When we experience the positive connection of amplified love, it increases the odds that we will respond positively in the future to the same person. This is why we can light up when we run into an old high school friend at the supermarket, connecting quickly and easily even though it has been a decade since we last saw each other.

GENERATING LOVE AND CONNECTION

So if our happiness and our success are best predicted by the quantity and quality of our relationships with others, and our relationships are built through these micro-moments of positive connection, the question remains: How can we best engineer lots of micro-moments of positive connection? There are many ways, but the best way is to become one of life's big givers.

WHAT WE GET WHEN WE GIVE

For starters, we know that giving people reap the most significant rewards in business settings. According to Adam Grant, professor at the Wharton School of Business and author of *Give and Take: Why Helping Others Drives Our Success,* givers develop superior networking, collaborating, evaluating, and influencing skills. So over the long haul, they tend to be the most successful.

We also know that helping others improves our physical health and longevity. People who volunteer tend to experience fewer aches and pains, and giving help to others protects overall health twice as much as aspirin protects against heart disease. People fifty-five and older who volunteer for two or more organizations have an impressive 44 percent lower likelihood of dying—and that's after sifting out every other contributing factor, including physical health, exercise, gender, marital status, and smoking. This is a stronger effect than exercising four times a week or going to church; it means that volunteering is nearly as beneficial to our health as quitting smoking!

We feel good when we give because we often get what researchers call a "helper's high," or a distinct physical sensation associated with helping. About half of participants in one study reported that they felt stronger and more energetic after helping others; many also reported feeling calmer and less depressed, with increased feelings of self-worth. This is probably a literal "high," similar to a drug-induced high. For example, the act of making a financial donation triggers the reward center in our brains that is responsible for dopamine-mediated euphoria.

Similarly, volunteer work substantially reduces symptoms of depression. Helping others and receiving help are associated with lowered anxiety and depression. Adolescents who identify a strong inclination to help others are three times happier than those who lack such altruistic motivation. Teens who are giving, hopeful, and socially effective are also happier and more active, involved, excited, and engaged than their less giving counterparts. Generous behavior reduces adolescent depression and suicide risk, and several studies have shown that teenagers who volunteer are less likely to fail a subject in school, get pregnant, or abuse substances. Teens who volunteer also tend to be more socially competent and have higher self-esteem.

Although it may be that happier and healthier people are more likely to volunteer in the first place, it is important to note that experiments have demonstrated again and again that the effects of kindness on our health and happiness are *causal*. It isn't just that kind people also tend to be healthier and happier (and that might be why they are kinder in the first place), but kindness toward others actually *causes* us to be happier, improves our health, and lengthens our lives. Being kind to others strengthens our social bonds. Giving to others also increases our sense of self-worth—heightening our sense that we have something to offer the world—which makes us feel more satisfied with our lives. But that's not all that is at work here.

Most of us know from experience that when our own worries take center stage—*What did she think of me? Will I get there on time? Will I have enough money this month?*—we stress ourselves out. Heart attacks and other stress-related illnesses are highly correlated with how much people reference *themselves* in interviews, using words like I, me, my, mine, myself. In one study, patients with severe disease were more self-focused and less other-focused.

Indeed, giving to others makes us healthier and happier because it makes us less preoccupied with ourselves, thereby reducing stress and reversing its damaging effects on the body. "One of the healthiest things that a person can do is to step back from self-preoccupation and self-worry, as well as from hostile and bitter emotions," writes altruism expert Stephen Post; and "there is no more obvious way of doing this than focusing attention on helping others."

One study showed, for example, that people who were feeling worried and stressed about their finances felt better when they offered social support to others. Another study found that people who tend to help others are *far* more resilient in the face of stress than non-helping people. Kindness redirects our energy toward things that make us feel good, reducing the toll that negative feelings have on our health and happiness.

HOW TO BECOME ONE OF LIFE'S BIG GIVERS

All of us have three primary resources to give to others: our time, our love and positive thoughts, and our money. Below are seven ways we can give in all three of these domains:

(1) **Just contemplate giving to others.** I always think it's a good idea to make life changes in small increments, and becoming a giver is no exception. Simply thinking about giving seems to have an effect on health and happiness that is similar to actually giving. Volunteers who were asked to watch a film about Mother Teresa helping orphans showed a significantly strengthened immune system, particularly when, after the video, they focused their mind on times when they had been loved or loved someone else. Similarly, praying for others reduces the harmful impact of health difficulties in old age for those doing the praying. And *remembering* helping someone else can induce health benefits for hours or even days.

When I'm feeling stressed or overwhelmed or just a little sorry for myself, I make a conscious effort to think like a giver. I imagine helping someone else, or I remember a time when I was acting less self-centered and more helpful, or I simply send loving thoughts to others.

the power of well wishes

When Barbara Fredrickson and her colleagues want to study what happens when people increase their daily diet of love, they simply ask people to do a loving-kindness meditation once a day. This is a private, quick, no-contact-with-others way to give. If you are going to do only one thing in this chapter to bring more love and connection into your life, I recommend you do this.

Why?

Because research demonstrates its incredible power: This stuff is more effective than Prozac for many people. Also called *metta,* loving-kindness meditation is the simple practice of directing well wishes toward others.

Over a nine-week period, research showed that metta substantially increased people's experiences of positive emotions. (Which means there is a buy-one-get-one-free special running here. If you are working on improving your ratio of positive to negative emotions, start with metta!) Loving-kindness meditation puts people on "trajectories of growth," leaving them better able to ward off depression and "become ever more satisfied with life." More than that, though, doing a simple loving-kindness meditation can make us feel less isolated and more connected to those around us. One study showed that a single seven-minute loving-kindness meditation made people feel more connected to and positive about both loved ones and total strangers, *and* more accepting of themselves. (Imagine what a regular practice could do!)

how to do it

The general idea is to sit comfortably with your eyes closed, and imagine what you wish for your life. Formulate your desires into three or four phrases. Traditionally they would be something like this:

May I be healthy and strong.
May I be happy.
May I live with ease.

Loving-kindness meditation is a simple repetition of these phrases, but directing them at different people:

1. Start by directing the phrases at yourself.

2. Next, direct the *metta* toward someone you feel thankful for or someone who has helped you. (I usually visualize whomever I'm directing the blessings toward.)

3. Now think of someone you feel neutral about—someone you neither like nor dislike. This one can be harder than we think because we can be quick to judge people as either positive or negative in our lives.

4. Ironically, the next one can be easier: Visualize the people you don't like or with whom you are having a hard time. When someone in my life is causing me a bit of trouble, I tend to feel tremendous peace after sending them love.

5. Finally, direct the *metta* toward everyone universally: "*May all beings everywhere be happy.*"

I've found it can help to download a guided loving-kindness meditation (see christinecarter.com for free downloads) to do this the first time. Another good resource is Sharon Salzberg—she wrote *Loving-Kindness: The Revolutionary Art of Happiness*. But you don't need to read a book to do this now. Loving-kindness meditation isn't complicated. People write books about it because it is so powerful. It really isn't anything more than using your imagination to send love and well wishes.

Even if you aren't likely to sit in meditation every morning sending good thoughts to yourself and others, you can use *metta* throughout the day as a tactic to increase your feelings of well-being, compassion, and connection. Perhaps put a sticky note on your bathroom mirror or refrigerator door or car dashboard—wherever you tend to be most exhausted or overwhelmed or isolated—to remind you to pause and cultivate a loving thought or two.

(2) Give thanks. We sometimes forget that gratitude is another one of our most powerful positive emotions, and it's a great way to give to and connect with others. (If I thank you for doing me a favor, even a favor as small as picking up a pen I've dropped, you'll tend to like me a little better. That increases the odds that we'll experience positivity resonance.) So start giving thanks wherever you can. Text a thank-you if that is all you have time for, or pick up the phone, or send a note.

Gratitude letters are one of the most powerful interventions ever studied by the positive psychologists. Volunteers write a letter to someone whom they've never properly thanked for something (usually non-material) and then they read the letter out loud to the person. This brave act has been shown to bring most people a major boost of happiness—one that lasts as long as six months! Gratitude is a very social emotion, and when we give it freely, it dramatically increases our sense of connection to others.

A tip for giving good gratitude: When you thank someone for something they've done for you, be specific about the deed or gift you are giving thanks for *and* the qualities of the person you are praising. So if your husband puts away all the laundry because he knows that you hate this task, say something like, "Thank you so much for putting the laundry away. It was really thoughtful of you to do it, knowing I don't like to." Or if you see a child pick up a piece of litter, you could say, "Thank you for helping to clean up our park. You must really care about the earth, too." Or you could thank a colleague for helping you get a job by saying, "I really appreciate all the time you took to look over my résumé and help me practice interviewing. I know you are busy; you are one of the most generous people I know. Thank you for being such a great mentor."

(3) Give a micro-moment of love, care, or warmth.
I think the most important thing I've learned from Fredrickson's work on positivity resonance is that nearly every interaction we have with others holds the potential for a positive interaction. Strangers, neighbors, dogs, the local mail carrier, or the grocery bagger—all the people we meet in our day-to-day life can be approached with warmth, fondness, or compassion. Giving love is far easier than we tend to make it out to be; it can be as simple as touching a student on the shoulder, making eye contact and saying hello to a homeless person, giving a neighbor a hug, or petting a dog.

taking it too far, perhaps

My own attempts to love everyone around me have gotten so extreme that I have a reputation in my neighborhood. I recently met someone at a party who looked familiar; she suddenly exclaimed (interrupting herself mid-sentence), "I know you!" I assumed she'd been reading my blog or books. Instead she continued, "You're the friendly jogger! Our family calls you the friendly jogger!" I make an effort to make eye contact with and say hello to everyone I pass on my morning runs. I'm shooting for neighborly, but apparently I'm also quite loud and perhaps a bit too enthusiastic first thing in the morning. (I've since turned down my iPhone music; that should help with the volume level of my voice.)

Remember, there are two important conditions for us to be able to give and receive love: our safety, and a live connection. When we feel safe, we are able to move from trying to keep ourselves alive and well to the more happiness-producing goal of keeping *others* alive and well.

The live connection allows our warmth to amplify into positivity resonance. It allows us to use touch—our primary language for communicating love—as well as our body language, our voices, and our eye contact to express our interest and concern for others.

Touch is a particularly high-leverage area for giving, as the benefits to those we touch are so profound. When someone touches us warmly—by giving us a hug, a fist bump, or just a pat on the back—we tend to feel calmer and more resilient in the face of stress. Touch soothes cardiovascular stress by activating the vagus nerve and, if the touch goes on long enough, by triggering the release of oxytocin, a neurochemical nicknamed "the love hormone." It can even strengthen our immune system.

Because touch signals safety and trust, it helps us build cooperative relationships. Don't believe me? How about this amazing statistical analysis: The NBA basketball team players who touch one another most during games *also tend to win most often*. Similarly, psychologists can use touch to influence the outcome of games in which volunteers choose to cooperate or compete with others for money. When an experimenter quickly pats participants on the back as they are starting to play the game, they become far more likely to cooperate and share money with their partner than if they aren't touched.

Premature babies who get three daily fifteen-minute massages for about a week gain 47 percent more weight than those who receive only standard medical treatment. People who are anticipating a painful procedure tend to show brain activity in the regions associated with threat and stress—unless they have a romantic partner with them stroking their arm, in which case they show no re-action at all. And students whose teachers pat them in a friendly way are more likely to speak up in class: Touch gives them confidence.

All of this is to say that one of the easiest and most powerful gifts we can give others is our warm touch.

(4) Do a handful of favors that take five minutes or less each week. There are countless things we can do for others that take very little of our time. We can make an introduction, help a fellow traveler with their luggage, hold a door open, send a helpful article to a friend who's looking for information. We can do the Earth a favor by using a reusable shopping bag or water bottle. My friends ask me all the time to post information about their work on my social-media pages. It usually takes me less than five minutes, but it is a way I can give to my friends by supporting their work.

Acknowledging other people can also be a great gift. Public recognition is, for many people, the highest form of praise. So take two minutes to send an email to a co-worker who is doing great work, and copy the rest of your team. Or make a card for your kid's teacher, and invite the whole class to write on it something they love about him or her.

Five-minute favors, a term coined by Adam Grant, include random acts of kindness. Google the phrase "random acts of kindness" for literally millions of ideas. For example, check out the 26 Acts of Kindness (https://www.facebook.com/26acts/info) campaign related to the Newtown school shooting, where people did twenty-six small acts of kindness to honor the victims. They also built a community around giving, sharing their acts, and encouraging others to act.

Compile a list of easy things you can do in your day-to-day life, and consider doing them in clusters. Although cluster-giving like this may take you past the five-minute mark, research shows that people tend to get more bang for their happiness buck when they do a bunch of five-minute favors together once a week than just one a day. My kids and I call the times when we string together a dozen or so five-minute favors "kindness scavenger hunts." We make a nice long list of random acts of kindness (things like distributing care kits to homeless people and bringing vegetables from our garden to our neighbors) and then do as many as we possibly can in one afternoon, or a whole weekend if we are really into it.

A fun fact: *Asking for favors* can also strengthen your connections to other people. Because giving to others brings the giver such huge benefits, when we give others the chance to help us out, we are also giving them the opportunity to reap the benefits of being a giver. But asking people for favors also strengthens our connections by increasing our own likeability. Although we typically assume we do favors for people we like, it turns out that we also report liking someone more once we do them a favor! This phenomenon has been dubbed the "Franklin effect" because Benjamin Franklin once said, "He that has once done you a kindness will be more ready to do you another than he whom you yourself have obliged." Franklin was right.

(5) See if you can also fit in one or two fifteen-minute favors a month. Some favors aren't as effortless as a five-minute favor or random act of kindness, but they deliver a lot of bang for the buck. Multiple sclerosis (MS) patients who were trained to provide compassionate, unconditional, positive regard for other MS sufferers through monthly fifteen-minute telephone calls "showed pronounced improvement in self-confidence, self-esteem, depression and role functioning" over two years. These helpers were especially protected against depression and anxiety.

How can you help someone in a way that will take about fifteen to twenty minutes? Can you help your niece with her job search by reviewing her résumé? Listen attentively to a friend who's feeling a little isolated? Walk your neighbor's dog when he or she is under the weather?

(6) **Show compassion for strangers.** Although we seem to be inclined, biologically, to connect most easily with people who are most similar to us, we benefit tremendously when we extend our love to a diverse community of people whom we don't necessarily know. Nice people do nice things for their friends, family, and coworkers; truly giving people give significant chunks of their time, love, and money to people they don't even know.

The first step in becoming one of these Olympic-level givers is to be aware of other people's needs. To do that, we need to slow down enough to actually notice what those needs are. Over the holidays, an elderly friend of a friend I had met before but didn't really know kept leaving me vague indications that she'd like to talk to me "sometime." I gave her my cell phone number, "just in case." Finally she called. It turns out that she was thinking about her brother who had recently passed away, and she simply wanted to tell me a quick story about him because she thought I would appreciate his approach to life. Sometimes people's needs are surprising—and surprisingly easy to fill.

We need to expose ourselves to other people's suffering in order to understand what they really need. As Wendell Berry once said, "You have to be able to imagine lives that are not yours" to feel true compassion. Typically, we protect ourselves from pain and suffering (our own and other people's pain), but when we do this we also shelter ourselves from others' needs. Consider the counterintuitive notion that compassion is a positive emotion strongly correlated with happiness—but in order to feel compassion, we must also feel another person's suffering. In this way, we become connected to others.

Gregory Boyle, the Jesuit priest who founded Homeboy Industries, a chain of businesses that employ only gang members, and the author of the astonishing book *Tattoos on the Heart: The Power of Boundless Compassion*, writes:

> Compassion is not a relationship between the healer and the wounded. It's a covenant between equals . . . Compassion is always, at its most authentic, about a shift from the cramped world of self-preoccupation into a more expansive place of fellowship, of true kinship.

Compassion requires that we see our common humanity with those whom we might not previously have admired or even seen. In return, it delivers the profound and life-altering experience of oneness.

What does it mean to show compassion for strangers, practically speaking? Obviously, this deeper level of giving takes more time than a handful of five- or fifteen-minute favors. First notice and let yourself feel other people's needs, and then give what you have to help them. This might be work as a mentor, or volunteering in a soup kitchen. I do my regular work (speaking and writing) pro bono for people and organizations that don't have the budget to pay my regular fees. For me, this is much easier logistically than volunteering at a homeless shelter (although I do that whenever I can, too) even though it takes more time. I'm just better set up to do my regular work pro bono. Giving ourselves—showing compassion— doesn't have to be hard; sometimes it is the easiest thing.

(7) **Finally, give money.** This doesn't mean you need to be wealthy. It means you need to give generously from what you already have, even if it is not a lot of money in absolute terms.

Giving away money, no matter how little you have to

give, is an easy route to bliss if you do it from a place of generosity. Most of us have made a donation, say, to our college reunion committee because we felt badgered into it. Although this is not exactly the spirit of generosity I'm advocating, research shows that even that type of financial giving can make us happier. Even when we *think* that we'll be happier if we save our money, or we spend it on ourselves, we're usually wrong in this assumption. Giving money is one of the lowest-effort ways we have to feel happier.

This is pretty counterintuitive to Americans, most of whom pursue financial wealth like it is the holy grail. Most of us believe that when it comes to money and stuff, *more is better* and *there isn't enough* to go around. (These are two of what Lynne Twist calls the "three lies" that create feelings of scarcity.)

The feeling or perception of *lack* creates tremendous stress for us human beings that disrupts our focus, diminishes our self-control, and even lowers our IQ. Sendhil Mullainathan, a professor of economics at Harvard and recipient of the MacArthur Foundation "genius grant," does research with Princeton psychologist Eldar Shafir about what happens when people believe *there isn't enough*. The perception of scarcity "taxes our cognitive capacity and executive control, thus diminishing intelligence and impulse control, among other things," they write. So ask yourself: Do you think that you *don't have enough* money to give some of it away to a person or organization that needs it to further the greatest good of the world? To help someone else less fortunate than you?

If so, consider that there *is* enough, that you have enough, and find a way to give away some of your bounty. Remember that everything is relative; if you think that you don't have enough to give away or to make a difference, perhaps you are comparing yourself to people who seem like they have more than you. Instead of measuring or analyzing how much you have, try experiencing yourself as having enough. Can you give one dollar to the next homeless person you encounter? If not, can you give a warm smile and a blessing and a quarter? We always have enough to give something to others; the trick is in experiencing our own abundance.

Similarly, do you think it would be *better if you had more* money before you started giving generously? Twist describes the toxic myth that *more is better*:

> More of anything is better than what we have. It's the logical response if you fear there's not enough, but *more is better* drives a competitive culture of accumulation, acquisition, and greed that only heightens fears and quickens the pace of the race. And none of it makes life more valuable. In truth, the rush for more distances us from experiencing the deeper value of what we acquire or already have . . . *More is better* is a chase with no end and a race without winners.

The truth is that more of a good thing is not necessarily better. Often having just what we need is more meaningful and more enjoyable. When we appreciate that we actually do have what we need now, and we do have enough to give to others, we bring greater ease into our lives. More than that, we see that money is a tool we can use to express our highest values. Our perception that more would be better or we don't have enough is "an unexamined and false system of assumptions, opinions, and beliefs from which we view the world as a place where we are in constant danger of having our needs unmet," writes Twist.

The "more would be better" belief system that our culture fosters is demonstrated by a series of studies by researchers in Vancouver, British Columbia. In one study, the researchers asked people two things: If they were given five dollars or twenty dollars, would they be happier if they spent it on themselves or spent it on someone else (or a charity)? Second, would they be happier if they got twenty dollars rather than five dollars? The majority felt they'd be happier if they spent the money on themselves, and *more money would be better.*

But another study shows us how wrong most people are. This time people were given either five dollars or twenty dollars and were randomly instructed to spend the money on themselves or on someone else. Before they were given the money in the morning, participants took a quick test to assess their happiness. In the evening, the researchers called the study participants to assess their happiness again. You can probably guess by now who ended the day happier: the folks instructed to give their money away. By contrast, the people who received a gift of money to spend on themselves ended the day feeling measurably less happy than when they started it! Interestingly, the amount of money that participants got or gave made no difference whatsoever.

For all the research out there that attempts to determine whether or not money buys happiness, you'd think by now we'd realize that our happiness depends at least as much on *how we spend our money* as it does on how much money we have. Spending money on other people and making donations to charity reliably make us happier, while spending money on ourselves does not. So the next time you are tempted to think that it won't make a difference if you give just a small sum of money, remember: It *will* make a difference, especially for you! Givers— and our world's happiest people—give money to others.

And no matter how much money we have, there is plenty to be done without giving away one's own dollars.

My daughter's seventh-grade class is spectacularly re-
sourceful at *raising money to give away*. They have bake
sales regularly, and are making a real difference in our
community with their donations. Not only does our wider
community benefit from their efforts and donations, but
their school community is built in the process. When we
pool our money (and our efforts), we create a caring community of positive connections. More and more, these
caring communities are popping up and have a tremendous impact, from the 26 Acts of Kindness Facebook
page referenced above, to the One Fund Boston, created
to help victims of the Boston Marathon bombings. Only
nine days after the bombings, it had raised $20 million-
plus and had 50,000 donors.

You can also count your fund-raising efforts as financial giving. When you work to raise money to give away,
or plan events that generate money and donations for a
cause, or ask others to make financial donations, you are
giving some portion of your own finances, too, even if
only in the form of the time you could have been padding
your own wallet. I've served on the board of a school in
Ojai, California, long enough to witness (and participate
in) fund-raising for two capital campaigns. The sheer
amount of work it takes to raise funds for new buildings
and programs is striking. Very few philanthropists donate
without first being solicited. The work of cultivating and
soliciting donors is vital to the financial health of an organization. If it weren't for the fund-raisers who engage the
donors, the donations would likely never be made.

If you take only one thing away from this chapter, I hope it is
this: If you are feeling down, or sick, or unproductive, or unsuccess-
ful, a sure way to get your mojo back is by helping someone else.
The times when we are feeling low are precisely the times when
we benefit the most by doubling down on how much we give to
others.

THE EASIEST THING:
SMILE AT THE BARISTA

If you are feeling intimidated by the idea of becoming an Olympic-level giver in order to make your life feel easier, you aren't alone. Perhaps the thought of hugging everyone everywhere kinda grosses you out. No worries: You hardly have to spend any time at all to start reaping the benefits of giving love.

Researchers sent people into a Starbucks with five dollars each to buy themselves a latte. Half were instructed to get their beverage as fast as they could, to "get in, get out, go on with the day." The other half were instructed to "have a genuine interaction with the cashier"—to smile and initiate a brief conversation. The folks who smiled at the barista left Starbucks feeling more cheerful. In the words of the study authors Michael Norton and Elizabeth Dunn: "Efficiency, it seems, is overrated."

The takeaway is that often the easiest way for us to connect with others is to slow down *just enough* to make eye contact with someone, smile, and, if we're feeling brave, start a little conversation.

Feeling blocked? We humans often badly want better relationships, but we knock ourselves down before we are even out the gate. Our connections are incredibly important for our health, happiness, and success, but sometimes we push others away rather than deepening our connections with them. The next chapter is about how we can build stronger connections even in the situations where we tend to push other people away.

CHAPTER 7

mending ruptures

The only things that really matter in life are your relationships with
other people.

—George E. Vaillant

In *Triumphs of Experience*, George Vaillant writes that "there are
two pillars of happiness revealed by the seventy-five-year-old Grant
Study. . . . One is love. The other is finding a way of coping with life
that does not push love away."

We all do things—perhaps daily—that push the people we love
away from us. We sneak "harmless" glances at our smartphones
while playing games with our children. We forget to take thirty seconds to greet our spouse warmly when we haven't seen her or him
all day. We decline a call from our friend or grandmother because
we don't feel like mustering the energy to truly listen. This modern
world we live in is full of common situations and experiences which,
if not handled well, create resistance rather than ease, impairing
the strength that a relationship brings us. Tiny unrepaired ruptures
in our relationships drive love and connection *out* of our lives. I
think of these behaviors as "connection dis-ease." One small behavior doesn't necessarily indicate that a relationship is diseased, of
course, just that our precious connection with another person is
experiencing friction or fray. We saw in the last chapter that our
relationships have tremendous potential to make our lives easier
and more joyful. But when our connections rupture a little—as *all*
relationships do from time to time—they can cause more strain

than ease. Consider this chapter your guide to preventing these ruptures—and to repairing day-to-day relationship rifts.

CONNECTION DIS-EASE #1: TECHNOLOGY MISUSE

You know the feeling: You're having a drink with an old friend, and her cell phone keeps buzzing. She's left her thirteen-year-old daughter home alone, so she keeps checking her phone, just to make sure everything is okay. But then a text comes in from one of her colleagues who is working late on a problematic project. Your friend feels the need to answer her questions. In the end, you feel you had only half her attention. It was good to see her, but the friendship isn't what it once was.

Or you are having dinner with your extended family, and everyone is excited that the college kids are home and wants to catch up with them. But throughout dinner, the kids can't resist the pull of Snapchat, laughing at photos that school friends send and trying to share them before they fade. Soon, all the adults have their phones out, too, just to check what's happening on *their* social media feeds or to post a picture of the college students on their Facebook page. No one really gets to catch up with the kids.

Or you've taken your kids to the beach on their day off from school—something you promised you'd do ages ago. Ten minutes into the outing, someone from work calls, and instead of listening to the family audiobook you'd selected for the road trip, you spend the time in the car on the phone. The kids are fine with this—they have video games to play. Once at the beach, the kids play while you try to work from your phone, caught in a snare of texts and emails. You spend the day squinting at a spreadsheet on a tiny screen instead of building castles in the sand.

In all these situations, and many others we've all experienced, our smartphones and laptops and tablets and all the social media they carry disrupt the very social connections they promise to create. They make us available to work 24/7, which might seem like a bonus to our relationships because now we can have our work and our family time at the beach, too—in theory. But actually, technology can damage our relationships *and* our work. We don't really experience our family time, and the work we do at the beach isn't our best. Rather than bringing us together, new technologies often create an illusion of togetherness, but without the joys, benefits, and, frankly, the challenges that real relationships bring.

Our technology addiction erodes the most important pillar of our ease—connection with others. Each time our phone dings, we get a nice hit of dopamine, a neurochemical that activates the reward system in our brain. It feels good, but it also makes us less willing to return to the much more demanding world of live conversation. Real-life friendship has a lot of benefits, but instant gratification is rarely one of them. Our live relationships can be exhausting compared to our online "friends." At the end of the day, it is so much less taxing to text a friend than to actually call her. It is so much less draining to update our Facebook page and reap the instant satisfaction of dozens of "likes" than to share our ideas and interests with our actual neighbors. In the *short* run, it seems easier to connect with others through technology, but we need to be clear that this is a *false ease*. In the *long* run, these behaviors have little power, and they introduce strain into our relationships.

Sherry Turkle, an MIT sociologist and author of *Alone Together*, writes:

[We] *avoid the vulnerability and messiness of "real" contact and intimacy while getting the sweet satisfaction of a neurochemical high from being connected digitally to more and more people. We can hide from each other, even while we are tethered together.*

This hiding from others (and sometimes from our own feelings) that technology can facilitate is a pernicious poison. Fortunately, the technology itself is not at all the problem. We need only to use it differently.

THE ANTIDOTE: USE GADGETS TO FACILITATE REAL-LIFE CONNECTIONS

Turkle ends her book with a call to be more *deliberate* in our technology use. Technology *can* foster true connection, of course—Skype and Google Hangouts have been a real breakthrough for me in the way I connect with the people I work with. *Deliberate* technology use is about using technology strategically; for most of us, that means using it less. Here's how:

> **Carve out sacred spaces** to be truly present with your own feelings and the people you are with. See Chapter 5 for more about this, but the gist is to create technology-free zones and times in your life when you can pay mindful attention to what is happening in real time. Being really present with people means that when we are on the phone with them, we don't do anything else. It means initiating real, face-to-face conversations with people, even though they can bring conflict, even though they can be tiring. When we are really present, we stop interrupting ourselves and others all the time. It might be gratifying to sneak a peek at your texts, but we don't *have* to react to our devices all the time. We can command them instead of always letting them command us.
>
> We can *choose* to act on our highest values rather than on our desire for gratification. The other day I was talking to my mom on the phone; she had been traveling in Cuba and I hadn't seen or spoken with her in a while. She called in the middle of the workday, and I answered my cell phone at my desk. It was dang hard for me to stop going through my emails while she told me about her trip, so it was also difficult for me to really listen to her, even though I was just deleting promotional emails. But then I stopped myself, realizing that I was introducing dis-ease into my own life and into my connection with my mother. I also realized how annoyed I'd be if *she* was

cleaning out her email inbox while I was telling her about a recent adventure. What hit me was that she would *never* do that: She values our relationship too much. She's too interested in what I have to say. Ultimately, I changed my behavior because of my values. I stepped away from my computer with the conviction that my relationship with my mother deserved more than just 70 percent of my attention.

Practice being alone. When we don't learn how to tolerate (and even relish) solitude, we often feel lonely. "Solitude—the ability to be separate, to gather yourself—is where you find yourself so that you can reach out to other people and form real attachments," explains Turkle. "When we don't have the capacity for solitude, we turn to other people in order to feel less anxious or in order to feel alive. When this happens, we're not able to appreciate who they are. It's as though we're using them as spare parts to support our fragile sense of self."

Spend time alone at home and in the car unconnected. Learn to tolerate the initial boredom that may come; it will pass. Go on a hike or to the beach without a cell phone. Deep down I think we all have a deep, dark terror of being alone, and that we are hardwired to stay with our clan. But when we experience our ability to turn inward—which we can do only when we find the silence and stillness of solitude—we realize that we are never really alone. We feel our innate connectedness. So we need to catch ourselves when we "slip into thinking that always being connected is going to make us feel less alone," writes Turkle. "It's the opposite that's true. If we're not able to be alone, we're going to be more lonely."

Limit the time you spend in virtual worlds. Virtual realities, video games, and social media are addictive. In the short term it can be far more rewarding to spend time in a fantasy world—rewarding in the way that a sugary soda is rewarding (but very unhealthy if over-consumed). Virtual realities allow us to put on our best performances, showing the world the moment when we looked (or imagined ourselves to look) pretty or felt proud. If we're feeling lonely, we can easily "connect" with dozens of online "friends." More than that, we can avoid the problems of real people and real relationships in all their untidiness and vulnerability and pain (and all our own messiness, as well).

But the reality (no pun intended) is that our vulnerabilities create real intimacy and draw us together, and when we avoid the messiness that real-life relationships require, we end up isolated and disconnected. So be very deliberate: Use online games, social media, and virtual realities to facilitate *live connections with real people,* choosing real connections and real people over fake ones. Use Facebook to deepen your connection with a faraway friend by sharing articles, photos, and videos that you think she will appreciate. Play online games with your son rather than a stranger. Use Match.com to make new connections, but then actually meet those connections live, in person, instead of constraining your relationships to online forums.

CONNECTION DIS-EASE #2: BUSYNESS AND OVERWORK

Time starvation is a nearly universal complaint among working parents. We just don't have enough time to maintain our friendships. We want to spend time with our kids when we get home from work, and we don't have the energy to deal with the hassle of lining up a sitter on the weekends. Not to mention the complexity and logistical nightmare that scheduling with other parents can be.

If this is you, ask yourself: Is my busyness adding to my sense of connectedness, or is it preventing me from maintaining friendships and relationships with my family? For some people, busyness—long commutes and long work hours and endless time in the car driving kids to lessons and practices—leaves them little time for positive connections. Other people may be just as busy—they work and volunteer and go to their kids' games and see their friends regularly—but their activities *facilitate their friendships* rather than hinder them. This type of busyness is evidence of a dynamic and connected life rather than a life that is too busy for friendship.

THE ANTIDOTE: FIND FRIENDSHIP EFFICIENCIES

I love looking for efficiencies in my relationships—things that bring ease to what is often a scheduling nightmare. I'm a big fan of "ritualized relationships"—relationships that are maintained through predictable time together. I'm in a discussion group that meets on the first Monday of every month. I have lunch with a good friend most Thursdays, and I hike every Saturday morning with another friend. My husband and I have date nights every other Saturday and every other Monday. We have dinner with my parents every other Wednesday night, and with Mark's mom and sister's family every other Sunday. I work out with a friend on Tuesday and Thursday mornings. I get together with my whole group of best friends reliably four times a year: for a Christmas party the Saturday before Christmas in San Francisco; for our annual gratitude fest the weekend before Thanksgiving in Chico; for a three-day camping trip on Indigenous People's Day weekend in Santa Cruz; for a five-day vacation in May.

All these "ritualized relationship" events are on "repeat" on my Google calendar. They took time and effort to establish but now are fairly automated. Does this mean I never miss a date or a lunch or a hike with a friend? Honestly, because of my travel schedule and the vagaries of life with four children, I probably miss more than I actually attend. But I also know that I see my friends lots more than I would if I didn't already have time carved out on the calendar with them. Our full lives can make scheduling a hassle, and this tactic makes it all a heck of a lot easier.

Also in the friendship efficiencies department, many of my friendships are multi-tasking ones. I'm usually either getting some exercise or eating with my friends. And as long as we are truly present wherever we are—meaning we aren't texting during the time we scheduled to be with our spouse, or we aren't trying to work during an outing with our friends—the killing-two-birds-with-one-stone approach to friendship can bring efficiency and ease. We have to eat lunch anyway, so why not eat with a friend? Why not catch up with your neighbor while you walk the dogs? Why not make friends with the people you volunteer with, so that volunteering becomes built-in social time?

CONNECTION DIS-EASE #3: ENVY

We've all felt it: the sting of envy and jealousy, of wanting what another already has. Jealous feelings also come from a scarcity mindset (which has an evolutionary basis; scarcity was a major reality for eons), a belief that *more is better* and *there is not enough* in the world for you and me *both* to be successful, or wealthy, or beautiful—or whatever it is that we envy. Jealous feelings make us feel competitive and separate from others instead of connected and loving.

THE ANTIDOTE: CELEBRATE OTHER PEOPLE'S SUCCESS

First, try shifting your perspective from one of scarcity to one of sufficiency, or abundance. Do this by recognizing that there are enough resources in the world for you to have or be what you ultimately long for. For example, when we recognize success, beauty, or strength in another person, we can acknowledge that we are working toward the same thing in our own lives. Recently, a happiness expert was featured on national television, and a half dozen friends called me to share their vicarious envy. "It should be you," they said.

"Your work is so much more substantive and practical."

"She's so annoying."

"Doesn't it drive you crazy to see her up there?"

I did what I do whenever this sort of thing happens. I take the success of other happiness experts as signs from the universe that similar success is coming to me. I can find ample evidence that there is room for the success of *many* happiness experts in this world. More than that, I genuinely appreciate the success I have already found, and I feel like it is enough. It is just right for me right now—I have a lot of work, and I like having as much time with my family as I do. This doesn't mean I lack ambition or don't want to continue to grow in my career. It just means that I feel grateful for how far I've already come, for friends who think so highly of my work, and for how much I've already achieved. I actually sometimes have to tell my friends all this out loud—because sometimes I have to remind myself, too—and allow them to laugh it off along with me.

Some of you are probably thinking, *Easy for you to say, Carter. You're a published author who's been on TV!* So what if you haven't experienced "success" in the same way I have? Work with the small voice of jealousy in your head. What do you have that others envy? When it comes down to it, what are you grateful for in your own life?

This perspective frees us up to celebrate when other people succeed or are beautiful or strong. It's not that I don't feel an initial hit of envy; I'm human. But after I acknowledge how I'm feeling, I can choose to celebrate in response, to participate in another person's happiness. This is something that one of my favorite happiness teachers, James Baraz, coauthor of *Awakening Joy,* calls "vicarious joy": when our emotions mirror the expansive happiness of others. (And by the way, vicarious joy is a great way to increase the flow of positive emotions in your life, as discussed in Chapter 2.)

In our closest relationships we can choose to take this a step further and actively celebrate our loved one's successes. Researchers have noticed that happy couples do this: They yell things like "Woo-hoo!" when their partner shares good news. We know to do this with the children in our lives, but for some reason we think that adults don't need this kind of celebration. Wrong. One "Nicely done!" can go a long way.

There are two key pieces of advice to take away from that finding. The first is when you have good news, share it because it will make you happier. This is Savoring 101. Positive emotions are amplified when we share them with others.

The second piece of advice concerns how to *respond* to good news from our friends and romantic partners, and it's a key to making our relationships happier. When a friend or spouse shares positive news with us, we don't actually have to whoop or cheer, as my mother and I are prone to do, but we do need to respond enthusiastically. It isn't enough to be positive and loving but not particularly emotive. It's not enough to smile quietly and assume that our loved one knows we are glad for them. Silent support doesn't count in this realm. Our response to good news needs to be *active*. We need to articulate our joy and support verbally, and maybe even demonstrate it physically with a hug or excited body language.

Enthusiastic responses—such as saying "I'm really happy for you!"—make people feel even better about the event or news they are sharing, and it puts the sharer into a better mood. Couples who make a big deal celebrating positive things in life score higher than others on intimacy and relationship satisfaction. They are also less likely to break up.

So pop open a bottle of champagne when that hard-earned promotion comes. Take a walk together to celebrate a particularly wonderful day. Jump up and down a little—and hug—when your partner reaches his or her exercise goal, commending their great effort or strategy or hard work (rather than their innate talent). They feel loved and we benefit from the connection we are nurturing; life feels just a tad easier in the wake of the shared moment.

And what about when things go wrong and the news isn't so good? Still, be very responsive. Make sure that your friends and spouse feel understood, their abilities and opinions are valued, and you've made them feel cared for.

CONNECTION DIS-EASE #4:
DISAPPOINTMENT

We've all felt it: disappointment when our best friend *doesn't* celebrate our success or our spouse forgets our birthday, or frustration when our children seem to take us for granted, or hurt when our lover isn't nearly as romantic as the guy next door seems to be. We can start to feel entitled in our closest relationships—which means that we are more likely to feel disappointed or frustrated when our nearest and dearest friends and family members don't act the way we want them to, rather than grateful when they do. This sort of disappointment can—and often does—have the opposite effect from what we are looking for: It pushes love away from us, making life feel harder.

THE ANTIDOTE: CONSCIOUSLY PRACTICE GRATITUDE (AGAIN)

My buddy Jack recently stopped by for tea to show me his wedding pictures and tell me all about his new love—a whirlwind sixty-something romance, a second great love after the death of his beloved wife of twenty-five years. My friend has written books about relationships and has actually figured out how to make a marriage great. He said something that really struck me.

"I text her several times every day," he said, his voice emotional. "I say, 'I love you.' 'You are beautiful.' 'And *thank you*.'"

"I'm so grateful," he told me, "to have a new partner in my life. I feel that every day. It isn't hard for me to find reasons that I love her, or to tell her that I find her beautiful. I'm just so grateful to have her in my life."

Similarly, the late Lee Lipsenthal—a wonderful doctor and teacher of work-life balance—told me and some colleagues about his gratitude for his wife a few months before he passed away. "I'm so grateful for the love in my life," he told us repeatedly. "I have had a great marriage."

For years—maybe a decade—Lee had a very specific way of cultivating his gratitude for his wife (with whom, by the way, he didn't always see eye to eye, so much so that he once almost left her, as he disclosed in *Enjoy Every Sandwich*). Every morning, he would wake up and meditate. But instead of getting out of bed, he would open his arms, and his wife would roll over onto his chest and go back to sleep. Lee would then do a forty-five-minute "gratitude meditation" with her on his chest as he thought about her and all that he appreciated about her.

Lee may or may not have expressed his gratitude out loud to his wife; I don't know if he did. The key thing was that he *cultivated his own deep feelings of gratitude for her* on a daily basis. Research suggests that it is *feeling* gratitude for our partner—not necessarily expressing it to him or her—that predicts how satisfied we feel with our relationship and how satisfied our partner feels as well.

Let me say that again. When we cultivate feelings of gratitude toward people, we feel more satisfied with our relationships, and—amazingly—our friends and partners feel more connected to us and more satisfied with the relationship, too. We are taught to think that our feelings of love or affection or fondness are entirely dependent on the character and behavior of the other, but the truth is that we can cultivate these feelings.

This doesn't mean that we should skip telling our partner how much we appreciate him or her: Research also suggests that expressing gratitude to a romantic partner (or a close friend or colleague) can make us feel more satisfied with the relationship and increase our sense of responsibility for our partner's well-being. But the real takeaway, in my mind, is that simply feeling gratitude can improve our relationship.

I have to confess to something: After I talked with these two amazing men about their deep gratitude for their wives, I felt disappointed and frustrated with my husband. The subtext of my sentiment: *I'm a great wife. I'm entitled to more. More would be better. What I do have isn't enough.* I did take notes about how to practice gratitude in my own relationship, but I also wanted *my husband to express more gratitude for me.*

Relationships are hard. People (usually unintentionally) disappoint us all the time. They forget to acknowledge us when we most need acknowledging. They forget to bring us what we need, or do what they said they were going to do. Even when unintended, it hurts our relationships nonetheless.

But what I've learned about gratitude's role when we feel disappointed with another is this: Connection starts within our own self. When we consciously foster feelings of appreciation for our loved ones—whether by doing a gratitude meditation about them every morning or by deliberately focusing on specific things we love about them—our relationship is less strained by daily disappointments.

CONNECTION DIS-EASE #5: PREDICTABILITY AND BOREDOM

One of the greatest things about our long-term romantic relationships is that they can provide comfort and predictability in this wild world. But let's face it: Long-term relationships can get a little boring. Within nine to eighteen months, research suggests, 87 percent of couples lose that knee-quaking excitement they felt when they first fell madly in love. It isn't that these relationships are *bad,* necessarily; they are just stale. Still edible, but not nearly as delectable as they were fresh out of the oven.

It isn't just in our romantic relationships, either. In most aspects of our lives, we get used to the surroundings and circumstances that stay the same; researchers call this "hedonic adaptation." What was once new and exciting—be it a lover, a new pair of shoes, a new neighborhood, or a new job—nearly always loses its luster over time.

The key word there, though, is *nearly:* 13 to 20 percent of people in long-term marriages successfully keep the fires of passion alive. (This doesn't mean that 80 percent of couples are unhappy; it just means that their relationships aren't particularly sexy or passionate.) And although we adapt to most things in life, we tend *not* to adapt to circumstances and situations that involve "variable, dynamic, and effortful engagement." So we tend not to succumb to hedonic adaptation when we do things like take an engaging class or while we are learning a new sport, according to researcher Ken Sheldon, who studies the phenomenon.

All this means that the very predictability that makes our long-term relationships comforting can also make us feel bored and uninterested in our spouses—which, of course, causes disconnection and even conflict. The destructive way to deal with relationship boredom is to seek romantic excitement and novelty outside the relationship. Fortunately, there are better solutions to this common problem.

THE ANTIDOTE: SHAKE THINGS UP. MAYBE A LOT

The good news is that it's *fun* to stoke the fires of your relationship. The bad news is that you'll have to give up some of the comfort (or, if not that, the complacency) that has settled into your relationship. Here's how:

- **Make yourself vulnerable** (just like you probably were on that first date!). Vulnerability can be uncomfortable because it involves, by definition, emotional exposure, uncertainty, and risk. (Remember: Vulnerability is not weakness! See Chapter 9 if you struggle with that.) Vulnerability allows trust and intimacy to develop and deepen.

  A simple (if not always easy) way to make ourselves vulnerable in our relationships is to bare ourselves emotionally. What can you reveal to your long-term love that he or she doesn't already know about you? Ask your beloved intimate questions to which you aren't sure you know the answer. (I put a little rubber-banded pile of preprinted question cards from the *TableTopics Couples* game in my purse for just this purpose. My husband always rolls his eyes and resists at first, but I persist and we actually manage to talk about something other than work or the kids.)

  Or do something mildly risky. Go on an adventure for your next vacation, to an unknown place that feels a little daunting. Visit a karaoke bar for your next date night, and actually sing. Try a new sport (where you risk feeling silly or uncoordinated). Do something thrilling, like ziplining or bungee-jumping.

Vulnerability works in part because it creates a similar biochemistry and physiology as when you and your beloved were first falling in love. Researchers think it is likely that we tend to conflate the high arousal induced by doing something risky with the high arousal of intense attraction. The two states feel similar. Either way, an adrenaline rush is good for a relationship that has lost momentum.

- **Routinize variety.** As you saw in Chapters 3 and 4, I'm a huge fan of productive routines and positive habits, and I advocate them in relationships as well, with one caveat. Your relationship habits routinely need to introduce variety, or you'll start feeling entitled and bored. A variety habit. Think that's an oxymoron?

It isn't. You may have a gratitude ritual at bedtime, where you tell your love before sleep something you appreciate about them. Challenge yourself to come up with something new every day. Or perhaps you have a weekly date night. It might be cozy and comfortable to always go to the same Italian restaurant on the corner, but you're gonna need to shake it up a little bit. Keep the date night, but always do something different. Vary the restaurant, vary the activity. Do what you'd do to impress a new date.

Even if you aren't up for the risk of an adventure or the intensity of emotional exposure, make sure there is a little *excitement* in your relationship routines. When researchers have couples create lists of things that they find exciting to do (maybe skiing, or trying a new restaurant, or going to a part of the city they rarely visit), the couples who actually did something together from their list of exciting activities were more likely to agree with statements like "I feel happy when I am doing something to make my partner happy" and "I feel 'tingling' and have 'an increased heartbeat' when I think of my partner."

- **Surprise your significant other** (and maybe yourself at the same time). This is no more complicated than making an effort not to be so predictable. Throw them off their game a bit by blindfolding them on the way to your date night. Similarly, a good friend and her husband trade off date-night planning, and don't tell the other anything about the date. They might not end up doing anything outlandish, but the element of surprise makes the situation novel and exciting. Research shows that when ambiguity is introduced into something positive, the uncertainty in and of itself tends to increase our pleasure.

  While you're at it, look for unintended surprises in your significant other. You might be doing something you've done with her 1,001 times, but challenge yourself to find something new about the way she is doing it. Our brains are pattern finders, and they often see only what they expect to see. We find new people and situations more interesting and exciting because we don't know yet what patterns we'll find in their behavior (researchers call this the "lure of ambiguity"). When we find something new about a familiar person, we'll tend to find him or her more interesting.

In romantic relationships, all these strategies can be tried in the bedroom, of course. Lovemaking is one of the most significant ways that most couples stay connected, but like the relationship itself, it can get stale over time. Shake things up in your sex life by making yourself vulnerable, taking risks, changing up your routines, and adding elements of surprise.

Finally, do these things as a way to deepen your connection and closeness in your relationship rather than to avoid conflict or rejection. When our relationship goals are positive (for example, we want to have fun) rather than negative (we're trying to avoid a fight or prevent someone from leaving us), we tend to be much more satisfied with our relationships and feel less lonely and insecure. And there's nothing boring about that.

CONNECTION DIS-EASE #6: ANNOYANCES AND IRRITATIONS

Too often, many of us find ourselves annoyed by our nearest and dearest. Our spouses can be a nearly endless source of irritations, as can our children and co-workers. They leave their dirty laundry in the wrong places, they make too much noise, they don't do what we want them to do when we want them to do it, and they complain or give us those *looks* when we are watching the TV shows that happen to fit our particular demographic and fancy.

When the people around us bug us, many of us lash out. "Turn that down!" "How many times do I have to ask you to clear your dishes!?" "Please just be quiet!" When we nag and criticize, we often create distance between ourselves and our loved ones and co-workers. We make them defensive and resentful, and often equally annoyed with us. We may not particularly like ourselves in these times, but it's hard not to take the bait.

THE ANTIDOTE: ACCEPTANCE

Because I'm a highly sensitive person, I'm also easily irritated, and so I've had to develop ways of coping that don't push the people I love the most away from me. It hasn't been easy, and my children would definitely confirm that I'm not perfect! But it is a relief to have ways of coping that don't involve making other people feel bad.

When someone is bugging me, my first step is always to simply focus on my breathing and my physical experience. Where am I feeling the irritation in my body? Where is the tension? Simply feeling my feet on the floor and connecting back to my physical self grounds me in the present moment.

If you have trouble feeling irritation (or emotion) in your body, try using 3-1-6 breathing: Breathe in for three slow counts, hold for one count, and then exhale deeply for six counts. Repeat this at least three times.

The key is to put the brakes on any fight-or-flight response that might be brewing due to the irritation. To this end, I make a conscious attempt to slow and deepen my breathing, look for humor in a given situation, and cultivate compassionate feelings toward myself and the target of my irritation.

Compassion comes more easily when we give others the benefit of the doubt for their irritating behavior. What is a reasonable explanation for their totally annoying conduct? Sometimes others simply have a bad habit that is proving hard to break despite their positive intentions. Other times people do irritating things because they are rushed or stressed (like kids who forget to clear their dishes before they leave for school) or worried or preoccupied with something unrelated (like the spouse who forgets to make the bed before leaving for work). In these cases, we can give them the gift of compassion and forgiveness. Stress doesn't feel good to anyone, and most people have experienced the frustration of not being able to break a bad habit.

Sometimes our annoyance with others is actually displaced anger or irritation with ourselves. I am never so frustrated with my children's dawdling as when I haven't left enough time for myself. My good friend Ginger gets angriest with her husband when she feels inadequate herself. In these cases, we do best to direct the compassion toward ourselves, not necessarily as a way to feel better but because it is the *most effective way* to handle this sort of situation (see Chapter 10 for more about how and why to practice self-compassion).

Other times, we just need to own the irritation as a sign of our own unmet needs. I'm rarely annoyed with my family when I'm well-fed and well-rested, but when I'm hungry and tired, I tend to get what my kids call "hangry." (As in, "Someone get Mom a snack. She's hangry and about to make us clean our rooms.") Mindfulness still helps here, as does self-compassion. But the main thing is that I figure out what I need in order to feel less irritable, and then make that happen.

My husband gets irritated with the kids when they sing or play games too loudly (with four kids and all their friends, our household gets very loud very quickly). In cases like this, the best policy is to embrace the imperfections of others as what makes them beautiful—while also acknowledging that whatever (and whoever) is bugging us will not last forever. This perspective is what the Japanese call wabi sabi, or the aesthetic of finding beauty in an object or a person's flaws. In his book *Wabi Sabi Simple,* Richard Powell writes that wabi sabi "nurtures all that is authentic by acknowledging three simple realities: nothing lasts, nothing is finished, and nothing is perfect." The loud, totally unconscious singing of the kids is what makes them beautiful. It is temporary—neither their singing nor their time at home with us will last. And it is both unfinished and imperfect; their singing will improve (possibly) as they grow, but for now the children (and their singing) are works in progress.

Researchers call a similar tactic "mental subtraction." When someone or something is irritating you, imagine your life without it. How would you feel? What would you miss? What if the kids were too anxious or unhappy to sing all the time? Or worse, what if they didn't live with us at all? Imagining something "subtracted" from our lives tends to make us profoundly grateful that it is in our life at all, even if that same thing is a little irritating at times.

I find the wabi sabi perspective to be the ultimate form of acceptance. Acceptance is a form of surrender to *what is* and to the present moment that can bring us profound peace where before there was irritation. As neuropsychologist Rick Hanson, author of *Hardwiring Happiness,* writes:

Accepting people does not mean agreeing with them, approving of them, waiving your own rights, or downplaying their impact upon you. You can still take appropriate actions to protect or support yourself or others. Or you can simply let people be. Either way, you accept the reality of the other person. You may not like it, you may not prefer it, you may feel sad or angry about it, but at a deeper level, you are at peace with it. That alone is a blessing. And sometimes, your shift to acceptance can help things get better.

Irritations are inevitable, but they don't need to block love from our lives. When we accept people along with all their annoying habits and behaviors, and manage our own feelings, we strengthen our connection with them.

CONNECTION DIS-EASE #7: UNRESOLVED CONFLICT

Sometimes our irritation is more profound, and we experience conflicts with our friends, neighbors, family, or co-workers, many of which can be quite wounding. Often, conflict begins as criticism; criticism is destructive to relationships when we turn a specific complaint into a global one, or when we attack someone's character ("You always forget to call! You are so self-centered!"). People who receive destructive criticism report greater anger and stress and say that they are likely to handle future disagreements with the person who criticized them by avoiding or resisting the person (rather than through collaboration and compromise). Recipients of destructive criticism also tend to set lower goals and perceive themselves as less efficacious. In other words, harsh criticism doesn't work.

Nor is it productive to seek revenge or stuff down your hurt feelings. And avoiding conflict altogether seldom works. Given that differing opinions, conflicting needs, hurt feelings, and even nasty arguments can happen in even the closest relationships, it is critical that we adopt ways to handle conflict constructively. The news here is good: Most of the time, we have considerable *choice* in how we act and feel in the face of a conflict.

THE ANTIDOTE: PROBLEM-SOLVE *TOGETHER*

When you're trying to resolve a conflict with someone, it can help to begin by understanding what type of problem it is. There are really only four types of conflicts:

(1) **One-time, solvable problems.** I think many of us bullheaded people assume that all problems are solvable.

They're not. But some are. These tend to be the types of conflicts that arise from a unique situation rather than differences in our personalities.

Say you and a co-worker disagree about a marketing strategy. This is a solvable conflict. You may disagree or even argue about it, but eventually you'll come to a decision.

(2) Cyclical conflicts. If it turns out that the marketing strategy conflict is actually about how to treat competitors, however—your boss is aggressively competitive by nature, and you are a natural collaborator—it won't be a one-time, solvable conflict. Marriage researchers and counselors John and Julie Gottman call these problems among married people "perpetual issues." Unlike solvable problems, they are based on fundamental differences in your personalities, emotional needs, or ideas about how you'd like to live life—and they will never, ever go away. Period. Accept that now.

They can become workable, however. The classic example of this is the slob who is married to a neatnik. She wants the house hospital-clean; he leaves piles everywhere. Being neat is hard (and potentially unimportant) for him but easy and essential for her.

Even if he commits to putting his stuff away, she can't turn him into a neatnik, so this is a problem that will wax and wane. His efforts to be neat will gradually fade as he gets busy or stressed or just lazy. She'll get frustrated, and the conflict will resurface. He'll redouble his efforts, and the conflict will fade again, and so on.

The question is not whether you can get the problem to go away completely—you can't—but whether or not you can establish a constructive dialogue about it and make periodic headway toward solving it.

In other words, can you arrive at a workable solution, knowing that you will continue to revisit this throughout your time together? Cyclical conflicts can actually create connection and intimacy. You've worked together to improve a problem, and that feels good.

(3) If you can't work with a recurring conflict, either because your pair hasn't found a solution or someone in the pair doesn't want to, you've got a **deal-breaker** issue on the table. Abuse, for instance, is a deal breaker that sometimes masquerades as a cyclical conflict.

Other deal breakers aren't so obvious. I have a friend who didn't feel close to her husband except when she was very upset and let him come to her rescue. She got tired of having to be stressed-out (or freaking out) in order to feel connected to him, and she realized that this was a deal breaker for her. If they couldn't move the problem into a different category—making it a cyclical conflict based on their personality differences—she didn't want to be in the relationship.

(4) Wounding problems are similar to cyclical ones in that they can be fights you have with someone over and over and over. The difference is that you never really make any headway on the issue.

Wounding problems generate frustration and hurt, they get worse over time, and they lead to feeling unloved, unaccepted, and misunderstood. These conflicts are characterized by the presence of the four things that the Gottmans have long found to predict divorce: defensiveness, contempt, criticism, and stonewalling (think of talking to a stone wall. The other person is totally disengaged).

Many people can move their wounding problems into the cyclical conflict category by learning how to fight differently (see below). When we raise our conflicts with genuine respect and appreciation, we tend to engage in radically different discussions than when we launch headlong into a fight and hope to "win" it, blaming and vilifying the other and going right for the jugular.

It's more constructive—and less stressful—when confronting a conflict to frame it not as picking a fight but rather *collaborating on a problem-solving effort.* Here is the method I've devised using John Gottman's research to initiate problem solving without actually starting a knock-down-drag-out.

HOW TO PICK A FIGHT (WITHOUT PICKING A FIGHT)

If you are the one with the gripe, what you'll essentially be doing is issuing a complaint. This is very different from offering criticism. A complaint is specific to one particular situation and can be raised in such a way that doesn't trigger fight or flight in the other person. Criticism, on the other hand, can feel like character assassination and lead to other behaviors that destroy connection: defensiveness, stonewalling, and contempt.

There are three things to keep in mind when you are about to issue a complaint. Say your partner has not been pulling his or her weight in the kitchen lately, and you are starting to feel frustrated and resentful every time you find yourself cleaning up the dinner dishes while he or she watches TV.

(1) **Start with an appreciation AND an "I statement."** How you begin is important. According to John Gottman, 96 percent of the time the first three minutes of a conversation can determine the fate of it all— whether or not a massive fight erupts, constructive solutions are found, or apologies are issued and accepted. Express gratitude, and then use that same "I statement" that we ask kids to use ("I felt X when you did Y because . . ."). *The key is not to strike a match, even if you are angry.*

WHAT NOT TO SAY:

"You never help me in the kitchen anymore, you lazy jerk."

AN APPRECIATION + AN "I STATEMENT":

"I appreciate how much time you are spending at work. I know you are putting in long hours for our family, and I'm grateful for that. I want you to be able to relax at the end of the day. But I felt angry and resentful tonight when you didn't help me clean up the kitchen because I *also* want to relax."

(2) Remain calm. Or find a way to calm down. Remember, you have a problem you need to solve. For that, you'll need the more evolved part of your brain to be in good working order, which it won't be if you are primed for a fight-or-flight response. The adrenaline rush and physiological changes that occur when we are attacking or being attacked (emotionally, intellectually, or physically) make creative, sophisticated thought rather difficult. If you are feeling super emotional, angry, or defensive—or if you know on some level that you're being a little irrational—stop yourself and take a break.

MAKE AN EFFORT TO:

Agree on a time to revisit the discussion later when you (and the person you are having the conflict with) are feeling more calm. Then go for a walk or do something that will help you relax and feel more centered.

CHOOSE NOT TO:

Go off into some corner to sulk or plot out your winning arguments. (I've been known to jot down key bullet points to make my argument airtight. This is not a good way to reduce the adrenaline coursing through my veins. It is also not a good way to collaborate.)

how to apologize

According to Aaron Lazare, who has studied the psychology of apologies extensively, effective apologies include some or all of the following: (1) a clear and complete acknowledgment of the offense; (2) a nondefensive explanation; (3) an expression of remorse; and (4) reparation.

Say you called your husband a lazy jerk before you read this chapter and realized it would be more effective to start with an appreciation and an "I statement." Here's how to fix that:

First, acknowledge your offense without mentioning what you were mad about. Say, *"I'm sorry I called you a lazy jerk,"* not, *"I'm sorry I called you a lazy jerk, but you really do nothing to help out around here anymore."* For an apology to work, the offender needs to fully confess to the crime without hemming, hawing, or making excuses.

Second, offer an explanation if you want, especially if you truly didn't intend to hurt the other person's feelings or if the offense isn't likely to reoccur. If you do choose to offer an explanation, again, remember that your apology needs to include an actual confession, and anything that makes it seem like you aren't taking responsibility for your mistakes will nullify your apology. For example, *"I know it sounded like I called you a lazy jerk, but actually I meant to say hazy clerk, which is what the kids call a person who is relaxed"* isn't going to build trust in your relationship. But it could help to say, "I was annoyed and not thinking clearly, and I really regret saying that."

Third, express remorse, guilt, or humility that recognizes why your comment might have hurt the other person. Finally, good apologies often include a reparation of some kind, either real or symbolic. Perhaps you lean in for an apologetic smooch, or offer to help with something you know he needs as a peace offering.

(3) Accept the other person's influence. This is how to go from being a complainer to being a problem solver. The key here is not to counter everything your partner says but instead to demonstrate empathy. The person you are in conflict with is not your opponent; you are partners solving a common problem. Remember your common goals—to create a thriving business, to raise happy kids, to have a stable and fulfilling relationship. To solve your common problem, you'll both need to make an effort to meet the other person's needs. To do that, you'll need to accept their influence.

MAKE AN EFFORT TO:

Agree on at least some points that the other person is making. (Perhaps you agree that, yes, you are able to clean up the dinner dishes more quickly than he is, and that, yes, he did the grocery shopping this weekend and that was helpful.)

CHOOSE NOT TO:

Continue to pursue the issue after an apology has been made and a solution proposed. For example, if your spouse says, "I'm sorry, honey. You're right, it isn't fair that you're doing all the work. I'm going to help you tomorrow," one way of accepting influence is simply to accept an apology: "Thank you for your apology. I'm looking forward to your help tomorrow."

I know this tip seems obvious, but when we are feeling emotional, a quick resolution can feel unsatisfying or too easy. Don't stir the pot by reminding your spouse *again* how they haven't been carrying their weight, or retorting, "Yeah, well, you don't *seem* that sorry." (I say this only because I've been known to, um, *express doubt* that an apology is sincere and that tomorrow will be different. When I do that, I'm sabotaging my own efforts.)

Finally, if it is *you* who needs to make the apology (yes, you), know that making good apologies is both science and art. The first thing is to apologize sincerely. If we can't be sincere about it, we shouldn't do it at all, as insincere apologies make people angrier than if there had been no apology in the first place.

Relationships, even really good ones, are often messy, especially when we respond reactively to conflict. Key to all this is that we choose to raise the issues we have with our nearest and dearest in a conscious way, with a clear intention to resolve a problem—rather than in an effort to be right, gain moral high ground, or otherwise feel superior.

CONNECTION DIS-EASE #8: HOLDING A GRUDGE

Maybe you've initiated problem solving as detailed above, but you're still feeling resentful for all the years you didn't have any help in the kitchen (or with the kids, or the marketing, or the driving, or for the mean things that were said, or the ill will that was implied. The list of things that we can hold on to and feel angry about is truly endless. It's as if there's a wounded scorekeeper in each of us: *There she goes again*).

Here's the thing: We rob ourselves of ease when we hold on to anger rather than letting it go. We may have *very good reasons* for being angry and for the grudges we hold, but the *in*ability to forgive hurts *us*. Often understandably, we feel angry and hostile toward the people who hurt us, and our thoughts turn to revenge (or justice). Hostility harms our health (putting us at increased risk of heart disease, for example). Wanting revenge rather than forgiveness creates more conflict with the person who hurt us, which increases our anger and anxiety.

Lingering resentment is a zero-sum game. When we hold on to negative emotions like anger, bitterness, and hatred, we block the experience of joy or gratitude.

THE ANTIDOTE: PRACTICE FORGIVENESS
Researchers find that unforgiving people tend to be hateful, angry, and hostile—making them anxious, depressed, and neurotic as well.

On the other hand, forgiving people have far more ease in their lives. In a study of Protestants and Catholics from Northern Ireland who had lost a family member to violence, for example, participants reported a 40 percent decline in depression after practicing forgiveness.

Forgiveness is something we do for ourselves to lead happier lives. Few people fully realize the huge impact that the ability to forgive can have on their happiness. Forgiving people tend to be happier, healthier, and more empathetic. Which means that they have more positive social connections.

Fred Luskin, director of the Stanford Forgiveness Project, has spent decades researching and teaching about forgiveness. Luskin emphasizes that forgiveness is not about forgetting, as the adage would have us believe, but about letting go.

Forgiveness is not about erasing the original hurt; it is about choosing positive emotions over negative ones. As such, it is a decision that results in an entirely different emotional experience. Luskin has developed a program to help people learn to forgive even the most heinous acts. I've translated his forgiveness program here into skills we can practice to become more forgiving:

- A good first step is to develop the ability to understand your emotions and articulate them when something is bothering you. Practice this by identifying, accepting, and talking about your feelings, particularly when you are hurting. (Chapter 10 has a long section on specifically how to do this.)

- Acknowledge how awful we feel when we ruminate about how we've been hurt and remind ourselves of all the positive benefits of forgiveness. When we feel hurt, it can help to recognize that what we are feeling is distress coming from what we are thinking and feeling right now, not from the original offense, whether it was months or just minutes ago.

- Remember that we suffer when we demand things that life is not giving us. We can hope for things, of course, and we can work hard to get what we want. But we cannot force things to happen that are outside our control. When we expect something outside our control to happen, and then it doesn't, we often feel hurt and wronged. Practice letting go of desire for things you have no influence over, and redirect your energy toward things you do have control over.

- Talk with someone neutral about your desire for justice, fairness, or revenge if that is holding you back. Remember that **the best revenge—or the greatest justice—is a life well lived.** When we focus on how we've been hurt, we give power to the person who hurt us because it causes us to continue hurting.

- Practice forgiving people by writing letters of forgiveness (that you may or may not decide to send). It can help to write about how you were affected by a hurt, and the bad feelings you are still experiencing. State what you wish the offender had done instead. End your letter with an explicit statement of forgiveness, understanding, and even empathy if you can muster it. For example: "I imagine that you didn't realize that what you said would be so wounding to me, so I forgive you for hurting me in the way that you did."

Forgiving is a tough business. It takes courage and resolve to let go of negative feelings when we've been wronged. Fortunately, this gets easier with practice—especially if we start with the small stuff—and it makes us stronger and better people.

CONNECTION DIS-EASE #9: WEALTH

Here's something totally weird: Wealth makes it less likely that we'll have meaningful and fulfilling relationships with others. Or, more accurately, gaining social status through wealth impairs our social and emotional intelligence, making us less interested in connecting with other people, hindering our ability to read other people's emotions, and making us less compassionate and less generous. More than that, a series of truly brilliant studies has proven the relationship between attaining high social status and all the negative attributes I just listed is *causal*. When researchers manipulate people's social status by making them feel inferior to others financially, they become more empathetic, better at reading other people's emotions. People made to feel superior start having a *harder* time empathizing with others.

Sadly, financial wealth makes us more likely to act like a jerk. One of the most striking studies of this documented how people driving luxury cars were less likely to stop for pedestrians in crosswalks or to stop at stop signs at all. Their "king of the road" attitudes showed up as a lack of concern for the safety of others.

It's ironic that social status makes us arrogant and disconnected from others. Many of us strive to be financially wealthy, thinking this will bring the lasting happiness we've been seeking. But if happiness is best predicted by the breadth and depth of our social connections, making more money is clearly not an automatic road to lasting joy.

Similarly, materialism—the pursuit of material objects such as a bigger house or nicer car or designer clothes—has been shown to damage relationships, partially because materialistic people spend more time pursuing wealth and possessions and less time with friends and family. It's worth noting that materialism doesn't just damage our connection to others, it also damages our self-esteem, increases our risk for depression and anxiety, and increases frequency of headaches.

THE ANTIDOTE: PAY IT FORWARD

If you are financially wealthy or have gained high social status, or if you are just a little on the materialistic side, the antidote is in the last chapter, in the section about giving. Stop thinking about yourself so much, and turn your attention to the things that really *will* make you happy. Realize that the stuff and experiences that money can buy may bring you a quick hit of gratification or pleasure— much like the hit of a drug—but the short-term pleasure can cost you your relationships and long-term happiness. See your wealth as a wonderful responsibility, an opportunity to be generous, and a tremendous resource for supporting your values.

Materialistic people tend to be insecure, and they look outside themselves to material possessions as a salve for their sense of inadequacy. Instead, look inside yourself for meaning, happiness, and fulfillment. What inner resources do you have that bring you contentment? Consider that your connections—to friends and family, to God and your spirituality, to nature and your community and even animals—are your most important resources. How can you nurture your connections?

Similarly, although research shows that compassion and empathy for others often arise more naturally when we are lower on the social totem pole, that doesn't mean that we can't consciously cultivate our desire and ability to really see and understand the people around us. If you are wealthy, be careful not to shelter yourself from the suffering that is all around you. Don't lose sight of how you may possess power to help those less fortunate than you, and receive in return the benefits that accompany compassion. Consciously attending to the needs of others—as when we become life's true givers—is a better route to the love we crave than the stuff that money can buy.

THE EASIEST THING: REPAIR A MINOR CRACK

The other day I got into a snitty little fight with my teenage stepdaughter. She was being oppositional with her father, and I was tired and hungry and *done* listening to them bicker. I started delivering ultimatums I couldn't possibly follow through on, which, as you know if you have a teenager, does not ever work. She saw my mistake and said some hurtful things. I stood there, stunned, mouth alternately gaping open and then closing like a fish, no actual words coming out.

We both stewed about the fight for a while. Hours later, at bedtime, she came into our bedroom where I was reading and sat down on my side of the bed, unusually chatty about something fun she'd just seen on YouTube. She was giving me a choice: I could engage in her light conversation and pretend that nothing had ever happened between us earlier in the day. Or I could lecture her about being respectful. Or I could repair the relationship.

"I'm really sorry about our fight earlier," I said quietly, putting my arm around her. "I love you a lot, you know."

"I'm sorry, too, Christine," she said, leaning in for a real hug. "I didn't mean what I said. I really love you a lot, too."

I really love you a lot. There are no more wonderful words for a stepparent to hear. All anger evaporated, and all I could feel was love.

Little cracks appear in our relationships all the time, and while we can certainly spend a lot of time and energy examining fissures and assigning blame—or pretending they aren't there or never happened—often the easiest thing is to *just repair the crack.* Without getting into it again, without raising past hurts, without projecting into the future. Often a hug and an "I love you"—or an apology and a heartfelt expression of gratitude—is all it takes.

When we repair a crack in one of our relationships, usually we end up feeling much closer to the person with whom we made the repair. My daughter Molly illustrated this beautifully the other day when she told me how she'd hurt her best friend Emma's feelings at recess by ditching her to play with another friend.

"What did you do when you found out how hurt she was?" I asked, concerned.

"I told her that I'd made a mistake by ignoring her. I know I should have told her where Amelia and I were playing, and so I said I was sorry for not doing that. I promised that next time I'd tell her, even if I know that she won't want to come and might try to convince us [to do something different]."

"What did Emma say? How does she feel now?" I wanted to make sure that Emma wasn't still hurt.

"Oh, Mom," Molly said with a sigh, as though she felt sorry for me for being so slow on the uptake. "Don't you know that when you make a mistake with a friend and apologize, they forgive you, and then you feel like you are *even better* friends?"

PART FIVE

tolerate *some* discomfort

No mud, no lotus.

—Thich Nhat Hanh

Given that life includes a boatload of disappointment, risk, discomfort, and even failure, we need to develop an ironic *comfort* with discomfort if we are to truly build strength and find ease. We need to make sure that every setback doesn't send us headlong into a massive fight-or-flight response. This means that we need to be able to do three things. First, we need to tolerate the discomfort that comes from difficulty and challenge inherent in *persuing mastery,* because mastery ultimately makes hard things easy. Second, we need to be able to cope with the discomfort inherent in our own vulnerability by *becoming brave* enough to follow our passion and purpose instead of the crowd. Finally, we need a plan for *bouncing back* when the going gets rough—which it inevitably will!

CHAPTER 8

making hard things easy

The sweet spot: that productive, uncomfortable terrain located just beyond our current abilities, where our reach exceeds our grasp. Deep practice is not simply about struggling, it's about seeking a particular struggle.

—Daniel Coyle, *The Talent Code*

We've all witnessed people who make a task that is very hard look easy. My friend Annie, an extraordinary mother, makes managing her household—which includes four daughters and a husband, all of whom play competitive hockey on traveling teams—seem like a cakewalk. Olympic snowboarders make something terrifying and death-defying look like a playground slide. My editor can read through one of these chapters, finding and suggesting fixes for all the problematic bits, in less than an hour.

The good news is that we are all developing mastery all the time. My buddy Alex has developed—through more than fifteen years of training and practice—the ability to diagnose complex learning disabilities in children. Kelly is a master friend and sister: She makes us all feel uniquely loved and needed. (I'm definitely not the only one who considers her a best friend.) My husband, Mark, could build a stunningly beautiful home in his sleep. I can write a well-researched blog post in a quarter of the time it took me when I first started blogging. We have all developed unique areas of mastery, and you probably have, too.

Even my children are gaining mastery every day. Macie makes horseback riding look like something even I could do with grace (I can't). Fiona has mastered dozens of difficult rock climbs. Tanner knows more about baseball and baseball players than anyone else I know (I'm not exaggerating). And Molly makes extraordinary jewelry that few people could imagine, much less actually create. I'm not telling you all this to brag about the unique talents of my children. Most people, no matter their age, are constantly developing mastery. Think of all the arenas in which you have mastered something or are developing mastery. What are some difficult things that you can now do with relative ease?

Mastery is, perhaps, the most pure example of the sweet spot, or the intersection between strength and ease. When we master an activity, we have great power with little strain. When we master a task or a skill, we don't have to *consciously* direct ourselves in doing it any longer; we perform it automatically. The bad news is that mastery is rarely easy to develop. In fact, mastery *requires* difficulty to develop, but it pays huge dividends in ease down the road.

MASTERY 101

We used to think that people developed mastery thanks to their genetic makeup—their inborn talents and innate passions. We called these people "gifted" and assumed that their success came from God-given talents more than from their efforts. This is because they display great command of their craft, or their sport, or their subject, but rarely evidence of pain or stress.

The belief that success—that mastery—comes from genetically-based talent is not only discouraging (what if you don't *feel* "gifted"?) but profoundly incorrect. Because researchers love to study achievement, we know that mastery doesn't spring from innate talent as much as it emerges from three things: (1) grit—or persistence, passion, and deliberate practice; (2) rest (yup, you read that right; mastery is not about working on something relentlessly or about being perfectionistic); and (3) good coaching and great teachers. Rarely can we teach ourselves something without also learning from the perspective of others.

(1) GRIT

Grit comes into play when we *aren't* operating in our sweet spot, when something throws us off our game. Even the best athletes don't succeed in every play. What they do when they *miss* the sweet spot has tremendous implications for what happens next. Grit gives us the ability to return to the sweet spot, to learn from our mistakes and grow. As such, grit predicts performance over the long haul better than IQ or innate talent.

Angela Duckworth, the celebrated psychologist who first defined "grit" as perseverance and passion for long-term goals, has a theory about mastery. Instead of seeing achievement as simply a by-product of IQ or intelligence or innate talent, Duckworth sees achievement as the *product* of skill and effort (*Achievement = Skill x Effort*) in the same way that we understand that *Distance = Speed x Time*. She explains:

> Distance [is] an apt metaphor for achievement. What is achievement, after all, but an advance from a starting point to a goal? The farther the goal from the starting point, the greater the achievement. Just as distance is the multiplicative product of speed and time, it seems plausible that, holding opportunity constant, achievement is the multiplicative product of skill and effort.
>
> Tremendous effort can compensate for modest skill, just as tremendous skill can compensate for modest effort, but not if either is zero.

Researchers across diverse fields have produced remarkably consistent findings that back up Duckworth's theory. They find that innate ability has relatively little to do with why people go from being merely okay at something to truly mastering it—to making something hard look easy.

This is hard for most of us to believe, but K. Anders Ericsson, a psychologist and author of several landmark studies on this topic, has shown that *even most physical advantages* (like athletes who have a larger heart or more fast-twitch muscle fibers or more flexible joints—the things that seem the most undeniably genetic) are, in fact, the result of certain types of effort. Even super-skills, like "perfect pitch" in eminent musicians, have been shown to stem from training more than inborn talent. Hard to believe, but entirely true.

It isn't just putting in any old effort that will build the right skills and lead to mastery. Masters tend to have three things in common: (1) They **practice** deliberately over time; (2) they are driven by **passion** and intrinsic interest; and (3) they wrestle adversity into success by **persisting** in the face of difficulty.

PRACTICE

Masters don't just practice a lot. They spend hours upon hours in deep and deliberate practice. This isn't just poking around on the piano because it is fun, or outlining a quick social-media plan, or trying a new form of discipline with your children once or twice. It is consistently practicing to reach specific objectives—say, to be able to play a new piece currently beyond your reach, or to be a social-media leader, or to see evidence that your children are clearly exhibiting self-discipline. Masters usually focus on a micro-skill, like a musical phrase or even a single measure, practicing the same bit again and again and again.

Masters also practice consistently over a pretty long period of time. Ericsson says that "elite performers in many diverse domains have been found to practice, on the average, roughly the same amount every day, including weekends." Spending a half hour jogging over the weekend isn't going to make you a great runner, but training every day might. Dabbling with your paints every once in a while isn't going to make you a great artist, but practicing your drawing every day for a decade might.

True masters gain experience over the long haul—specifically, ten years of dedicated work, or 10,000 hours of practice. Malcolm Gladwell, in his bestseller *Outliers,* made the "ten-year-rule" famous by colorfully writing about Ericsson's research. Most successful people average ten years of practice and experience before becoming truly accomplished. Even a child prodigy generally works at it for a decade or more before being considered a virtuoso. Bobby Fischer became a chess grand master at sixteen years old, but he'd been studying since he was seven. Tiger Woods had been working on his golf game for fifteen years when he became the youngest-ever winner of the U.S. Amateur Championship. We might not aspire to be an elite performer in our field, but these extreme examples show us the road to mastery—allowing hard things to become easy.

Why does mastery require so much effort? Because what we're really doing when we're honing a skill is strengthening a neural circuit. Each time we practice something we prompt nerves to fire in a particular order, building what is essentially an electric circuit. That circuit becomes uber-fast the more it is stimulated through a process called myelination. Myelin is a super insulator for our neural circuits; once a nerve is myelinated, it can fire 3,000 times faster. So although myelination develops slowly through consistent and deliberate practice, it is *the key* to making something hard feel easy.

PASSION

When we perceive a child as being innately talented or gifted, or as showing great promise for something, what we are really perceiving is interest, not talent. A four-year-old who pretends to play the violin with a stick and demonstrates an unusual interest in classical music does, indeed, show promise as a violinist. She does not, however, show talent yet. Her interest in the music at such an early age may stimulate a lot of things that lead her to virtuosity, like early music instruction and parents who encourage her to practice deliberately and consistently. But early interest is not the same as early achievement. Achievement takes both effort and skill, neither of which the four-year-old has had enough time to develop.

We need more than discipline to stick with our deliberate and consistent practice for the decade that it will take us to become virtuosos. We also need intrinsic motivation, or *passion*—and the space to pursue our passions. Like most people, I have always been most successful when I pursued work that interested me intrinsically. When I was graduating from college, I didn't look for work that I felt passionate about because I assumed there were no good jobs that would involve my interests. My intention was to get the most prestigious, high-paying job I could. At that time, corporations recruited on Ivy League campuses, and I interviewed for advertising and brand-management jobs that seemed to fit my internship experiences and creativity.

I landed a prestigious and high-paying job in marketing management. Unfortunately, I hated it. I didn't feel like I was actually *doing* anything but clocking in, checking tasks off a list, and heading home. I started therapy for anxiety. I didn't know who I was or what I wanted in life.

When I started studying the sociology of happiness six years later, my world was set ablaze. I left corporate America when I was too pregnant with Fiona to travel. In the fog that came with having a baby, I was somehow released from caring so much what other people thought of my career path. As I embarked on my Ph.D., an infant in tow, I felt free to pursue something that I was more naturally passionate about. No one else particularly thought my studying the sociology of happiness was a great idea; one professor told me to "at least stop calling it happiness" if I was studying "subjective well-being" because people were going to think that I was "not very smart." After my struggle with anxiety in corporate America, I had learned to pay more attention to my passion than to what other people thought I should be passionate about. And I paid *no* attention to what type of research was going to get me a tenured track position; I was too thrilled by all I was learning.

Passion is a pure and long-lasting fuel. Sure, other things motivate us—money, prestige, fear, social pressure—but these things run out and run us down. The practice and effort that lead to true mastery over the long run is fueled by intrinsic desire, not hard-driving parents or social expectations. In fact, my passion for the science of happiness probably developed better—and my chances for success increased—because there was no one pushing me to achieve. When we find something we are passionate about, that we love, we are naturally grittier, which in turn enables us to develop mastery.

Does this mean that we are born with all the intrinsic passion that we need to succeed in life? Not necessarily, actually. As Daniel

Coyle convincingly demonstrates in *The Talent Code,* our passions are usually ignited by something *in our environment:* a great coach or someone that we relate to that makes us think that we, too, could be masters in their domain. When twenty-year-old South Korean golfer Se Ri Pak won the McDonald's LPGA Championship she became a national icon—and ignited the passions of a country of women. A decade later (after they'd had time to practice), Korean women were winning one-third of all LPGA events. Before Pak, no South Korean had succeeded in golf.

My passion was ignited by my oldest childhood friend, Laura Beth Nielsen, a sociology professor at Northwestern University. LB got her Ph.D. in sociology a decade before I did, and always made me feel like my success in her old department at UC Berkeley was guaranteed if I worked hard enough. And my mentors and advisors, Arlie Russell Hochschild and Mike Hout, nurtured my focus on the sociology of happiness. Arlie is a master coach who kept my passion for public sociology ignited each time the going got rough.

Passion comes in especially handy when we consider another important ingredient to success: failure.

PERSISTENCE IN THE FACE OF FAILURE

Most masters don't just pile up one achievement after the next. Failure is a key part of growth and, eventually, mastery. J. K. Rowling's first Harry Potter book was rejected by twelve publishers (and before she wrote the book she suffered a stream of potentially devastating personal failures). Michael Jordon was cut from his high school basketball team. Abraham Lincoln, probably the most famous example of failure contributing to success, suffered a series of lost elections (along with some notable successes) before he went on to become one of our greatest presidents.

Consider that 75 percent of all people experience some form of trauma in life, and, within any given year, about 20 percent of all people are likely to experience a traumatic life event. So the odds are good that our lives aren't going to be free from pain and suffering, no matter how well off or well positioned we are.

Although we hate to think about the *benefits* of traumatic life events—I wouldn't wish cancer or a car accident on any of us, for example—adversity does bring with it the opportunity for personal growth. As William Zinsser wrote in his famous essay "The Right to Fail":

I'm not urging everyone to go out and fail just for the sheer therapy of it, or to quit college just to coddle some vague discontent. Obviously it's better to succeed than to flop . . . I only mean that failure isn't bad in itself, or success automatically good.

While there might not be anything good *in* misfortune, as Viktor Frankl wisely reminds us, it is often possible to wrench something good *out* of misfortune. We know that adverse life events—an accident, a scary diagnosis, a botched presentation, a breakup—can trigger depression, anxiety, and post-traumatic stress disorder. But what most of us don't realize is that post-traumatic *growth,* as researchers call it, can also awaken us to new strength and wisdom. Misfortune—even tragedy—has the potential to give our lives new meaning and a new sense of purpose. In this way, adversity also *contributes* to the passion part of the grit equation. Misfortune offers us the opportunity to choose new meaning and purpose.

Adversity plays a significant role in helping us develop the grit we need to develop mastery. With adversity comes stress. And a vast body of scientific research shows that the stress we experience as a result of adversity—and how we *respond* to that stress—tends to predict how much we will benefit from it. The people who show the most growth following hardship are *not* the people who deny feeling any stress in the face of adversity. Instead, the people who grow the most are actually the ones who are "shaken up," and even exhibit a degree of post-traumatic stress. So if we don't feel some stress in the face of a difficult situation, odds are we won't grow from it.

Why is this? Because myelination—the neural process that allows us to master a particular skill—seems to occur best when we make a mistake, when our learning process resembles a kid learning to ride a bike for the first time, when we are unsteady, out of our comfort zone, and willing to fall. The fastest way to develop a skill is to trigger myelination through what I think of as repeated "micro-failures." We attempt something hard that we haven't succeeded at before, testing ourselves, and we miss the mark. Micro-failures stimulate the neural circuit needed for the skill that we are developing. Focused, we try again. And again. And again—eventually getting it. Each time we engage in this mistake-riddled practice, we trigger myelination. "Struggling in certain targeted ways—operating at the edges of your ability, where you make mistakes—makes you smarter," writes Daniel Coyle, author of *The Talent Code*.

mastery mistake #1

Many millennials have grown up with "snowplow" or "helicopter" parents—parents who clear obstacles from their kids' paths, hovering close to them to protect them from making mistakes or from experiencing discomfort, disappointment, even boredom. People parented in this way don't tolerate discomfort or difficulty particularly well. Many snowplow-parented millennials even (unconsciously) feel *entitled* to a life free from discomfort, frustration, and disappointment—which means that they are more likely to cheat when the going gets rough, or blame other people for their own discomfort and their own failings. When challenges arise, snowplow-parented people don't often rise to the occasion. They tend to quit, and in the process they deprive themselves of the opportunity to develop mastery.

Guess what? Developing mastery is difficult. Deliberate practice is uncomfortable; it is often boring or frustrating or agonizing. Being at the bottom of the learning curve can be deeply humbling. Challenging situations—so needed for mastery—often lead to pain and failure. Mastery may be one of the purest forms of ease, but *developing* mastery is *hard*.

Adversity and failure in life are givens. Our success and happiness depend on our ability not just to cope with them but to actually grow because of it. Emotionally, intellectually, athletically, professionally, artistically, spiritually—we have the greatest potential to grow when we challenge ourselves just beyond our comfort zone. This means risking fear, embarrassment, errors, or even full-blown failure. And pushing through these things enables us to build new skills and abilities that contribute to our greater mastery and success in the future.

This doesn't mean that adversity—be it a disappointment, failure, or full-blown tragedy—doesn't hurt. The engine for post-traumatic growth is, after all, post-traumatic *stress*. But how we choose to deal with the hurt, or the stress, makes all the difference in the world. (The next two chapters are chock-full of concrete strategies for fostering post-traumatic growth.)

(2) REST

Just as masters are strategic about *what* they practice, they are also strategic about *how long* they practice. If you think that success requires practicing until your fingers bleed or your mind spins or your muscles give out, for hour upon hour upon hour of endless, relentless practice, I have some good news for you. Research suggests that that's not the way to get there. True masters also *rest* strategically. This is a *key* component of success, one that we often overlook in our 24/7 go-go-go culture.

What most people don't realize is that high achievers sleep significantly more than the average American. Even if, like me, you don't have your sights set on becoming an Olympian, here again we normal people can take a page from the book of elite performers. On average, Americans get 6.5 hours of sleep per night, even though studies show that 97.5 percent of the population needs between 7 and 9 hours of sleep a night. Elite performers tend to get 8.6 hours of sleep a night; elite *athletes* need even more sleep. One study showed that when Stanford swimmers increased their sleep time to 10 hours in a 24-hour period, they felt happier and more energetic—and their performance in the pool improved dramatically.

In his studies of truly great musicians, K. Anders Ericsson found that they practiced and *rested* a lot more than their good but not elite peers. For example, violinists destined to become professional soloists practiced an average of 3.5 hours per day, typically in three separate sessions of 60 to 90 minutes each. Good but not great performers, in contrast, typically practiced an average of 1.4 hours per day, with no deliberate rest breaking up their practice session.

mastery mistake #2

I work with several high-level executives in Silicon Valley, people who have been at the top of their fields for a long time now. They have "leaned in" a la Sheryl Sandberg, and they've had incredible professional success. They regularly do difficult things more quickly, skillfully, and with less effort than their juniors. But they don't make their jobs or their lives look easy.

These people are the opposite of the snowplow-parented millennials described in Mastery Mistake #1. Their pain tolerance is so high that they are able to work unceasingly, unrelentingly. They get into the office early and leave the office late, only to stay connected to their work via email and text at home. (One executive expressed annoyance to me that his children don't want him to bring his laptop to the dinner table; he felt they should be grateful that he was having dinner with them.)

Despite their incredible skills, success, and work ethic, these executives aren't masters. They are headed for burnout so deep they may never recover, and that's not mastery. There is no ease with their success. Although they may often display the raw strength of the sweet spot, it is paired with stress rather than ease.

If you are making this mastery mistake, the solution is simple: Just rest. Honor your animal nature, and call a day's work a day's work. Go home and play with your friends or children. Get enough sleep to refuel and rejuvenate for the next hard day's work. Take your weekends off. Go on vacation. Do these things knowing that this is how you will *sustain* your high performance—and find your groove at work *and* at home.

So it isn't *just* that elite performers work more than others; they rest more as well. The top violinists mentioned above *slept an hour a night more* than their less-accomplished classmates. They were also far more likely to take a nap between practice sessions—racking up nearly three hours of napping a week.

Mastery requires more sleep because it involves higher rates of learning and sometimes physical growth. Adequate sleep allows us to focus our attention on our practice when we are awake. When we are sleep deprived, our overworked neurons become uncoordinated, and we start having trouble accessing previously learned information.

When we sleep, our brain consolidates what we've learned while we were awake, making it part of our working memory that we can access later. Sleep allows us to remember tomorrow how to do what we've practiced today, and it enables us to recall the information and knowledge we've just learned.

It isn't just brain function that is influenced by our sleep patterns. "Sleep affects almost every tissue in our bodies," says Dr. Michael J. Twery, a sleep specialist at the National Institutes of Health. Sleep affects our heart and other major organs, like our lungs and kidneys. It impacts our appetite and metabolism and therefore how much we weigh. It determines our health by tweaking our immune function. Sleep influences how sensitive we are to pain. Lack of sleep slows our reaction times. And, as anyone with a sleep-deprived toddler or teenager knows, sleep has a dramatic impact on our mood.

The amount of sleep we get—and how disciplined we are about following our body's natural rhythms of rest and work—affects not just our health but our productivity and performance. We don't usually think of it as a necessary ingredient for mastery, but it is.

So developing mastery isn't about pushing yourself 24/7 toward your goals. It's about making progress toward your goals consistently and deliberately and in a way that works with our human biology, allowing for proper refueling and consolidation of knowledge.

when perseverance prevents mastery

If we want to develop mastery and reap the benefits of the ease that it brings, clearly we need to value hard work and practice. But it is a myth that "winners never quit and quitters never win." From a stress-management standpoint, we need to *know* when to disengage—and *be able* to disengage—when the cost of reaching a goal is outstripping the benefit. People who can't disengage from over-pursuing a difficult goal tend to show increased levels of the damaging stress-related chemicals in their bloodstream that are linked to diabetes, heart disease, and early aging. It doesn't matter if they eventually reach the goal or not; too much perseverance can elevate stress hormones and extract a high cost physically and psychologically.

People tend to feel better, both physically and mentally, when they disengage from a very difficult goal and *re-engage with one that is more attainable*. For example, in college my good friend Vanessa was failing calculus—despite lots of studying, tutoring, and other efforts—but was doing well in her other classes. Her adviser coached her to admit she was failing the class (passing was a mathematical impossibility at that point) and, instead of continuing to throw good effort at a lost cause, rededicate herself to the classes that she really enjoyed. Her adviser was concerned that she would spend so much time and mental energy on calculus that Vanessa would also tank in her other classes. That advice—to choose to fail—was revolutionary for Vanessa, and she'll never forget it. She left calculus behind and did very well in all her other classes from there on out. Moreover, she enjoyed college, went on to grad school, loves learning, and now laughs about calculus. Failing that one class had no negative impact on her life.

The social pressure *not* to quit can be tremendous, and for some people it takes a great deal of courage. If you are having a hard time quitting something that you know isn't serving you on your journey, ask yourself what is holding you back. Are you embarrassed to admit that you just can't do it? Are you so committed to persevering that you can't abandon a project or give up on a class that you've already paid for but can't follow through on?

Life is too short to keep our noses to the grindstone 24/7. Downtime, rest, play—and sometimes quitting—are not indulgences or a waste of time but are necessary for strength and growth. Not all mountains are worth climbing all the way to the top, especially if the costs of doing so are great. Sometimes the greatest cost comes from climbing the mountain to the top, only to look longingly down at another path you'll always wished you'd followed.

(3) COACHES, TEACHERS, MENTORS, AND CHEERLEADERS

Coaches and tutors also play very important roles in helping us go from good to great by helping us determine what strategies to take and what tactics to practice. Few (if any) people can develop mastery all on their own; most of us just don't have the perspective or the experience we need. Coaches ignite our passions, help us decide what to put our effort into practicing, and they help us see our failings and weak spots. Their feedback is critical to our success.

So if we are to achieve mastery, it is important for us to surround ourselves with people who have the knowledge, experience, and astuteness needed to guide our actions and practice. Furthermore, they must believe that with practice, we, too, can become masters. In a famous experiment, Harvard social psychologist Robert Rosenthal and South San Francisco Unified School District principal Lenore Jacobson examined what they called the Pygmalion Effect, named for the mythological Greek character Pygmalion, made famous by Ovid's narrative poem in which Pygmalion was a sculptor who could look at a piece of marble and see a vision of his ideal trapped inside it.

Rosenthal and Jacobson's hypothesis was that when kids have their own private Pygmalion—a teacher who sees something ideal within them—they fulfill higher expectations. They conducted their experiment in a public elementary school, telling teachers that certain children could be expected to be "growth spurters" based on their IQ tests. In reality, the students designated as "spurters" were chosen at random.

Rosenthal and Jacobson asked the teachers not to tell their students that they were "spurters." Teachers were told they were not to change their instruction for "spurters" in any way, or give them more (or less) attention. At the end of the year, all the students were administered IQ tests again, and the findings were remarkable. The IQ of first- and second-grade "spurters" went up dramatically. (The experiment worked most dramatically with the younger students, presumably because their reputations as students and their intellectual capabilities were relatively unknown, and so the designation as a "spurter" was highly believable by the teachers.) Kids randomly chosen as "growth spurters" actually *did* grow more intellectually than the rest of their class.

This experiment shows us that one person's expectations of another's behavior can come to serve as a self-fulfilling prophecy. Which begs the question: Who is, or can be, the Pygmalion in your life? Who sees your potential beneath the surface? That person will be your best teacher or coach.

Getting good coaching depends as much on our ability to *take the coaching*—to incorporate the feedback that other people give us. This can be really hard. Many of us deny our failings, pushing them out of view. This is not the tack I recommend taking, particularly because denial tends to travel with a couple of pernicious cousins: defensiveness and blame.

Perhaps you've said something that hurt your boss's feelings, and she is mad mad mad. You now have a choice about how you'll respond. You can maintain that what you said is true and deny that saying it out loud, the way you said it, was a mistake. You can blame her for being unreasonable and overly sensitive. I feel certain that there are any number of ways you can defend yourself (and maybe even your defensiveness).

The benefits of denial, defensiveness, and blame are clear: They preserve our self-esteem. It feels much better in the moment to make ourselves feel superior to those around us than it does to accept responsibility for our actions. But high self-esteem buys only *temporary* feelings of superiority. Believe it or not, having a heightened sense of self-esteem won't boost our performance at school or at work, or make us more attractive or effective leaders. And denial, defensiveness, and blame tend to make us uncoachable, to keep us from learning and developing mastery.

Kristin Neff, a prominent research psychologist and the author of *Self-Compassion: Stop Beating Yourself Up and Leave Insecurity Behind,* likens the benefits of preserving our self-esteem to eating a candy bar instead of having a healthy snack; we get a little sugar high, but then we crash. "And right after the crash comes a pendulum swing to despair as we realize that—however much we'd like to—we can't always blame our problems on someone else."

The obvious alternative to the destructive trio of denial, defensiveness, and blame is to look our weaknesses squarely in the face, even if it makes us feel vulnerable to do so. If you are having a hard time taking feedback or coaching, try swapping self-esteem for self-*affirmation*. Self-esteem comes from telling ourselves that we are wonderful—even in the face of evidence to the contrary. Self-affirmation comes from remembering and acknowledging what we truly value—the things "that constitute our true or core self," says Lisa Legault, a psychologist who researches self-affirmation. This is a form of mindfulness, not of our temporary thoughts or feelings but of our core identity, values, and self.

Brain imaging studies illuminate the power of self-affirmation. Taking a few minutes to reflect on who we are and what we value in life tends to reduce our anxiety and defensiveness after we make a mistake, or when we receive potentially threatening feedback from our spouse, boss, or even from an ordinary activity that isn't going as well as we'd hoped. Self-affirmation also makes us more likely to accept bad news about ourselves without denying it. It makes us more open to opposing views, which helps us see a bigger picture.

How do we practice self-affirmation? Take a moment to reflect on what is most important to you in life. Jot down a handful of things, and then rank them. Often the only thing we need to do to feel less anxious and defensive is to remind ourselves what matters most to us.

WHEN ACHIEVEMENT NEVER LEADS TO EASE

When we realize that achievement is the product of effort—not sheer God-given talent—some perfectionists are inclined to dig in and persevere to the bitter end, until they have outlasted all the competition and done everything *perfectly*.

All this emphasis on effort and hard work can be misleading, so I think it is important to clarify that there is a huge difference between mastery and perfectionism. I'm not advocating a mentality of put your nose to the grindstone and stick with it forever (see "Mastery Mistake #2," above). Remember, this book is as much about happiness as it is success. Sweating it out through the sheer force of your iron will isn't usually fun, and it's hard to be happy or truly successful if you aren't having fun.

the line between persistent practice and perfectionism

Perfectionism is the dark side of deliberate hard work. It produces a chronic feeling that nothing is good enough and the worst thing in the world is failure. The resulting elevated stress hormones coursing through perfectionists' blood make them prone to a host of health problems, including depression, severe anxiety, and a higher incidence of suicide.

A lot of people incorrectly assume that perfectionism propels kids to the top of their class and adults to the top of their fields. Although some of us no longer call it perfectionism—instead labeling ourselves or our kids or the people we admire as "super-focused" or "overachievers"—it can *seem* like a sure road to mastery. On the contrary, perfectionism detracts from success and happiness by creating a steady state of discontent fueled by a stream of negative emotions like fear, frustration, and disappointment. Perfectionists can't enjoy their successes because there is always something they could have done better.

All that fear diverts energy from more constructive things, making perfectionists less able to learn and be creative. Ironically, perfectionists expend a lot of energy on the things they are desperately trying to avoid—failure and the criticism they imagine it will create. This preoccupation has been shown to undermine performance in sports, academics, and social situations.

Perfectionism keeps us from taking risks and embracing challenge. For this reason, sometimes perfectionism leads to *under*-achievement. We give up or don't even try because we assume that we can't be good enough. And rising to a challenge—especially a challenge that doesn't come naturally at first—is one of the best ways to transform something hard into something easy.

Furthermore, perfectionism leads people to conceal their mistakes. In nearly every field—writing groups are a wonderful example—group critique and coaching are rapid ways to get better at something. But as a perfectionistic undergraduate at Dartmouth College, I was terrified of having my work read aloud by a professor or my paintings critiqued by a class. Though I couldn't prevent these things from happening except by skipping class, when I did have to endure group critiques I was so paralyzed by fear of judgment and having my mistakes exposed that I couldn't learn from (or even really hear) the constructive feedback being given to me.

Here's why I couldn't hear the feedback: My brain was operating on pure stress. Whether or not our fear is rational (in other words, whether or not we are actually in any danger), simply perceiving a threat unleashes a torrent of hormonal and chemical responses in our brain. Suffice it to say that what we think of as an "adrenaline rush" is actually a cascade of hormones and neurotransmitters wreaking havoc in our brain and body.

As discussed in Chapter 2, these chemical messengers suppress activity in the areas in the front of the brain that are responsible for short-term memory, concentration, inhibition, and, you guessed it, *rational thought*. Stress hormones also interfere with our ability to handle difficult social or intellectual tasks. And, adding insult to injury, all this neurotransmitter hullabaloo renders our short-term memory temporarily out of order while helping our long-term memory record the event for eons to come, ensuring that we remember to be *especially afraid* the next time a similar situation occurs.

This means that just when I should have been listening closely so that I could make improvements, I couldn't concentrate on what was being said. I struggled to control my impulse to leave the room.

I couldn't *think*—and I couldn't figure out how to respond grace-fully. I lost the opportunity to improve my writing and my painting because I couldn't hear anything except that my work wasn't per-fect.

The takeaway: The fear that perfectionism generates isn't func-tional. It will never make things easier for us. To develop mastery, we need to be persistent without being perfectionistic.

To be clear, perfectionism is not about setting high expectations or being successful in our endeavors. It is about being concerned about making mistakes and worrying about what others think. **The difference between perfectionism and mastery is the ability to risk, and even embrace, failure.**

> Perfectionism is not a quest for the best. It is a pursuit of the worst in ourselves, the part that tells us that nothing we do will ever be good enough.
>
> —Julia Cameron

We seek perfection out of fear—fear of not being good enough for others or ourselves. Perfectionists are absolutely terrified of vul-nerability because, like most people, they believe that allowing themselves to be vulnerable will make them look weak or stupid.

On the other hand, we pursue mastery out of passion. We are motivated both by passion and fear, but one brings ongoing and deepening mastery while the other just brings the next thing in a line of unceasing tests. Ironically, acceptance and love for ourselves as we already are underlies the motivation toward personal growth or our life's purpose—as opposed to relentless self-improvement.

So the core difference between pursuing mastery and pursuing perfection is **vulnerability.** Mastery requires us to be vulnerable; perfection can be equated with total vigilance against vulnerability.

The next chapter is all about vulnerability, and how to muster the courage you need for it.

THE EASIEST THING: FOCUS ON THE JOURNEY, NOT THE ACHIEVEMENT

I know from experience how easy it is to think thoughts like, "If I could just earn more money . . ." or "If I could just live in that city . . ." or "If I could just go to that school . . ." or "If I could just be there, then I could be happy." But more than three decades of research on this topic shows us that what truly makes us happy is letting go of our fantasies about the future and instead engaging in the journey, in the process, and in the present moment.

The simplest way to refocus on the journey is to practice mindfulness. Try being mindful right here, right now. What are you feeling in your body? Is it tense or relaxed? Are you feeling any emotions? If so, where are they showing up in your body? What is your breathing like right now? What themes do your thoughts keep returning to? Can you notice and label them?

Remember not to judge or resist what things you notice about your current state. Mindfulness is just about noticing. The ability to "know your state," as mindfulness researcher and teacher Shauna Shapiro calls it—to do a quick self-status check—is a critical skill. Mindfulness of our current mental and emotional state allows us to remain calm—or to return more quickly to calm—in the face of a stressor.

Feel like you need more than a moment of mindfulness to face your life? Does all this feel a bit daunting? Turn the page to learn more about fostering ease in the face of fear.

CHAPTER 9

how to be divergent

Becoming fearless isn't the point. That's impossible. It's learning to control your fear, and how to be free from it.

—Veronica Roth, *Divergent*

My daughter Fiona—and all her middle school friends—were obsessed for a while with the dystopia that Veronica Roth creates in her book *Divergent*. In it, the characters are allowed to develop and display only one character strength: intelligence, courage, honesty, peacefulness, or selflessness. People who demonstrate more than one strength are considered "divergent," which is seen as highly dangerous and threatening. The main character, Tris, is divergent—she is smart, brave, *and* selfless. Because the divergent are hard for the government to control, they are usually killed.

The appeal of *Divergent* to the middle school crowd is obvious, given the pressure that many teens feel to conform to a rigid set of standards set by their peers, parents, and schools. But I also see Roth's dystopia as a commentary on the adult world we live in, where most of us are constantly comparing ourselves to three common, and powerful, archetypes that display and develop only one strength: the ideal worker, the intensely involved mother, and the provider father.

I don't know anyone who has worked for a traditional business who hasn't run up against our cultural notion of what journalist Brigid Schulte calls the ideal worker: the perfect employee who—without the distractions of children or family or, well, *life*—can work as many hours as the employer needs. Ideal workers don't have hobbies—or even interests—that interfere with work, and they have someone else (usually a wife) to stay at home with sick children, schedule carpools, and find decent child care. Babies aren't their responsibility, so parental leave when an infant is born isn't an issue; someone else will do that. The ideal worker can jump on a plane and leave town anytime for business because someone else is doing the school pickups, making dinner, and putting the children to bed.

Most working parents can't compete—in terms of sheer hours of work—with these ideal workers, and they've got additional archetypes to cope with: intensely involved mothers and provider fathers. The intensely involved mother doesn't appear to work outside the home (if she does do paid work, it certainly doesn't interfere with her mothering or volunteering in her children's classrooms). The intensely involved mother always knows best. She was the one who breast-fed her children for *years,* after all, and so she (and she alone) knows what the babies need and when they need it. When her children reach school age, she becomes the ideal parent volunteer. She's a room parent, fund-raising worker bee, pizza-day helper, field-trip driver. She juggles so many roles that she seems omnipresent on campus. Her children are shuttled from every ideal enrichment activity available and are enrolled in the best summer camps. She takes lots of pictures, diligently documenting her children's carefully constructed childhoods, but she herself rarely appears in the photo albums. Her needs are seldom considered. How fulfilling she finds her job serving her family is not relevant.

Similarly, provider fathers—who focus on making as much money as possible for the benefit of their families yet rarely spend quality time with them—shame working dads who turn down promotions or take lower-paying work so they can spend more time with their kids.

Like the characters in *Divergent,* each of these stereotypical Americans can develop and display only one strength: the ability to work long hours, *or* the ability to be a great and selfless parent, *or* the ability to make a lot of money for the family.

But here's the thing: The ideal worker is not necessarily ideal. Nor is the intensely involved mother or the provider father. Reams of research show that people who work long hours, to the detriment of their personal lives, are *not* more productive or successful than people who work shorter hours so they can have families and develop interests outside of work. And nothing in the research indicates that intensely involved mothers are more successful raising happy or high-achieving children than moms who invest in activities that are not 100 percent centered on their children. In fact, there is plenty of evidence that kids do better when they are given more autonomy. And we know beyond a shadow of a doubt that children benefit hugely from having an involved father—even when the father earns less money than he would if he worked more.

In other words, if we are to be our most productive, successful, and happy selves—if we are to find our groove in our work and our home lives—we *must be divergent,* as threatening as this is to our cultural norms and the people around us who strive to be ideal workers, intensely involved mothers, and provider fathers. Divergence is especially threatening to the ideal workers who still run many of our corporations and government institutions. As in Roth's novels, people deeply wedded to the ideal archetypes will seek to control and, if necessary, discredit or undermine people dedicated to being good parents *and* good workers *and* community contributors *and* happy individuals.

To develop our multiple talents, we must stray from the herd of our cultural archetypes. As we know from Chapters 4 and 5, our nervous system is designed to keep us in a group, so straying from the herd can be terrifying and disorienting. In *Divergent,* the strong female main character, Tris, is forced to join a single-strength faction in order to hide her divergence. She chooses to become "dauntless"—the group that prizes bravery—even though she secretly knows that she also has a predisposition for the highly intelligent "erudite," or the selfless "abnegation." She knows that changing the world, and her life, will take a great deal of courage, and only when she has enough courage will she truly be able to help others or fully use her own intelligence.

Virtually every action or behavior I suggest in this book will, for some readers, require divergence from the herd, or courage, or both. Sometimes we need courage in our personal lives—to face a past trauma that is holding us back, or to demand more from (or leave) a mediocre relationship that is sucking the life out of us, or to insist that our partner help us with the child care or housework so we can get more sleep. Other times we need courage professionally, to tackle a major challenge, to risk making a mistake, to confront a co-worker who is blocking our progress, or to set out in a new career direction. Often (maybe always) we need courage to pursue the everyday changes that can get us into our groove. It can take courage to establish a gratitude practice or rules around smartphone use in our home. It takes pluck to love someone with our whole heart, and it takes bravery to forgive.

We will not find our groove by conforming to unrealistic ideals or outdated stereotypes. To find our groove, we must allow ourselves to be complex and divergent, to be our authentic selves. Authenticity in and of itself is a form of tremendous ease. It is easier—we ultimately have greater power and less stress—when we say "I don't know" instead of faking an answer, when we tell the truth about our preferences instead of pretending to like something we don't, or when we do the thing we want to do instead of the thing that others expect of us.

BECOMING DAUNTLESS

Brené Brown, author of *Daring Greatly,* may be the best guide out there to becoming dauntless. She writes about remarkable research into the power of vulnerability and shame, where she defines vulnerability as "uncertainty, risk, and emotional exposure." My friend Ben recently made himself vulnerable by applying to business school at the age of forty-three. Ben will have to tolerate the uncertainty of not knowing whether or not he'll be admitted and, if he is, if the financial investment will be worth it. Great athletes make themselves vulnerable every time they take a potentially game-winning—

or losing—shot. Engaging inevitably means risking the game. And every parent I know is vulnerable because having children and loving them unconditionally exposes you emotionally.

Our minds seem to easily link vulnerability to weakness. But do we think that great athletes, or people who make major mid-career moves, or all the parents out there who are so emotionally exposed by the love they have for their children, are *weak*? Does their vulnerability make them look feeble, disappointing, or like a failure?

Turns out, it's a big fat myth that vulnerability equals weakness. "Yes, we are totally exposed when we are vulnerable," Brown writes. "Yes, we are in the torture chamber that we call uncertainty. And, yes, we're taking a huge emotional risk when we allow ourselves to be vulnerable. But there's no equation where taking risks, braving uncertainty, and opening ourselves up to emotional exposure equals weakness."

One reason that we perceive vulnerability as weakness is that vulnerability is at the core of all our emotions. When we feel something—and especially when we show our emotions—we expose ourselves. When we feel, we become vulnerable. And when we see emotions as weak or "girly" (an insult to grown women and men alike), we are also likely to conflate vulnerability with weakness.

Let me say this one more time: Vulnerability is not a sign of weakness even while it is a sign of exposure. Vulnerability is a sign that *courage is at work*. And the only way that we divergent people can survive is to muster the courage we need to be vulnerable.

But how do we do this? Below are several tactics for mustering courage to benefit from vulnerability—to reap the benefits from the ease that vulnerability ultimately brings. For it is only when we are vulnerable that we gain true intimacy and deep connections, when we are able to take the risks that we need for mastery. Only when we allow ourselves to be vulnerable—when we expose ourselves emotionally—are we able to experience profound joy and gratitude and inspiration.

Choose one or more strategies that resonate with you and start practicing!

JUST DO IT IMPERFECTLY

There are basically two ways to just do something imperfectly, and often you can choose a method that suits your style. If you are getting into a cold swimming pool, are you most likely to actually make it all the way into the pool if you dive right in, or will you get there by inching your way in slowly? How are you with Band-Aid removal? Do you rip it off fast or peel it off slowly? Even though we've all probably approached both tasks in both ways, we usually have a preference.

I'm the dive-right-in, rip-the-Band-Aid-off-quickly type. When I need to muster the courage to get into a new or scary arena, I know that I can't inch my way toward something, or I'll overthink things, change my mind, decide the water is too cold, and never end up swimming.

My friend Casey is afraid to pursue her career as an artist and writer. She feels stuck in her family business and can't seem to muster the courage she needs to begin a career that speaks more to her creativity and huge heart than to her husband's business acumen.

Casey is an inch-into-the-pool kind of gal. So in this case, she can muster the courage to pursue her long-term goal of making a living through her art by starting slowly. Opening the arena gate by talking to other artists and writers. Taking one step closer to the center every day by making a little collage or writing a paragraph or two. Working her way up to taking classes at night.

Either method is fine, as long as we actually get into the arena and start playing. What we can't do is wait to get started "until we're perfect or bulletproof" because, as Brown writes, "perfect and bulletproof don't exist in human experience."

See your next foray into doing something scary as what writer Anne Lamott calls the "shitty first draft." Welcome the imperfection of this next attempt. Most great writers swear by this: All you have to do is get that crappy first draft down on paper, and you are more than halfway home. Shoot for a perfect first draft and you are screwed, though; most people are paralyzed by the impossibility of that task. The wise coach Martha Beck says this about welcoming imperfection into our lives:

Long experience as a profoundly flawed person has taught me this un-expected truth: that welcoming imperfection is the way to accomplish what perfectionism promises but never delivers. It gives us our best performance, and genuine acceptance in the family of human—and by that I mean imperfect—beings.

Ironically, when we walk into the arena embracing our imperfection—like the boy who decides to ask a cute girl on a date even though he's pretty sure he's going to stutter and say something stupid—we increase the odds that we will be successful. We remove the pressure on ourselves. We perform better, we win more friends, and we build our capacity for acting with courage. Life feels easier after we do something hard.

CONSIDER THAT YOUR FEAR ISN'T LEGITIMATE

Sometimes fear is more about excitement and thrill and passion than it is a warning that you are about to jump into a toxic waste dump instead of a swimming pool. As Maria Shriver writes in *And One More Thing Before You Go,* often "anxiety is a glimpse of your own daring . . . part of your agitation is just excitement about what you're getting ready to accomplish. Whatever you're afraid of—that is the very thing you should try to do."

When we face our fears, we sometimes catch a glimpse of Marianne Williamson's famous insight about fear:

Our deepest fear is not that we are inadequate. Our deepest fear is that we are powerful beyond measure. It is our light, not our darkness, that most frightens us. We ask ourselves, "Who am I to be brilliant, gorgeous, talented, fabulous?" Actually, who are you not to be? You are a child of God. Your playing small does not serve the world. There is nothing enlightened about shrinking so that other people won't feel

insecure around you . . . And as we let our own light shine, we uncon-
sciously give other people permission to do the same. As we are liber-
ated from our own fear, our presence automatically liberates others.

So look what you are afraid of straight in the eye. What is it that you are most scared of? Is it rejection? Ridicule? What is the very worst thing that could happen to you if your fear comes true? Can you handle that outcome?

Your self-grilling might go something like this coaching session between Martha Beck and Lissa Rankin, author of the *New York Times* bestselling book *Mind Over Medicine*. Rankin, a doctor much like work-life balance teacher Lee Lipsenthal, has rededicated her practice to teaching other doctors to become more holistic healers. One of Rankin's biggest fears was of not being in total control of things. In particular, she had a paralyzing fear of not being able to control things in hospitals—a place where it is, of course, impossible to control every outcome.

> **Beck:** So Lissa, what would happen if you [weren't in total control] in the hospital?
>
> **Rankin:** Someone might die.
>
> **Beck:** And then what would happen?
>
> **Rankin:** Then they'd talk about how I lost control at the Morbidity & Mortality conference, where doctors get to-gether to talk about patients who died when they shouldn't have.
>
> **Beck:** And then what?
>
> **Rankin:** Then, if they determined that I did something wrong, they'd report me to the California board.
>
> **Beck:** And then what?

Rankin: Then the California board would launch an investigation.

Beck: And then what?

Rankin: If they determined I was negligent, they'd take away my license.

Beck: And then what?

Rankin: Then I wouldn't get to practice medicine.

Beck: So your biggest fear is that if you lost control in the hospital, you wouldn't be able to practice medicine. And yet, Lissa, you made the decision in September to let your board certification lapse because you never want to practice medicine again. So the worst thing that could have happened if you lost control in the hospital happened—by your choice.

Rankin: Gulp.

Here's what is great about this dialogue: Not only did Rankin uncover her actual fear and face it, but she was able to experience the way that her fear was telling her what she most wants. Although most doctors might quite legitimately fear losing their license, deep down Rankin did *not* want to keep her license. Although she didn't want to lose it by making a mistake or hurting someone, she did give it up in order to focus full time on her doctor-training business.

Occasionally when we face our fear, we find that the "worst possible outcome" that we are so afraid of is actually the outcome that we are looking for!

SEEK A SMALLER POND

I have a friend, whom I'll call Alan, whose wife wants him to be more romantic, but romance does not come easy to him; it is not, as

he puts it, "in my bailiwick." He's frightened of the emotional exposure that occurs when he is expressive about his love for someone
else; to him, the vulnerability of this emotional exposure seems to
outweigh the reward of his wife's satisfaction with their relationship.

One way for Alan to muster the courage to be more vulnerable in
this arena, and therefore more romantic, is to start expressing his
feelings in other ways with other people who don't make him feel so
exposed. I think of this as the big duck in a small pond strategy.
Psychologists call it the "inoculation principle of graded exposure."
The idea is to create experiences that are outside your comfort zone
(in the direction you need more courage) but are not so intense that
they are super stressful. For example, Alan can:

- Tell his kids more specifically what he loves about them
  at bedtime.

- Talk about what he is grateful for at dinnertime, when
  perhaps the rest of the family also does this, and look for
  opportunities to express gratitude for other people. For
  example, by saying that he is grateful for his mother and
  all the ways she helps him be a better father.

- Verbally link the little thoughtful things he already frequently does for his wife to his love for her. He's started
  saying things like, "I ordered you new printer toner today
  because I know you hate dealing with stuff like that and
  I love you and I wanted to do something nice for you."

The key for Alan is to *just do these things* without overthinking
them. If he pauses to "think of something really profound to say at
dinner," he makes romance feel hard again. The point is to practice
in a smaller pond and let go of the outcome. By stepping into these
smaller ponds daily, Alan is building the courage to be a bona fide
romantic with his wife.

Similarly, another way to make our pond smaller when we are
building courage is to set the bar very low, so success is guaranteed

in the early rounds. My friend Vanessa doesn't have a lot of athletic skills and has to (heavily) coax herself into going to the gym. When trying a new activity or class, she has no aspirations for herself other than just showing up and making it through the class. She can be terrible at the activity and still walk out feeling like it's a win— which gives her more courage to head back the next day.

The idea is to muster the courage to do things that are initially hard for us so that we reap huge gains in the ease department. Alan may never find romance *easy*, for example, but his life is way easier when his wife is happy and his relationship is strong.

REMEMBER WHEN YOU'VE BEEN BRAVE BEFORE

Write down a list of times when you've shown real courage. List things you were afraid to do but are glad you did anyway. Note especially the things that you did imperfectly but are *still* very glad you did. Also note the times when you were forced to do something that made you very vulnerable (like when your spouse asked for a divorce that you didn't want, or when you were pressured to speak for all your siblings at the funeral of someone dear to you all) but you showed tremendous courage anyway.

My friend Dan Mulhern, a leadership coach and professor at UC Berkeley's Haas School of Business, designed this "Analysis of a Scary Situation" exercise to help his students remember when they've been brave:

- Briefly, write or think about a situation or circumstance in which you felt afraid, and what you were afraid of specifically.

- Now, jot down or remember the action you took even though you were afraid.

- Write or think about what happened. Did what you feared materialize? If so, how? How did you respond? Were there unintended results or consequences that you could not have predicted?

- Now, look over your list again or mentally run through the times when you showed real courage. See, you are more courageous than you thought!

THINK COURAGEOUS THOUGHTS

Our thoughts profoundly influence what we feel and what we do. When we think about times when we've been a coward, we are likely to feel like a coward and then behave like one again. Or if we think about times when we've done poorly at something, we are likely to feel insecure and weak, upping the odds that we'll actually do something insecure and weak.

It's important to remember that the hard things we have to do or say are rarely what make us uncomfortable. It is the *fear* that makes us uneasy. Fear is the thing that actually makes actions hard, not the action that we think we are afraid of. Not doing something because we are afraid is actually not the easy way out in the long run. Though it might seem counterintuitive, it is finding the courage to try, or push ahead, or speak up, or make a change that will help us find our groove. When we do the hard thing, ultimately we find more ease.

That said, trying to control what we *don't* think about doesn't work. (Consider the old experiment where researchers tell their subjects not to think of a white bear: Most people immediately start thinking about a white bear.) It doesn't work to say to yourself, "I have to stop thinking about all the ways that I might fail" or "I have to stop being afraid; it's the fear that's making this difficult" even though it is true that you won't become braver by thinking about all the ways that you might fail.

Instead, take a two-pronged approach to thinking brave thoughts. First, simply pay attention. If you notice yourself having an insecure or an undermining thought, simply label it as such: "Oh, there's a fearful thought." For example, you are trying to get yourself to ask a question at a conference, but you are too afraid to raise your hand, and you notice yourself imagining that the presenter thinks your question is totally dumb. Say to yourself, *That is a thought that will make me feel afraid to ask my question,* and take a deep breath. Noticing your not-brave thoughts can give you the distance you need to *not* act according to that thought and the feeling it produces.

(Note: Don't skip the "take a deep breath" part! Breathe in through your nose and fill the bottom of your lungs, pushing your tummy out. This can trigger your vagus nerve, which will have a calming effect.)

Second, actively fill your mind with courageous thoughts. Consider times when you've been brave before. Focus on how people just like you have done what you are mustering the courage to do. Think about how the last time you did it, it wasn't that hard. Think about how you'll regret it if you don't do it. Think about how the worst-case scenario is something that you can deal with.

Simply reminding yourself what your long-term goals are is a way of thinking bravely. If you are depressed, for example, it can take real courage just to get out of bed in the morning, but your life depends on it. What are your hopes for your life? Remind yourself what you— and the world!—stand to lose if you can't muster the courage. As Meg Cabot so wisely said, "Courage is not the absence of fear, but rather the judgment that something else is more important than fear."

Play around with the thoughts that make you feel most courageous, and the ones that lead you to act bravely. Then make the best thought your mantra. Write it on sticky notes that you place around you strategically (like the bathroom mirror, the kitchen clock, your computer screen, your car dashboard) so you'll be reminded of your mantra when you most need it.

THE EASIEST THING:
SWAP STRESS FOR COURAGE

There you are, freaking out in front of your colleagues when you should be calmly giving a presentation. Or you're sweating bullets in the ER, waiting for the doctor to bring you news about your daughter's high fever. Descending into a full-blown fight-or-flight response is not going to help, and it's just going to drain you, but what can you do?

Amazingly, we can actually shift our physiological stress response from "I'm freaking out right now" to "I'm facing a challenge right now." When we do this, we prevent the deleterious effects of a fight-or-flight response.

Our bodies and minds are tightly linked. When we use our minds to "reappraise our stress response," as scientists call it, from stress to challenge, we can actually change the typical physiological response itself from a stress response to a challenge response. In a typical stress response, our heart rate elevates and our blood vessels constrict, which increases our blood pressure and *decreases* the efficiency of our heart. Anticipating defeat, our heart protects the cardiovascular system by contracting. In a challenge (or courage) response, the heart rate elevates but the blood vessels don't constrict, which *increases* the efficiency of our cardiovascular system. Researchers have found that when people reframe the meaning of their physiological response to stress as something that is improving their performance, they feel more confident and less anxious. Moreover, their physical response to the stress actually *changes* from one that is damaging to one that is helpful.

How does this work? Through our emotions. When we are afraid, we trigger a physiological response, which is more often than not unhelpful and damaging. When we are courageous, we trigger a different, more constructive, response.

So sometimes the easiest thing in a difficult situation is to see our physical response as a sign that we are engaged and our body is helping us meet the challenge. Our heart is pumping more blood sugar and oxygen to our muscles and brain so that we can respond more quickly.

CHAPTER 10

a short guide to getting your groove back

We must accept finite disappointment, but never lose infinite hope.

—Martin Luther King Jr.

Life is difficult; there's just no getting around that fact. Sure, life is more difficult for some people than others—but no matter how hard we try or how privileged we are, it is not possible, or even desirable, to lead a life free from discomfort and difficulty. As we've seen in the previous two chapters, the best way to find our groove is to accept, and even welcome, discomfort and failure into our lives.

Yeah sure, I can hear you saying. All of that is well enough in the abstract, but what does it really mean in practice to "welcome failure" or "accept difficulty" when we're struggling? How can we best navigate when we are thrown off our game? How can we get our groove back when we can't find our sweet spot? Most of us need—but few of us naturally develop—a specific plan of approach for when the going gets rough.

How we cope with discomfort and adversity depends, of course, on the severity of the particular setback we are dealing with. How we respond to making an embarrassing mistake will differ dramatically from learning that we have breast cancer to feeling discomfort when arriving at a party where we don't know anyone. The setbacks we face in the course of our day-to-day life exist on a continuum from mild discomfort to profound pain. The tactics outlined below are versatile enough to scale up or back depending on the situation.

After thirty-five years of emotionally whipping myself after even the slightest misstep, I have finally disengaged from the tangle of fear, embarrassment, and tension that every little setback created in me. You can build these important skills, too.

STEP ONE: FEEL WHAT YOU FEEL

We are living in an age of anxiety, and when we feel stressed-out (or sad or disappointed or bored or frustrated), our world offers up a host of ways to numb those negative feelings, ways to dull the pain. We drink alcohol and take drugs; we overeat and gossip; we have affairs and go shopping for things we don't need; we keep ourselves too busy to feel anything, compulsively checking our phones and email and Facebook.

Unfortunately, when we numb unpleasant feelings, we numb *everything* that we are feeling. There are two problems with this. First, our emotions are how our heart talks to us, how it tells us what choices to make. As Omid Kordestani, one of the first Google employees, reminds us, "In life you make the small decisions with your head and the big decisions with your heart." So to make good decisions, to know who we are and what we want in life, we need to be able to listen to our emotions.

Second, to completely feel the positive things in life—to truly feel love, or joy, or profound gratitude—we must also let ourselves feel emotions like fear, grief, and frustration. So if you are feeling anxious or embarrassed or hurt, the first step to getting your groove back is to let yourself *feel* that emotion.

Even though it can be scary to expose ourselves to our strongest emotions, neuroscientist Jill Bolte Taylor teaches us that most emotions don't linger more than ninety seconds. What you'll probably find is that if you can sit still with a strong emotion and let yourself feel it, even the worst emotional pain rises, crests, breaks, and recedes like a wave on the surf.

The key to not getting sucked into an undertow of cyclical rumination and emotional retriggering is acceptance. Lean into your feelings, even if they are painful. Take a moment to be mindful and narrate: *I'm feeling anxious right now,* or *this situation is making me tense.*

See if you can describe the emotion you are experiencing as though it is an object. Where in your body does it live? Is it in the pit of your stomach? In your throat? What, really, does it feel like? Can you give it a shape or a texture or a color? Hang in there with unpleasant feelings at least long enough to acknowledge them.

For instance, I was trying to work on this chapter, and one of my kids was singing in the kitchen *really loudly.* Because the kitchen is adjacent to my office, I asked her to pipe down, which she did. For about one second. And then she started up again. Which I found really, really irritating, even though I also recognized that my irritation is irrational. She's just happy and has a song stuck in her head. I want her to be happy and comfortable singing in the kitchen while she empties the dishwasher. But instead of letting my irrational irritation spin me into a spiral of escalating annoyance and guilt, I notice and label it. *I'm feeling SUPER irritated by the sound of her singing that SUPER annoying song. I feel the irritation in the tops of my shoulders and behind my eyes. It is orange and red and spiky. It moves around and is sharp but static-y.*

This is the foundation of emotional intelligence: We label what we are feeling, and we validate those feelings, no matter what they are. Accepting what we are feeling isn't the same as resignation; we aren't deciding to *keep* feeling the same thing in perpetuity. That is *defeat,* not acceptance. Surrendering to what we are feeling in the present moment might mean accepting the present—and therefore finite—disappointment. But when we surrender, we open ourselves up to something much greater and much more powerful—hope for something better in the future.

It may help to understand that letting ourselves feel what we feel is a form of mindfulness. Most people associate mindfulness with monks sitting calmly in meditation, but mindfulness is not necessarily a lack of emotion or a state of blissed-out calm. We can feel terrified, and mindfulness enables us to have that experience. We can be yelling or howling in pain and still pay mindful attention to that experience. We can be sitting calmly, quietly anxious in a concerning situation, and at the same time be mindful of our worry.

STEP TWO: UNTANGLE YOUR THOUGHTS

Sometimes it is not our feelings about a difficult situation that keep us down, but our thoughts. Perhaps when you read above that emotions last only ninety seconds, you thought, *No way! I let myself really feel my feelings when [insert painful/heartbreaking situation here] and I felt [devastated/frustrated] for way longer than a minute and a half!* You've experienced your thoughts at work here. Physiologically, emotions pulse through us rather quickly. Neurotransmitters related to an emotion we feel really will be cleared out of our system in a matter of about a minute and a half. We experience emotions as lasting much longer, however, because often we keep re-stimulating them with our thoughts. Something painful happens, and we feel an emotion. Then we think about what happened, and we feel the emotion again. And then we think about it again . . . you get the idea.

Susan David, a Harvard psychologist, and Christina Congleton, a consultant who advises companies around the world, write compellingly about how sometimes when we figuratively trip we stay down because we get tangled in unproductive thoughts. "We see leaders stumble not because they *have* undesirable thoughts and feelings—that's inevitable—but because they get *hooked* by them, like fish caught on a line." We get hooked by our thoughts in a couple of ways. First, we can treat unproductive thoughts like unquestioned facts: *"It was the same in my last job . . . I've been a failure my whole career."* We then often apply these faulty thought-facts more broadly to other situations. This leads us, David and Congleton write, to *avoid* situations that might evoke similar thoughts and feelings—so a mistake at work can lead us to pass up a challenging project or not apply for a promotion.

Instead of buying into negative, spiraling thoughts that can come following adversity, we first need to identify the thoughts we might be tangled in and separate out the benefits—and costs—of the thought. Perhaps you accidentally missed an important teacher conference at your child's school, and you feel "hooked" by the thought *I am too involved with my work to be a good parent*. Ask yourself: Is that thought productive? Will it help me be a better parent? Is it helping me at work? Will it help me remember future meetings at the school? The answer, of course, is no.

Next, decide whether you are treating your unproductive thought as a fact, or if you are avoiding situations that will lead to similar thoughts. If you feel guilt or shame about your performance as a parent, you've likely bought into it, and that might make you more likely to avoid emails from the school, for example, or to procrastinate calling a teacher back—neither of which will help the situation. If you've bought into the thought, question the truth of it. Is it a *fact* that you work too much to be a good parent? Can you *absolutely know that it is true*? Maybe it is. If so, accept that, and proceed to step three ("Take Responsibility and Course-Correct," below). If it isn't a fact—perhaps you know many great parents who work as much as you—acknowledge that your thought is just a thought, and not necessarily absolutely true.

Or perhaps you are pushing the thought aside with the rationale that *All working parents miss important meetings at the school sometimes. I'm a great parent who is more involved than most*. While it might be true that you *are* a great parent, missing important meetings with teachers is probably not evidence of it; moreover, your desire to prove that you are a good parent might lead you to make up for your mistake in unproductive ways (think of the parents who buy their kids presents when they feel guilty, or don't uphold legitimate and important standards like bedtime or limiting screen time). Instead of avoiding the difficult thought, acknowledge it. Is it useful information? How does it make you feel when you think that thought? Can you lean into *that* feeling?

When we acknowledge and question our thoughts, we can often gain the perspective we need to untangle ourselves from them, something researchers call "emotional agility." Emotional agility is a skill that has been shown to reduce stress and future errors, increase innovation in businesses, and improve our job performance.

We need to pay particular attention to self-critical thoughts. These are the most unproductive ones of all. If you are anything like me, making a mistake can generate a fair amount of self-flagellation. Somehow I think—or act as if I think—that if I'm really hard on myself, I'll be less likely to make the same mistake again, or I'll motivate myself toward better performance in the future.

But **self-criticism doesn't work.** It doesn't actually motivate us. Instead, self-criticism is associated with *decreased* motivation and future improvement. Kristin Neff, the psychologist who has done pioneering research on self-esteem and self-compassion, explains how this works:

Self-criticism is very strongly linked to depression. And depression is antithetical to motivation: It causes us to lose faith in ourselves, and that's going to make us less likely to try to change . . . If every time you fail or make a mistake you beat yourself up, you're going to try to avoid failure at all costs. It's a natural survival instinct.

Self-criticism conditions us for failure in two ways. First, it makes us risk-avoidant, which compromises our potential for growth. Instead of challenging ourselves—something essential for improving performance—we hedge our bets by taking the easy route. Second, self-criticism makes it extra painful for us to see our weaknesses and failings for what they are, ensuring that we won't learn from our mistakes but rather that we'll repeat them. According to Neff, when we beat ourselves up over a mistake our "subconscious pulls every trick in the book to not have to own up to [our] weaknesses."

So self-criticism isn't an effective way for us to prevent ourselves from repeating a mistake in the future; instead, it increases our stress and prolongs our negative feelings. (The same is true for the majority of criticism of others, too. This is food for thought the next time you think you are motivating your children, spouse, or employees through criticism or critique.)

Neff's research demonstrates the benefits of *self-compassion* over self-criticism, especially in the face of our flaws. She also offers us an easy way to enter into this mindset. Self-compassion, she writes, is simply "treating yourself with the same type of kind, caring support and understanding that you would show to anyone you cared about . . . In fact, most of us make incredibly harsh, cruel self-judgments that we would never make about a total stranger, let alone someone we cared about."

Self-compassion—being warm and supportive toward ourselves, and actively soothing ourselves—has many benefits over self-criticism. It leads to less anxiety and depression, and greater peace of mind. Neff herself was "surprised by how strongly the links were between self-compassion and well-being."

Self-compassion also builds our capacity to hear useful feedback from others. In one study, Neff and her colleagues asked college students to make a video to introduce and describe themselves. They were told that they would be given feedback on how "warm, friendly, intelligent, likeable, and mature" they appeared. The feedback was fake—participants randomly got negative, neutral, or positive feedback—but the self-compassionate people were relatively unflustered by the task and the feedback they got. People high in self-esteem but not in self-compassion, however, tended to take offense when they didn't get positive feedback. They couldn't even take in neutral feedback, but instead tended to deny that the feedback was due to their own personality. Instead they blamed it on the shortcomings of the person giving them feedback. Self-compassionate folks could attribute feedback to the job they did without blaming the messenger.

Contrary to what you might think, there is more to practicing self-compassion than just being kind to yourself. Neff's research shows that self-compassion also involves mindfulness, as discussed in step one, and having a strong sense of our common humanity. We can cultivate this sense of common humanity simply by remembering that imperfection is "part of the shared human experience"—that we aren't alone in our suffering.

So, follow the logic and the psychology toward ease. When we drop judgment and just pay mindful attention to our feelings and thoughts and reactions, when we comfort ourselves with the knowledge that "to err is human" and in this way we are connected to a common humanity, we allow ourselves the space to relax. We allow our nervous system to operate in "pause and plan" mode, which dramatically increases the odds that we'll recover from our error more gracefully than if we were in a state of fight or flight. This is when we find our groove.

In this process of untangling ourselves from our critical thoughts we're simply noticing. This involves a kind of discipline through which we are *not* chastising ourselves—or other people—for *making us* feel how we feel. We are experiencing. We are not shifting into a cause-and-effect inquiry.

Generally speaking, this sort of acceptance without judgment *isn't* our default mode. At least, it's not mine, and it's not the default mode of most people I know. Instead, most of us tend to be quite judgmental of ourselves and those around us, particularly when the chips are down.

a little reminder

One thing Neff always teaches about self-compassion: Don't expect, or hope, that self-compassion will relieve your pain or make difficult feelings go away. (But that's not to say there isn't a way to feel better. It's coming, I promise.) We don't practice self-compassion to make ourselves feel better. We practice self-compassion *simply because we are suffering*. This ability to acknowledge problems, negative feelings, and toxic thoughts while still being kind to ourselves is a key skill for becoming comfortable with discomfort.

STEP THREE: TAKE RESPONSIBILITY AND COURSE-CORRECT

Although sometimes we don't play any role whatsoever in the difficulties we face, often our difficulties and disappointments do come from our own mistakes and weaknesses. If we can allow ourselves to be honest, that's just a fact. For example, we overcommitted and are now in a jam, or we did do something that we told our teenager or our spouse we would stop doing. How we respond to the blunders we bring upon ourselves determines whether or not we are able to overcome them.

Before we can grow from an adverse situation, we need to acknowledge whatever role we played in the setback. We can't learn from a mistake or prevent it from happening again when we are still blaming *someone else* for causing it. This mature step is about acknowledging the role *we* play in difficult situations. Accepting responsibility allows us to take back some of the control, and not feel so victimized.

When we hold ourselves accountable, we put ourselves in a better place to course-correct. What can we do differently the next time so that this doesn't happen again? And how can we repair relationships that may be damaged due to the mistake or challenging situation? To whom do we need to make an effective apology? Who do we need to forgive? What conflict do we need to resolve? What skills do we need to build? Ask yourself these questions, and already life will be a little easier.

LEARNING FROM DIFFICULTY 101

Most mistakes, failures, and difficulties follow a particular pattern:

- Something happens.

- We react to it emotionally: We feel embarrassed, horrified, struck with fear, et cetera.

- We have predictable thoughts about the event that lead us to continue to react emotionally or to avoid our emotions altogether.

- We accept our feelings and untangle our thoughts, and the negative emotion dissipates. The sting of the mistake or misstep clears, the grief wanes, the situation blows over.

Now, *finally,* the opportunity arises for us to grow and become a better or more skilled person from the adversity we just faced. Although once we are feeling better it often is far more appealing to move on fully without re-examining what went wrong, when we skip this last step we walk away from the greatest prize. Adversity almost always carries with it a gift—the opportunity to learn something that we couldn't have learned any other way, or a change in perspective that fundamentally shifts our actions or our values.

Don't worry, there isn't a large time commitment to taking that last step. Take just a few minutes—or longer if you need to and can make more time—to reflect and problem-solve. What can you do to improve a difficult situation tomorrow? Who else can help? Whom do you need to forgive before you'll feel better? How can you be better prepared, or what better approach can you take next time? Do you simply need to try harder?

Put a plan into place now, while the issue or uncomfortable situation is still fresh in your mind. Be as specific about your next action steps as possible. This is your best bet for improving future outcomes.

Now, take a moment to reflect. What have you gained from the adversity you've faced? How have you grown? What new perspective have you gained?

When we've recovered from a blunder or come through a very difficult time, wonderful things can happen. We try again with our new strategy or learning, and we succeed. Or we gain the confidence that comes from having tried, failed, and learned something important. As South African adventurer Boyd Varty writes, "Confidence that comes from never having been burned is different from confidence that comes from having been in situations where it all went wrong."

COURSE CORRECTING WITH THE SWEET SPOT EQUATION

As I've been copyediting and putting the finishing touches on this book, I've also been moving homes. And moving. And moving and moving and moving. We cleaned out our garage and all our closets in May, and painted and replaced old carpeting in June. In July, we put most of our stuff in storage and staged our house, and moved in with relatives. But then our Realtor recommended that we not put our house on the market over the summer after all, so we moved back home—without our stuff. In August, we moved back out and put our house up for sale. As I write this, we finally have a plan to move in mid-September, provided our new house is ready.

As you might imagine, living with most of our stuff in storage for nearly three months has really thrown me off my game. I've lost my groove a zillion times. But I also keep *finding* my groove again, using the Sweet Spot Equation:

(1) **Take Recess.** Knowing that I'm more likely to feel overwhelmed and frustrated during this move, I've had to make sure to add a lot of positive experiences and emotions back into my life to keep my ratio of positive to negative emotions high (see Chapter 2). I'm spending more time in nature with my kids, going to movies with my husband, making art, and playing with my dog.

(2) **Return to Routine.** Even though it is difficult, my kids and I have been trying to maintain our carefully constructed morning and evening routines. We always feel

more in the groove when we return to our routines; they are a natural stress reliever.

(3) Ease Overwhelm. Though I've been free from physical clutter this summer, the uncertainty surrounding our move has been a recurring, low-level stressor. I've found that making a plan (page 96) is the best way for me to feel less overwhelmed. Even though I've had to continually adjust my well-laid plans, it's strangely comforting to have a plan where before there was uncertainty.

(4) Connect with Friends. Every time I start feeling particularly unsettled and sorry for myself, I try to reach out to someone who needs support. I have several friends who, unfortunately, are struggling with divorce and serious illness right now, so helping them helps me feel connected and loving, and gives me perspective on my own discomfort.

(5) Tolerate the discomfort that comes with growth. I've continually needed to follow the three steps I've outlined in this chapter. First, I've let myself feel what it is I'm feeling. As uncomfortable emotions arise, I notice and label them: *I feel profoundly unsettled* or *I feel really frustrated that I don't have an office right now.*

And although my first instinct is to criticize myself (*Why in the world did we start moving so early!?* Or, *Why am I so upside down? We are only moving—such a first-world problem!* are some frequent unproductive thoughts) I've also been practicing self-compassion, which helps *a lot.*

Finally, I've continually refocused myself on what I can learn from this unsettling time, what I will do differently next time, and what I'm gaining from the difficulty. The famous words of Thich Nhat Hanh, "No mud, no lotus" have become my mantra.

THE EASIEST THING: GO HAVE FUN

Off your game? Having a hard time? This is the time to call up one of your besties—or even just a friendly acquaintance who might be up for having a few laughs—preferably someone who can help lift you up, rather than someone you can easily drag down with your sad tale. This gives distant aquaintances—people you don't know well enough to share your pain with—an advantage.

I know, I know, you don't feel well. You don't want to call someone or plan something fun. That's the last thing you want to do. You want to hole up and cry yourself to sleep, or cower in a corner somewhere and wallow in your sorrows. Perhaps you are experiencing doldrums so deep that you can only sit and stare into space. It's rough.

I don't mean to seem uncompassionate, but someone needs to tell you. You can opt out of life—or your sweet spot—for only so long, my friend, before you are going to need to get your groove back. So spend another hour with your therapist, go through the three steps above, and then make an honest effort to go do something fun.

Pop quiz: What's the best way to reset your nervous system after you've been feeling bad? (Hint: See all of Chapter 2.) You need a hit of positive emotions—of gratitude or hope, of compassion or love, of faith or passion, of inspiration or awe. (We don't call these emotions elevating for nothing.) When I say "go do something fun," I mean this loosely. Technically, you could do anything that is likely to help you feel a positive emotion.

Watch a funny movie. Read your favorite poem—but not

the one about death, unless you find death poems inspiring, as I do (see Chapter 1 for more about that). Go for a walk in the woods. Give someone a hug. Go dancing. Perform a random act of kindness. Write a thank-you note. Have an orgasm.

Extra credit: Do one or more of these things with another human being. Remember how our positive emotions are amplified—how they get bigger and more powerful? (No? Please reread Chapter 6.) Do something *fun with a friend*. Or, again, maybe a stranger—just someone with a pulse. So go to it. Really. Put the book down. Get out of here. Go play.

CONCLUSION

making the final shift

> Don't aim at success. The more you aim at it and make it a target, the more you are going to miss it. For success, like happiness, cannot be pursued; it must ensue, and it only does so as the unintended side effect of one's dedication to a cause greater than oneself.
>
> —Viktor Frankl, *Man's Search for Meaning*

Most Westerners chase money, fame, sex, power, happiness, and success. We don't question whether or not we are chasing things that will ultimately make us feel satisfied or content. We don't question whether or not these things will enable us to sleep at night without worry or existential loneliness, help us live with ease and health, help us live from that sweet spot where great personal power emerges without stress or strain. We usually don't stop and think: Will this help me find my groove? We know, on some level, that money and other outward signs of success won't ultimately make us happy—perhaps because we know wealthy or famous or powerful people who are deeply *un*happy—but on another level we really don't believe it. *Money might not buy other people happiness,* we think, *but I know I'd be happier living in a bigger house in a better neighborhood driving a nicer car.*

Perhaps we aren't directly chasing fame or fortune; instead, we pursue happy experiences. We buy things that delight us and cheer us up, we buy tickets to events and parks that promise entertainment. But will these pleasant or fun experiences make us feel that our life is, in the end, meaningful?

Compelling research indicates that the pursuit of pleasure and gratification won't ultimately bring us ease and it most certainly won't bring us strength. The pursuit of pleasure won't allow us to live and work in our sweet spot. Although we claim that the "pursuit of happiness" is our inalienable right and the primary drive of the human race, we humans do better pursuing fulfillment and meaning—creating lives that generate the feeling that we matter. Social psychologists define meaning, as it applies to our lives, as "a cognitive and emotional assessment of **the degree to which we feel our lives have purpose, value and impact.**" Among other things, meaning is **a belief** about our lives.

What we believe about ourselves—our physical and mental health, our life's purpose and impact, our ability and intellect—has the potential to change everything. A mountain of research shows us the many ways that our beliefs dramatically change our outcomes, even when our environment or life circumstances stay the same. Consider, for example, phenomena like the placebo effect, where the belief in a treatment alone heals the body and the mind.

THE POWER OF THE PLACEBO

Placebos are sham treatments, like a sugar pill with no medicinal properties, used in studies to determine whether real medicines have additional effects. Until the 1940s, nearly all Western medication relied on the placebo effect—the patient's *belief* that the pill the doctor prescribed would heal them. In reality, doctors were essentially prescribing sugar pills in different forms and colors. Even though today we have real medicines that often have dramatic effects (and side effects), our belief about our treatment and our confidence in our doctors still hold great power. Consider that 42 percent of bald men started to regrow hair using a sham hair growth tonic. Or that when researchers rubbed the arms of people who were extremely allergic to poison ivy with a harmless leaf with no allergenic properties, 100 percent of those told that the harmless leaf was poison ivy broke out in a rash. On the other hand, only 15 percent developed an allergic reaction when rubbed with *real* poison ivy that they were told was harmless. Physician Lissa Rankin set out to understand how she could use placebo effects to better heal her patients. She turned to the medical literature to learn more. This is what she writes about her discovery:

> *I found that nearly half of asthma patients get symptom relief in the form of a sham inhaler or sham acupuncture. Approximately 40 percent of people with headaches get relief when given a placebo. Half of people with colitis feel better after placebo treatment. More than half of patients studied for ulcer pain have resolution of their pain when given a placebo. Sham acupuncture cuts hot flashes almost in half . . . As many as 40 percent of infertility patients get pregnant while taking placebo "fertility drugs."*
>
> *In fact, when compared to morphine, placebos are almost equally effective at treating pain. And multiple studies demonstrate that almost all of the happy-making responses patients experience as a result of antidepressants can be attributed to the placebo effect.*
>
> *It's not just pills and injections that work wonders when it comes to symptom relief. . . . [S]ham surgeries can be even more effective.*

Dr. Rankin's fascinating book *Mind Over Medicine* documents these and many more of her findings. She makes one thing strikingly clear: Our beliefs have tremendous power. *Believing* that we are sick when we are not can make us ill. Believing that we are being healed is sometimes enough to stimulate actual healing. Why? Although we don't know precisely how placebo effects work, we know that the brain triggers a cascade of effects in our bodies when our beliefs about the immediate future are altered. Researchers refer to this as "expectancy theory." However it works, here's the marvelous opportunity it lays at our feet: A simple belief can generate both strength and ease. Healing and improvement can occur without effort or strain.

maybe you *don't* need to hit the gym

Placebo effects aren't confined to medicine. Consider this study of hotel maids: Room attendants working in seven different hotels were tested for a variety of measures of physiological health—the measures that are most affected by exercise, like blood pressure and body mass index. Half were told how their work cleaning hotel rooms meets the surgeon general's recommendations for an active lifestyle—essentially, that their work counts as good exercise. The other half, the control group, weren't given any information about their work's exercise value. One month later, all the room attendants had their health measured again. Amazingly, those informed that their work counted as exercise showed a decrease in weight, blood pressure, body fat, waist-to-hip ratio, and body mass index. Their jobs hadn't changed, but their beliefs about their jobs changed—and so did their bodies!

GETTING YOUR HEAD IN THE GAME

But wait, there's more. Our beliefs have the power to change more than just our physiology or our health. They also dramatically change our overall happiness levels and our performance. Sometimes the best way to develop mastery, for example, is to take a long, hard look at what we believe—what we are thinking about ourselves and our performance—in a moment of adversity. More specifically, why do we think we are facing difficulty?

Do we believe that we are inherently not good at whatever it is we are pursuing? If so, we have what psychologists call a "fixed mindset," and that fixed mindset is holding us back. Research on mindsets was pioneered by Carol Dweck, now at Stanford, over thirty years ago. According to Dweck, a mindset is a belief about why someone is successful (or not). There are two really powerful mindsets. People with a **fixed mindset** believe that talents and personalities are more or less inborn, carved in stone. People with a **growth mindset** believe that success is a result of effort as much as or more than aptitude.

Most of us describe our personalities in fixed-mindset ways. Perhaps you are good at languages, "just like your grandmother," but terrible at math, like your father. Tennis seems to come naturally to you, but you simply can't carry a tune. Here's the thing: We consistently perform more poorly and give up more quickly when we believe that our intelligence (or athletic ability or anything else) is innate rather than believing that talent is something we can develop. The fixed mindset is a poison pill. *I'm terrible at details,* you might think. Or *only young people can learn a new language or do a flip turn in a pool.* These sorts of fixed mindsets are every bit as much a self-fulfilling prophecy as a placebo pill because they keep us from doing the work that will lead to mastery.

Our beliefs about why we or someone else is successful—or not—dramatically change how engaged and passionate we are about our activities, how much effort we put into them, whether or not we engage in deliberate and consistent practice, and, consequently, our performance. In short, our mindset powerfully affects how much grit we have in any given situation, and therefore whether or not we achieve mastery.

For example, Dweck's research team did an experiment where they gave kids a short nonverbal intelligence test (basically, puzzles) and then one line of praise. They either said, "Wow, that's a really good score. You must be smart at this" (fixed mindset), or they said, "Wow, that's a really good score. You must have worked really hard" (growth mindset). After the first test, the researchers offered the kids either a harder puzzle that they could learn from, or one that was easier than the one they completed successfully. The majority of the kids praised for their intelligence wanted the easier puzzle.

They weren't going to risk making a mistake and losing their status as "smart." On the other hand, more than 90 percent of the kids praised for their growth mindset chose a harder puzzle.

Why? When we believe that effort and hard work lead to achievement, we want to keep engaging in the process. We aren't diverted from what we're doing by a concern about how smart—or dumb—we might look.

When we praise the people around us by attributing their success to innate gifts, we hand them a prescription for anxiety and joyless achievement. In Dweck's study, during the first puzzle, pretty much everyone had fun. But when the kids who had been told they were "smart" were given a harder puzzle, they said it wasn't fun anymore because it's no fun when your special talent is in jeopardy. Besides making them insecure and crushing the fun of learning something new, telling kids how smart they are actually hinders performance. In another study, praising kids' smarts actually lowered their IQ scores! On the other hand, the effort-praised kids continued to have fun even when they weren't doing as well.

Our beliefs about success influence our performance and enjoyment as adults, too—at work and at home. For example, managers with a fixed mindset are less likely than growth-mindset managers to seek or welcome feedback from employees. And because they believe that people are not really capable of change, they are also less likely to mentor their employees. (Once they are schooled about having a growth mindset, however, such managers tend to give more useful advice and coach their employees more.)

Similarly, our mindset influences the quality and longevity of our friendships and romantic relationships. People with a growth mindset are more likely to address problems in their relationships and try to solve them. Because people with a fixed mindset are more likely to believe that people don't really change or grow in meaningful ways, they lack confidence that confronting concerns in their relationships will do any good. This attitude makes seeking the help of a counselor less likely and the likelihood of breakups more frequent.

Keep in mind that we can have different mindsets in different arenas. You work with a growth mindset on the job, knowing that you can figure out pretty much anything that you put your mind to. But at home, your wife is trying to get you to run a 10K with her, and you keep saying fixed-mindset things like "I'm just not built like a runner."

Fixed mindsets, particularly when we use them to label ourselves or others ("I'm not a runner"), can shackle us, becoming an excuse to give up. So if we want to be courageous and authentic and gritty, if we want to develop mastery and find ease, we need to believe that with the right strategies, coaching, and deliberate practice, we will improve.

Counterintuitive as they might be in some ways, mindsets are less mysterious to us than placebo effects because we understand how they influence our behavior and therefore our outcomes. But like the belief in a sugar pill's medicinal properties, mindsets are still only a simple belief. Although they operate like facts, mindsets are cognitive and emotional assessments—subjective opinions, not facts—about the degree to which we feel that our ability is innate rather than self-made through effort. We don't really know how good we are at the puzzle, or if a relationship is salvageable, unless we try.

CHASING MEANING

Similarly, our happiness and productivity as we work are dramatically affected by the *social* meaning—our belief about how something benefits others—that we assign to our activities. In a stunning series of studies, Adam Grant proved that briefly showing people how their work helps others increases not only how happy people are on the job but also how much they work and accomplish. Grant's most famous study was conducted at a call center with paid fundraisers tasked with phoning potential donors to a public university. As anyone who's ever made cold calls knows, work in a call center isn't easy. People receiving calls are often annoyed and can be downright rude. Employees must endure frequent rejection on the phone and low morale at the office—all in exchange for relatively low pay.

Not surprisingly, call-center jobs often have a high staff turnover rate.

In an effort to see if he could motivate call-center fund-raisers to stay on the job longer, Grant brought in a few scholarship students (who presumably had benefited from the fund-raisers' work) for a five-minute meeting where callers could ask them questions about their classes and experience at the university. In the next month, that quick conversation yielded unbelievable results. Callers who had met the scholarship students spent twice as long on the phone as the fund-raisers who had not met any students. They accomplished far more, bringing in an average of 171 percent more money. In another study, Grant found that having fund-raisers read an account from scholarship students about how they had been helped by the fund-raisers' work significantly increased the amount of money they raised. But reading an account from a previous fund-raiser about how the callers *themselves* benefited from their work as a fund-raiser did *not*. The difference? A shift in the callers' beliefs about the *social meaning* of their work, and an increased sense of their purpose, value, and impact.

Grant replicated his call-center studies with swimming pool lifeguards—a job that is often so boring that it's hard to keep people at it. He gave lifeguards something to read; one group got a paragraph written by a predecessor explaining how he or she had personally benefited from being a lifeguard, and a second group read about cases where lifeguards had saved lives. The first group's work didn't change—they stayed on the job the same amount of time as those who hadn't read about the benefits of being a lifeguard. The second group, who had been reading about lifeguards who prevented fatalities, worked 40 percent more hours than the others. Moreover, they reported being more dedicated to their jobs, and their managers said they were more helpful. What motivated them? Their increased perception of their impact on others, and an increased sense of their social worth.

These studies are remarkably counterintuitive. We assume that Westerners are best motivated on the job by our *own* interests—

money, prestige, what's in it for us, what we'll *get,* not what we *give.* But actually, these studies show clearly that we humans are best motivated by our *significance to other people.* We'll work harder and longer and better—and feel happier about the work we are doing— when we know that someone else is benefiting from our efforts. It turns out that one sure path to ease is to find the social meaning in your daily activities.

Long-term studies of grandparents find similar results. Those who report being able to help out their adult grandchildren in practical ways—with chores, transportation, advice, money—show significantly fewer symptoms of depression than those who are just the receivers of help from their grandchildren.

The final shift, then, is "a shift from the cramped world of self-preoccupation into a more expansive place of fellowship, of true kinship," to quote Gregory Boyle again. It's a shift in the meaning of our lives, in our beliefs about ourselves. Our significance in life comes from our relationships with other people and the ways that we give to others. As leadership and management professor Satinder Dhiman writes in *Seven Habits of Highly Fulfilled People,* "Success is about getting; significance is about giving: we make a living by what we get; we make a life by what we give." In the end, finding our groove is about finding meaning—our purpose, value, and impact—in what we do.

MEANING IS AN INSIDE JOB

Here's the kicker: The best way to make the final shift away from the "cramped world of self-preoccupation" is, ironically, to turn inward. Let me explain.

For the most part, the meaning that we assign to any given thought, feeling, action, experience, or environment is entirely our choice. Our rapidly changing world can feel wildly out of control (even as, if you are anything like me, you madly try to control most everything around you). As Viktor Frankl wrote in *Man's Search for Meaning:*

Man can preserve a vestige of spiritual freedom, of independence of mind, even in such terrible conditions of psychic and physical stress. We who lived in concentration camps can remember the men who walked through the huts comforting others, giving away their last piece of bread. They may have been few in number, but they offer sufficient proof that everything can be taken from a man but one thing: the last of the human freedoms—to choose one's attitude in any given set of circumstances, to choose one's own way.

The reality is that we can really control *only* the thoughts and beliefs running loose in our heads. We can *influence* the people around us and the situations we live and work in, of course, but ultimately we cannot really control them. We *can* control, however, the meaning that we assign to any given thought or feeling or situation. And the beliefs we choose have the power to transform us: from sick to healthy, from fat to fit, from stressed to courageous, from defeated to gritty, from bored to engaged.

Success, sex, power, prestige, fame, money, artificially stimulated happiness, the appearance of youth (when we're old), store-bought beauty—these are external rewards. And a mountain of research shows us that the pursuit of external rewards makes us more anxious, depressed, drug-abusing, and physically sick than when we pursue goals with intrinsic meaning (such as deep, enduring relationships).

Meaning is an inside job. In order to find meaning, we need to turn inward, to quiet our chatty verbal mind so that we can listen to our heart, listen to the still, small voice inside us that gives us direction, that points us toward the truth of our own significance.

In other words, the way to chase meaning is to end the chase. We need to step off the hamster wheel and look inside ourselves. We need to stop focusing on our dreary workplace or our annoying colleagues, frustrating spouse, complaining kids, or stressful commute, and start focusing on ourselves. Not focus on ourselves in a selfish way, but turn inward in the sense that all great wisdom traditions, and now scientific research, advocate: in contemplation, prayer, meditation, or simple attention to our own sensory experience of the present moment.

SILENCING THE CHATTER

While I've long known about the neurological benefits of meditation and other contemplative practices, it wasn't until I read brain
scientist Jill Bolte Taylor's book *My Stroke of Insight* that I realized
that we best experience meaning—a deep connection to something
larger than just ourselves—when we quiet the *verbal* part of our
brains.

Researchers are actually able to *see* this phenomenon inside the
lab. Tibetan meditators and Franciscan nuns praying or meditating
inside a brain scanner pulled a cord when they felt a shift in their
consciousness "away from being an individual to feeling that [they]
were at *one* with the universe (God, Nirvana, euphoria)." Researchers were able to identify corresponding shifts in the neurological
activity in the meditators' and nuns' brains. Activity in their language centers (on the left side of the brain) quieted down to next to
nothing, and activity ceased in the area of the brain, also in the left
hemisphere, that helps us identify our personal boundaries and
makes us feel like separate individuals.

Feelings of profound meaning, intense connection, and inner
peace are created when neurological circuitry, located in the right
hemisphere of our brain, is activated. Unfortunately, activity in this
area of our brain is often overruled by noisy activity in the verbal left
hemisphere. So in order to discover our purpose, intrinsic passion,
and significance as part of something larger than ourselves, we must
choose to silence our left brain's constant chatter—at least for a
while. Fortunately, just as we can shift our beliefs in ways that dramatically bring more ease into our lives—think of the placebo effect
and the growth mindset—we can shift our brain activity such that
we experience the *ultimate sweet spot:* transcendent inner peace.

How? Virtually every religious tradition offers practices that
quiet the verbal mind: prayer, yoga, meditation, fasting, prostration.
To be honest, none of these practices really appeals to me because
silence is *not* a state I naturally seek. I'm extroverted. I'd rather be
with people, preferably talking. And as an avid reader and a profes-

sional writer, I tend to fear—not cultivate—a loss of words. But I've long known the incredible benefits that research shows come from quieting the thoughts in my head, and this knowledge motivated the academic in me to want to tap into my right brain more effectively.

To quiet my noisy verbal brain, I frequently look to Martha Beck, who humbly calls herself a life coach (but really, she is a modern-day shaman). Beck teaches practices for what she calls "deep wordlessness." Here's what she writes about wordlessness in *Finding Your Way in a Wild New World*:

To master Wordlessness . . . you must unlearn almost everything you were taught in school about what it means to be intelligent. The sharp focus you were told to sustain is actually a limiting, stressful, narrow attention field—something animals only use in the moment of "fight or flight." Dropping into Wordlessness moves the brain into its "rest and relax" state.

One of the practices for dropping into wordlessness that works for me is simply to follow the feeling of my own bloodstream. You can try it by focusing your attention on your heart in the space between breaths. After you exhale deeply, pause your breathing and find the feeling of your heart beating. Take another breath while following the sensation of your heartbeat. Once you're following your heartbeat, see if you can feel your circulatory system elsewhere—in your ears or toes or hands, your head and organs, or your entire body. Hang out for a while in this meditative state.

If this doesn't appeal to you, no worries. There are literally hundreds of ways to quiet your verbal mind. Most forms of play will do it, and music can help, too. Try getting into a flow state while you're at work, playing with your dog, or dancing. Even just singing along to a favorite song can do it.

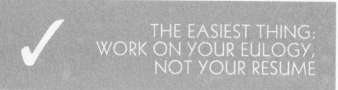

THE EASIEST THING:
WORK ON YOUR EULOGY,
NOT YOUR RESUME

This year at Wisdom 2.0, a conference where some of the wisest humans alive today give their best advice for living well, Arianna Huffington gave the audience fantastic directions for finding greater meaning and fulfillment in life: Start working on your eulogy, and stop working on your résumé. She elaborated:

It is very telling what we don't hear in eulogies. We almost never hear things like:

The crowning achievement of his life was when he made senior vice president. Or

He increased market share for his company multiple times during his tenure. Or

While she didn't have any real friends, she had six hundred Facebook friends, and she dealt with every email in her in-box every night.

After we've passed away, people will recount the ways that we made a difference in their lives and in the world. They will tell stories and recount memories of time we enjoyed together. They will talk, in essence, about the meaning we found in this lifetime, about our value, our impact, and our purpose. When we start working on our eulogy, we reorient our efforts toward meaning and away from achievements. We look away from the glitter of external rewards: the decadent meal, the Botox, the designer shoes, the higher paycheck, and the more prestigious title. We look inside ourselves to see what really lights our fire, what really brings us peace.

Does working on our eulogy rather than our résumé mean that we leave a high-paying job for a more meaningful but possibly lower-paying one? Perhaps you are an unfulfilled lawyer with a large house in a tony suburb, a stay-at-home spouse, three kids, a housekeeper, and annual vacations to Aspen and Aruba. Should you give it all up and become the seventh-grade math teacher you thought you would become when you were, well, a seventh-grader?

I'm a huge fan of making major life changes when they're appropriate and needed. Often, the best move for finding our groove is to totally upend something—a marriage, a career, a household—and start again. But for most of us, I don't think focusing on our eulogy is really about making a major life change. It's about finding meaning right where we already are. If you are the unfulfilled lawyer, my best advice is to find a way to unleash your inner math teacher at your existing job. Can you mentor a junior colleague who lacks confidence in his math skills? Can you start a tutoring program in partnership with a local school? Hire a high school student for a summer job? Try not to think of these possibilities as adding tasks to your already long to-do list. Rather, think of them as ways to live and work from your sweet spot by tapping into something that brings you joy and meaning.

We humans find our calling in *all* types of work—as janitors and ministers, as executives and hairdressers, as artists and parents and mail carriers and farmers. One study found that among administrative assistants, one third considered their work a job (they focused on their paycheck—not the meaning or enjoyment they derived from the work), one third considered it a career (mostly a series of ascending achievements), and another third considered it a true calling (they felt that their work was interesting, socially useful, and truly worthy of their time and energy). Researchers have found the same results in other occupations. People tend to be more or less equally distributed in each of the categories of job, career, and calling.

What this means is it isn't the job description or title that determines meaning—whether we consider it a job, a career, or a calling. It's the person. It isn't about the prestige or even the helping nature of our work. It's about the meaning we personally find in it and express through it, and the effort and commitment we give to it.

So ask yourself what meaning you find in your work, and in your life. What are you passionate about? What do you find most interesting, important, and worthy of your time and energy? How are you adding value? What positive impact are you having on the world and other people? What, in other words, are you giving your eulogizers to work with? Do your time and effort reflect your commitment to the work you value the most? To paraphrase Kierkegaard: Eternity will not ask about your wife and what she made of her life. It will ask about *you*.

People will remember you for all the ways that your strength arose with little strain. They will remember the happy times in your life. They will remember how you transcended the addictive siren song of technology to nurture real-life people. They will recount your quirky habits, the things that made you the most *you*. They will remember the times you chose to repair relationships that were crumbling, and they will remember how you held yourself accountable for your mistakes. They will remember the many non-material gifts that you showered on your family, your friends, your community—the world.

They will remember you for your passion. But more than that, they will remember you for your courage. They will recount your mastery in every arena where it emerged. They will most certainly tell of the times you tolerated discomfort or you broke with the herd in order to serve something larger than yourself. And, finally, they will remember your awe, your gratitude, your generosity, your optimism, and especially your love and compassion.

What do *you* want them to remember?

ACKNOWLEDGMENTS

I could not have written this book were it not for the three most important men in my life: my brother Tim, my dad, and my husband, Mark. They've consistently shown me what it looks like to be in the groove both at home and at work; without their examples, I'm not sure I'd have truly believed that an easier life—where I didn't have to sacrifice happiness for success or vice versa—was actually possible.

This book would not have been so fun to write were it not for all the people who helped me with it, especially Dan Mulhern, who was there from the beginning hearing every idea and reading every word. Liza Veto, Melissa Raymond, and Samantha Carter were also important readers who made this book far better. And, of course, my editor Marnie Cochran has been an important collaborator, supporter, and friend. I am so grateful and lucky to have all of you in my life!

A special shout-out to Marielle Echevarria Reading, who makes it possible for me to be in the groove at work. I love working with you!! Thanks also to Cathy Dai and Iris Agrafiotis for your research assistance, and to Monica Jane Albe for all you've done to support this work over the years.

Thanks to all who believed in this book from the beginning and helped shape it: Amy Rennert, Dacher Keltner, Rick Hanson, Claire Ferrari, and Joshua White—and Marielle again. Thanks also to everyone over at the Greater Good Science Center, especially Jason, for all the ways you make my work better.

Last but definitely not least, thanks to the many other friends and family members, who supported this project. Thanks Mom, LB, and Annie & Coley, for your love and support. Thanks to my amazing women's group—Emiliana, Cassi, Jennifer, Lynn, Michelle, and Claire—for your insights and profoundly loving wisdom. Very special thanks to the Turducken crowd, especially Kelly and Mike, Kendra and Joey, Scott and Loren, Alex and Tracy, Melissa and Brion. And thank you one more time to Kelly, Kendra, and Claire for all your magic. I hope each of you knows how you individually helped shape the ideas in this book or furthered its progress in some way—I am so grateful and lucky to have your unending love, support, and loyalty.

NOTES

Introduction: Stepping Off the Treadmill

xi We all have a sweet spot Peter Bregman. "Find Your Sweet Spot—And Stay There." *Forbes* (February 4, 2012). http://www.forbes.com/sites/peterbregman/2012/02/04/find-your-sweet-spot-and-stay-there.

xi Only 17 percent of the adult Keyes, Corey L. M. "The Mental Health Continuum: From Languishing to Flourishing in Life." *Journal of Health and Social Behavior* 43, no. 2 (June 2000): 207–22.

xii If you're lucky enough Sara Robinson. "Why We Have to Go Back to a 40-Hour Work Week to Keep Our Sanity." *AlterNet* (March 13, 2012). http://www.alternet.org/story/154518/why_we_have_to_go_back_to_a_40-hour_work_week_to_keep_our_sanity.

xii And think about the fact Schulte, Brigid. *Overwhelmed: Work, Love and Play When No One Has the Time* (London: Bloomsbury Publishing, 2014).

xii For most of the twentieth century Sara Robinson. "Why We Have to Go Back to a 40-Hour Work Week to Keep Our Sanity." *AlterNet* (March 13, 2012). http://www.alternet.org/story/154518/why_we_have_to_go_back_to_a_40-hour_work_week_to_keep_our_sanity.

xiv Not familiar with Katrina Alcorn. "Letter from Baltimore." *Working Moms Break* (December 1, 2010). http://www.workingmomsbreak.com/2010/12/01/letter-from-baltimore.

xvi Consider that our conscious brain Dijksterhuis, Ap. "Think Different: The Merits of Unconscious Thought in Preference Development and Decision Making." *Journal of Personality and Social Psychology* 87, no. 2 (November 2004): 586–98.

xxi [*Sufficiency isn't*] *a quantity* Lynne Twist. *The Soul of Money: Reclaiming the Wealth of Our Inner Resources* (New York: W. W. Norton & Company, 2006).

xxi As Mary Oliver once wrote Mary Oliver. "The Summer Day." In *New and Selected Poems, Vol. 1* (Boston: Beacon Press, 1992).

Chapter 1: From Working Overtime to Enjoying the Seasons

4 Everyone asks Wayne Muller. *Sabbath: Finding Rest, Renewal, and Delight in Our Busy Lives* (New York: Bantam, 2000).

5 Csikszentmihalyi unintentionally induced Mihaly Csikszentmihalyi. *Flow: The Classic Work on How to Achieve Happiness* (London: Rider, 2002).

5 *The results were almost immediate* Daniel Pink. *Drive: The Surprising Truth About What Motivates Us* (New York: Riverhead Books, 2009).

6 **We are poisoned** Wayne Muller. *Sabbath: Finding Rest, Renewal, and Delight in Our Busy Lives* (New York: Bantam, 2000).

6 **Li will be counted** Shai Oster, "They're Dying at Their Desks in China as Epidemic of Stress Proves Fatal." Bloomberg News (June 30, 2014). http://www.bloomberg.com/news/2014-06-29/is-work-killing-you-in -china-workers-die-at-their-desks.html

6 **The Japanese call** Katsuo Nishiyama and Jeffrey V. Johnson. "Karoshi—Death from Overwork: Occupational Health Consequences of Japanese Production Management." *International Journal of Health Services* 27, no. 4 (1997): 625–41.

6 **Stressed and exhausted employees** Mark Hamer, Romano Endrighi, Shreenidhi M. Venuraju, Avijit Lahiri, and Andrew Steptoe. "Cortisol Responses to Mental Stress and the Progression of Coronary Artery Calcification in Healthy Men and Women." *PloS One* 7, no. 2 (January 2012): e31356.

8 *When we are increasingly* Wayne Muller. *A Life of Being, Having, and Doing Enough* (New York: Harmony, 2011).

9 **This means they try** Collins, Jim, and Morten T. Hansen. *Great by Choice: Uncertainty, Chaos and Luck—Why Some Thrive Despite Them All* (New York: Random House, 2011).

13 *Some cures require* Lee Lipsenthal. *Enjoy Every Sandwich: Living Each Day as If It Were Your Last* (New York: Harmony, 2011).

Chapter 2: The Stress/Success Tipping Point

15 **The world obeys** Barbara Fredrickson. *Positivity: Top-Notch Research Reveals the 3-to-1 Ratio That Will Change Your Life* (New York: Three Rivers Press, 2009).

17 **If you were a zebra** Robert M. Sapolsky. *Why Zebras Don't Get Ulcers.* 3rd ed., (New York: Holt Paperbacks, 2004).

17 **Second, and even more significantly** J. M. Koolhaas, S. M. Korte, S. F. De Boer, B. J. Van Der Vegt, C. G. Van Reenen, H. Hopster, I. C. De Jong, M. A. Ruis, and H. J. Blokhuis. "Coping Styles in Animals: Current Status in Behavior and Stress-Physiology." *Neuroscience and Biobehavioral Reviews* 23, no. 7 (November 1999): 925–35.

19 **When we crack a grin** Dacher Keltner. *Born to Be Good: The Science of a Meaningful Life* (New York: W. W. Norton & Company, 2009); V. Surakka and J. K. Hietanen. "Facial and Emotional Reactions to Duchenne and Non-Duchenne Smiles." *International Journal of Psychophysiology* 29, no. 1 (June 1998): 23–33.

19 **Striking a "power pose"** Dana R. Carney, Amy J. C. Cuddy, and Andy J. Yap. "Power Posing: Brief Nonverbal Displays Affect Neuroendocrine Levels and Risk Tolerance." *Psychological Science* 21, no. 10 (October 2010): 1363–68.

19 **Meditation lowers** Elisa H. Kozasa, João R. Sato, Shirley S. Lacerda,

Maria A. M. Barreiros, João Radvany, Tamara A. Russell, Liana G. Sanches, Luiz E. A. M. Mello, and Edson Amaro. "Meditation Training Increases Brain Efficiency in an Attention Task." *NeuroImage* 59, no. 1 (January 2, 2012): 745–49; Robert Keith Wallace. "Physiological Effects of Transcendental Meditation." *Science* 167, no. 3926 (March 1970): 1751–54.

19 Massage and other forms V. Morhenn, L. E. Beavin, and P. J. Zak. "Massage Increases Oxytocin and Reduces Adrenocorticotropin Hormone in Humans." *Alternative Therapies in Health and Medicine* 18, no. 6 (November-December 2012): 11–18; Dacher Keltner. *Born to Be Good: The Science of a Meaningful Life* (New York: W. W. Norton & Company, 2009).

19 This is why Barbara Fredrickson: Barbara L. Fredrickson, Roberta A. Mancuso, Christine Branigan, and Michele M. Tugade. "The Undoing Effect of Positive Emotions." *Motivation and Emotion* 24, no. 4 (December 2000): 237–58.

19 *Applying considerable time pressure* Barbara L. Fredrickson. *Positivity: Top-Notch Research Reveals the 3-to-1 Ratio That Will Change Your Life* (New York: Three Rivers Press, 2009).

20 Fredrickson's team then Ibid.

20 It was the volunteers Barbara L. Fredrickson, Roberta A. Mancuso, Christine Branigan, and Michele M. Tugade. "The Undoing Effect of Positive Emotions." *Motivation and Emotion* 24, no. 4 (December 2000): 237–58; Barbara L. Fredrickson and Robert W. Levenson. "Positive Emotions Speed Recovery from the Cardiovascular Sequelae of Negative Emotions." *Cognition & Emotion* 12, no. 2 (1998): 191–220.

21 For example, in one study Adam K. Anderson, Kalina Christoff, David Panitz, Eve De Rosa, and John D. E. Gabrieli. "Neural Correlates of the Automatic Processing of Threat Facial Signals." *Journal of Neuroscience* 23, no. 13 (July 2, 2009): 5627–33.

21 Fredrickson calls this Barbara L. Fredrickson and Christine Branigan. "Positive Emotions Broaden the Scope of Attention and Thought-Action Repertoires." *Cognition & Emotion* 19, no. 3 (May 1, 2005): 313–32; Barbara L. Fredrickson. "The Broaden-and-Build Theory of Positive Emotions." *Philosophical Transactions of the Royal Society of London. Series B, Biological Sciences* 359, no. 1449 (September 29, 2004): 1367–78; Barbara L. Fredrickson. "The Role of Positive Emotions in Positive Psychology: The Broaden-and-Build Theory of Positive Emotions." *American Psychologist* 56, no. 3 (March 2001): 218–26.

22 Fortunately, something remarkable Corey L. M. Keyes. "The Mental Health Continuum: From Languishing to Flourishing in Life." *Journal of Health and Social Behavior* 43, no. 2 (June 2002): 207–22.

22 Everything we do in life Rick Hanson. *Hardwiring Happiness: The New Brain Science of Contentment, Calm, and Confidence* (New York: Harmony, 2013).

22 This is why more than two hundred studies Sonja Lyubomirsky, Laura King, and Ed Diener. "The Benefits of Frequent Positive Affect:

Does Happiness Lead to Success?" *Psychological Bulletin* 131, no. 6 (November 2005): 803–55.

22 **Although the math** Fredrickson, Barbara L. "Updated Thinking on Positivity Ratios." *American Psychologist* 68, no. 9 (December 2013): 814–22.

23 **Positive psychology pioneer** Barbara Fredrickson. "Are You Getting Enough Positivity in Your Diet?" Greater Good Science Center (June 21, 2011). http://greatergood.berkeley.edu/article/item/are_you_getting_enough_positivity_in_your_diet.

24 **By contrast** Alicia A. Grandey. "When 'The Show Must Go On': Surface Acting and Deep Acting as Determinants of Emotional Exhaustion and Peer-Rated Service Delivery." *Academy of Management Journal* 46, no. 1 (February 2003): 86–96.

25 **Studies report long laundry lists** Emiliana R. Simon-Thomas. "A 'Thnx' a Day Keeps the Doctor Away." Greater Good Science Center (December 18, 2012). http://greatergood.berkeley.edu/article/item/a_thnx_a_day_keeps_the_doctor_away.

26 *Contemplate death and destruction* Araceli Frias, Philip C. Watkins, Amy C. Webber, and Jeffrey J. Froh. "Death and Gratitude: Death Reflection Enhances Gratitude." *Journal of Positive Psychology* 6, no. 2 (March 2011): 154–62.

26 **Similarly, simply imagining** Minkyung Koo, Sara B. Algoe, Timothy D. Wilson, and Daniel T. Gilbert. "It's a Wonderful Life: Mentally Subtracting Positive Events Improves People's Affective States, Contrary to Their Affective Forecasts." *Journal of Personality and Social Psychology* 95, no. 5 (November 2008): 1217–24.

26 **Not surprisingly, research shows** Jordi Quoidbach, Elizabeth W. Dunn, K. V. Petrides, and Moïra Mikolajczak. "Money Giveth, Money Taketh Away: The Dual Effect of Wealth on Happiness." *Psychological Science* 21, no. 6 (May 2010): 759–63; Leif D. Nelson, Tom Meyvis, and Jeff Galak. "Enhancing the Television-Viewing Experience through Commercial Interruptions." *Journal of Consumer Research* 36, no. 2 (August 2009): 160–72.

28 **Awe comes with** Melanie Rudd, Kathleen D. Vohs, and Jennifer Aaker. "Awe Expands People's Perception of Time, Alters Decision Making, and Enhances Well-Being." *Psychological Science* 23, no. 10 (October 2012): 1130–36; Stacey Kennelly. "Can Awe Buy You More Time and Happiness?" Greater Good Science Center (August 17, 2012). http://greatergood.berkeley.edu/article/item/can_awe_buy_you_more_time_and_happiness.

28 **You can awe yourself** Patty Van Cappellen and Vasslis Saroglou. "Awe Activates Religious and Spiritual Feelings and Behavioral Intentions." *Psychology of Religion and Spirituality* 4, no. 3 (August 2012): 223–36; Stacey Kennelly. "Can Awe Buy You More Time and Happiness?" Greater Good Science Center (August 17, 2002). http://greatergood.berkeley.edu/article/item/can_awe_buy_you_more_time_and_happiness.

28 Optimism, hope, faith Laura A. King. "The Health Benefits of Writing About Life Goals." *Personality and Social Psychology Bulletin* 27, no. 7 (July 1, 2001): 798–807.

29 The power of this exercise Sonja Lyubomirsky. *The How of Happiness: A New Approach to Getting the Life You Want* (New York: Penguin, 2008).

30 A terrific way to evoke Luke Fortney and Molly Taylor. "Meditation in Medical Practice: A Review of the Evidence and Practice." *Primary Care: Clinics in Office Practice* 37, no. 1 (March 2010): 81–90.

30 After meditating daily Bruce Barrett. "Meditation or Exercise for Preventing Acute Respiratory Infection : A Randomized Controlled Trial." *Annals of Family Medicine* 10, no. 4 (July-August 2012): 337–46.

30 Fostering interest Heidi Grant Halvorson. "Nine Ways Successful People Defeat Stress." *Dr. Heidi Grant Halvorson* (December 13, 2012). http://www.heidigranthalvorson.com/2012/12/nine-ways-successful -people-defeat.html.

30 Now neuroscientists have shown Stephanie Khalfa, Simone Dalla Bella, Mathieu Roy, Isabelle Peretz, and Sonia J. Lupien. "Effects of Relaxing Music on Salivary Cortisol Level after Psychological Stress." *Annals of the New York Academy of Sciences* 999 (November 2003): 374–76.

31 Physical activity is even better Thomas Stephens. "Physical Activity and Mental Health in the United States and Canada: Evidence from Four Population Surveys." *Preventive Medicine* 17, no. 1 (January 1988): 35–47.

31 Happiness researcher Sonja Lyubomirsky. *The How of Happiness: A New Approach to Getting the Life You Want* (New York: Penguin, 2008).

31 Laughter lowers stress Mary Payne Bennett and Cecile Lengacher. "Humor and Laughter May Influence Health: III. Laughter and Health Outcomes." *Evidence-Based Complementary and Alternative Medicine* 5, no. 1 (March 2008): 37–40; Bennett and Lengacher. "Humor and Laughter May Influence Health. IV. Humor and Immune Function." *Evidence-Based Complementary and Alternative Medicine* 6, no. 2 (June 2009): 159–64.

31 Fred Bryant is Fred B. Bryant and Joseph Veroff. *Savoring: A New Model of Positive Experience* (Mahwah, N.J.: Lawrence Erlbaum Associates, 2007).

31 Boost your happiness Stacey Kennelly. "10 Steps to Savoring the Good Things in Life." Greater Good Science Center (July 23, 2012). http://greatergood.berkeley.edu/article/item/10_steps_to_savoring_the _good_things_in_life.

32 Hanson, who writes about Rick Hanson. *Hardwiring Happiness: The New Brain Science of Contentment, Calm, and Confidence* (New York: Harmony, 2013).

32 Practice actively looking Rick Hanson. *Buddha's Brain: The Practical Neuroscience of Happiness, Love, and Wisdom* (Oakland, Calif.: New Harbinger Publications, 2009).

33 Let it all sink in Ibid.

33 Facial expression alone Robert W. Levenson, Paul Ekman, and Wallace V. Friesen. "Voluntary Facial Action Generates Emotion-Specific Autonomic Nervous System Activity." *Psychophysiology* 27, no. 4 (July 1990): 363–84.

34 We exhibit microexpressions Paul Ekman and Wallace V. Friesen. "Nonverbal Leakage and Clues to Deception." *Psychiatry* 32, no. 1 (February 1969): 88–106.

34 Research shows that in adults Erik Peper and I-Mei Lin. "Increase or Decrease Depression: How Body Postures Influence Your Energy Level." *Biofeedback* 40, no. 3 (2012): 125–30; Dana R. Carney, Amy J. C. Cuddy, and Andy J. Yap. "Power Posing: Brief Nonverbal Displays Affect Neuroendocrine Levels and Risk Tolerance." *Psychological Science* 21, no. 10 (October 2010): 1363–68.

35 Here's the really astonishing thing Amy J. C. Cuddy, Caroline Ashley Wilmuth, and Dana R. Carney. "The Benefit of Power Posing before a High-Stakes Social Evaluation." Harvard Business School working paper no. 13-027 (September 2012); Dana R. Carney, Amy J. C. Cuddy, and Andy J. Yap. "Power Posing: Brief Nonverbal Displays Affect Neuroendocrine Levels and Risk Tolerance." *Psychological Science* 21, no. 10 (October 2010): 1363–68; Adam K. Anderson, Peter E. Wais, and John D. E. Gabrieli. "Emotion Enhances Remembrance of Neutral Events Past." *Proceedings of the National Academy of Sciences of the United States of America* 103, no. 5 (January 31, 2006): 1599–1604.

Chapter 3: Doing Without Trying

40 In his book Charles Duhigg. *The Power of Habit: Why We Do What We Do in Life and Business* (Random House, 2012).

40 For starters Daniel Goleman, Bruce H. Lipton, Gary Small, Jeanne Achterberg, Lynne McTaggart, and Daniel J. Siegel. *Measuring the Immeasurable: The Scientific Case for Spirituality* (Louisville, Ky.: Sounds True, 2008).

41 A lot of our actions David T. Neal and Wendy Wood. "Automaticity in Situ: Direct Context Cuing of Habits in Daily Life." In *Psychology of Action (Vol. 2): Mechanisms of Human Action,* edited by P. M. Gollwitzer, E. Morsella, and J. A. Bargh (Oxford: Oxford University Press, 2009).

41 As Jonathan Haidt artfully Jonathan Haidt. *The Happiness Hypothesis: Finding Modern Truth in Ancient Wisdom* (New York: Basic Books, 2006).

42 Moreover, our rider Ap Dijksterhuis. "Think Different: The Merits of Unconscious Thought in Preference Development and Decision Making." *Journal of Personality and Social Psychology* 87, no. 5 (November 2004): 586–98.

42 Your brain, unlike my mother Karl Spencer Lashley. "Basic Neural Mechanisms in Behavior." *Psychological Review* 37, no. 1 (January 1930): 1–24.

42 The mice learned Monica R. F. Hilário and Rui M. Costa. "High on Habits." *Frontiers in Neuroscience* 2, no. 2 (December 15, 2008): 208–17; A. Dickinson. "Appetitive-Aversive Interactions: Supercondi- tioning of Fear by an Appetitive CS." *Quarterly Journal of Experimental Psychology* 29, no. 1 (January 1977): 71–83; J. Lamarre and P. C. Hol- land. "Transfer of Inhibition After Serial Feature Negative Discrimina- tion Training." *Learning and Motivation* 18, no. 4 (April 1987): 319–42; P. C. Holland. "Differential Effects of Reinforcement of an Inhibitory Feature After Serial and Simultaneous Feature Negative Discrimination Training." *Journal of Experimental Psychology: Animal Behavior Processes* 10, no. 4 (April 1984): 461–75.

Chapter 4: Cracking the Habit Code

51 The good news Phillippa Lally, Cornelia H. M. Van Jaarsveld, Henry W. W. Potts, and Jane Wardle. "How Are Habits Formed: Modelling Habit Formation in the Real World." *European Journal of Social Psychol- ogy* 40, no. 6 (October 2010): 998–1009.

60 It's very painful to get up Sheina Orbell and Paschal Sheeran. "Mo- tivational and Volitional Processes in Action Initiation: A Field Study of the Role of Implementation Intentions." *Journal of Applied Social Psy- chology* 30, no. 4 (April 2000): 780–97.

60 A large meta-analysis Peter M. Gollwitzer and Paschal Sheeran. "Im- plementation Intentions and Goal Achievement: A Meta-Analysis of Effects and Processes." *Advances in Experimental Social Psychology* 38 (2006): 69–119.

62 Even if you aren't changing Bas Verplanken and Wendy Wood. "In- terventions to Break and Create Consumer Habits." *Journal of Public Policy & Marketing* 25, no. 1 (Spring 2006): 90–103.

64 One study even found Nina Mazar and Chen-Bo Zhong. "Do Green Products Make Us Better People?" *Psychological Science* 21, no. 4 (April 2010): 494–98.

67 As Kelly McGonigal Kelly McGonigal. *The Willpower Instinct: How Self-Control Works, Why It Matters, and What You Can Do To Get More of It.* (New York: Avery, 2011).

69 It *is* true Katherine Harmon. "Rare Genetic Mutation Lets Some Peo- ple Function with Less Sleep." *Scientific American* (August 13, 2009). http://www.scientificamerican.com/article/genetic-mutation-sleep-less.

70 A similar effect on our attention: P. M. Gopinathan. "Role of Dehy- dration in Heat Stress–Induced Variations in Mental Performance." *Archives of Environmental Health* 43, no. 1 (January-February 1988): 15–17.

70 When temptation is right Walter Mischel. "Processes in Delay of Gratification." In *Advances in Experimental Social Psychology,* edited by Leonard Berkowitz. Vol. 7 (New York: Academic Press, 1974): 249–92.

71 Compelling research demonstrates Nicholas A. Christakis and James H. Fowler. *Connected: The Surprising Power of Our Social Net-*

works and How They Shape Our Lives (New York: Little, Brown, and Company, 2009).

71 This is the elephant Chip Heath and Dan Heath. *Switch: How to Change Things When Change Is Hard* (New York: Broadway Books, 2010).

71 Chip and Dan Heath Ibid.

73 Research indicates that Jonah Lehrer. "Blame It on the Brain." *Wall Street Journal* (December 26, 2009). http://online.wsj.com/articles/SB 10001424052748703478704574612052322122442.

73 Say you've sworn off sugar G. Alan Marlatt and Judith R. Gordon. "Determinants of Relapse: Implications for the Maintenance of Behavior Change." In *Behavioral Medicine: Changing Health Lifestyles,* edited by Park O. Davidson and Sheena M. Davidson (New York: Brunner/Mazel, 1980), 410–52.

Chapter 5: Easing "The Overwhelm"

80 Before you allow Kristin van Ogtrop. *Just Let Me Lie Down: Necessary Terms for the Half-insane Working Mom*. (New York: Little, Brown, and Company, 2010).

80 Brigid Schulte, Brigid Schulte. *Overwhelmed: Work, Love and Play When No One Has the Time* (London: Bloomsbury Publishing, 2014).

80 First, feeling overwhelmed Ibid.; "E-Mails 'Hurt IQ More Than Pot.'" CNN (April 22, 2005). http://www.cnn.com/2005/WORLD/europe/04/22/text.iq.

80 Neuroscientists call Daniel Goleman. *Focus: The Hidden Driver of Excellence* (New York: Harper, 2013).

80 Say a researcher shows us Brigid Schulte. *Overwhelmed: Work, Love and Play When No One Has the Time* (London: Bloomsbury Publishing, 2014); see also Gregory S. Berns, Jonathan Chappelow, Caroline F. Zink, Giuseppe Pagnoni, Megan E. Martin-Skurski, and Jim Richards. "Neurobiological Correlates of Social Conformity and Independence During Mental Rotation." *Biological Psychiatry* 58, no. 3 (August 2005): 245–53; see also Elizabeth Landau. "Why So Many Minds Think Alike." CNN (January 15, 2009). http://www.cnn.com/2009/HEALTH/01/15/social.conformity.brain.

82 Saying 'no' Kevin Ashton. "Creative People Say No." *Medium: Thoughts on Creativity.* (March 18, 2013). https://medium.com/thoughts-on -creativity/bad7c34842a2.

83 I once saw Peter Bregman. *18 Minutes: Find Your Focus, Master Distraction, and Get the Right Things Done*. (London: Hachette UK, 2011).

87 *Distractions are costly* Tony Schwartz and Catherine McCarthy. "Manage Your Energy, Not Your Time." *Harvard Business Review* 85, no. 10 (October 2007): 63–73.

90 [A] *person in flow* Mihaly Csikszentmihalyi. *Flow: The Classic Work on How to Achieve Happiness* (London: Rider, 2002).

90 When I go through my pre-work ritual See, for example: "The Marvelous Properties of Gamma Brain Waves." *OmHarmonics* (April 15, 2012). http://www.omharmonics.com/blog/gamma-brain-waves.

94 Despite the many optimists Elizabeth D. Kirby, Sandra E. Muroy, Wayne G. Sun, David Covarrubias, Megan J. Leong, Laurel A. Barchas, and Daniela Kaufer. "Acute Stress Enhances Adult Rat Hippocampal Neurogenesis and Activation of Newborn Neurons via Secreted Astrocytic FGF2." *eLife* 2 (e00362) (April 16, 2013): 1–23; Firdaus S. Dhabhar, William B. Malarkey, Eric Neri, and Bruce S. McEwen. "Stress-Induced Redistribution of Immune Cells—from Barracks to Boulevards to Battlefields: A Tale of Three Hormones—Curt Richter Award Winner." *Psychoneuroendocrinology* 37, no. 9 (September 2012): 1345–68; Janet A. DiPietro, Matthew F. S. X. Novak, Kathleen A. Costigan, Lara D. Atella, and Sarah P. Reusing. "Maternal Psychological Distress During Pregnancy in Relation to Child Development at Age Two." *Child Development* 77, no. 3 (May-June 2006): 573–87; Jane Weaver. "Can Stress Actually Be Good for You?" (December 20, 2006). NBC News. http://www.nbcnews.com/id/15818153/ns/health-mental_health/t/can-stress-actually-be-good-you; Stephen M. Auerbach. "Trait-State Anxiety and Adjustment to Surgery." *Journal of Consulting and Clinical Psychology* 40, no. 2 (1973): 264–71.

94 Longtime stress researcher Robert Epstein. "Fight the Frazzled Mind: Proactive Steps Manage Stress." *Scientific American* (October 2011). http://www.scientificamerican.com/article/fight-the-frazzled-mind.

97 Harvard Business School professor Leslie A. Perlow. *Sleeping with Your Smartphone: How to Break the 24/7 Habit and Change the Way You Work* (Boston: Harvard Business Review Press, 2012).

97 There is something gratifying Charles B. Ferster, Burrhus Frederic Skinner, and Carl D. Cheney. *Schedules of Reinforcement* (Acton, Mass.: Copley Publishing Group, 1997).

98 Constant device checking Michelle Drouin, Daren H. Kaiser, and Daniel A. Miller. "Phantom Vibrations Among Undergraduates: Prevalence and Associated Psychological Characteristics." *Computers in Human Behavior* 28, no. 4 (July 2012): 1490–96.

99 [B]usy managers Leslie A. Perlow. *Sleeping with Your Smartphone: How to Break the 24/7 Habit and Change the Way You Work* (Boston: Harvard Business Review Press, 2012).

100 Designate the spaces "Contamination of Mobile Phones and Hands Revealed for Global Handwashing Day." London School of Hygiene & Tropical Medicine (October 14, 2011). http://www.lshtm.ac.uk/newsevents/news/2011/global_handwashing_day_2011.html.

102 Barry Schwartz Barry Schwartz. *The Paradox of Choice: Why More Is Less* (New York: Ecco, 2004).

102 The gist of what Schwartz's Sheena S. Iyengar and Mark R. Lepper. "When Choice Is Demotivating: Can One Desire Too Much of a Good Thing?" *Journal of Personality and Social Psychology* 79, no. 6 (December 2000): 995–1006.

102 Maximizers actually tend Sheena S. Iyengar, Rachael E. Wells, and Barry Schwartz. "Doing Better but Feeling Worse: Looking for the 'Best' Job Undermines Satisfaction." *Psychological Science* 17, no. 2 (February 2006): 143–50; Barry Schwartz, Andrew Ward, John Monterosso, Sonja Lyubomirsky, Katherine White, and Darrin R. Lehman. "Maximizing versus Satisficing: Happiness Is a Matter of Choice." *Journal of Personality and Social Psychology* 83, no. 5 (November 2002): 1178–97.

105 This advice is derived from Daniel Todd Gilbert. *Stumbling on Happiness* (New York: Alfred A. Knopf, 2006); Gilbert. "The Surprising Science of Happiness" (February 2004), *TED.com.* http://www.ted .com/talks/dan_gilbert_asks_why_are_we_happy.html.

105 Consider this experiment Matthew D. Lieberman, Kevin N. Ochsner, Daniel T. Gilbert, and Daniel L. Schacter. "Do Amnesics Exhibit Cognitive Dissonance Reduction? The Role of Explicit Memory and Attention in Attitude Change." *Psychological Science* 12, no. 2 (March 1, 2001): 135–40.

105 These data get even more Daniel T. Gilbert and Jane E. J. Ebert. "Decisions and Revisions: The Affective Forecasting of Changeable Outcomes." *Journal of Personality and Social Psychology* 82, no. 4 (April 2002): 503–14.

107 For these things Martha Beck. *Finding Your Own North Star: Claiming the Life You Were Meant to Live* (New York: Harmony, 2002).

112 *Overthinking ushers* Sonja Lyubomirsky. *The How of Happiness: A New Approach to Getting the Life You Want* (Penguin Press, 2008).

112 Or as renowned compassion Paul Gilbert. "How to Turn Your Brain from Anger to Compassion." Greater Good Science Center (September 4, 2013). http://greatergood.berkeley.edu/article/item/how_to_turn _brain_anger_compassion.

113 Scientific research on mindfulness Adam Moore, Thomas Gruber, Jennifer Derose, and Peter Malinowski. "Regular, Brief Mindfulness Meditation Practice Improves Electrophysiological Markers of Attentional Control." *Frontiers in Human Neuroscience* 6, no. 18 (January 2012): 18; Britta K. Hölzel, James Carmody, Mark Vangel, Christina Congleton, Sita M. Yerramsetti, Tim Gard, and Sara W. Lazar. "Mindfulness Practice Leads to Increases in Regional Brain Gray Matter Density." *Psychiatry Research* 191, no. 1 (January 30, 2011): 36–43; Thomas K. Houston and Jeroan J. Allison. "Culturally Appropriate Storytelling to Improve Blood Pressure: A Randomized Trial." *Annals of Internal Medicine* 154, no. 2 (January 18, 2011): 77–84; Shian-Ling Keng, Moria J. Smoski, and Clive J. Robins. "Effects of Mindfulness on Psychological Health: A Review of Empirical Studies." *Clinical Psychology Review* 31, no. 6 (August 2011): 1041–56; C. E. Kerr, S. R. Jones, and Q. Wan. "Effects of Mindfulness Meditation Training on Anticipatory Alpha Modulation in Primary Somatosensory Cortex." *Brain Research Bulletin* 85, nos. 3–4 (May 30, 2011); Jason Marsh. "A Little Meditation Goes a Long Way." Greater Good Science Center (February 9, 2011). http://

greatergood.berkeley.edu/article/item/a_little_meditation_goes_a_long
_way; Zindel V. Segal, Peter Bieling, Trevor Young, Glenda MacQueen,
Robert Cooke, Lawrence Martin, Richard Bloch, and Robert D Levitan.
"Antidepressant Monotherapy vs Sequential Pharmacotherapy and
Mindfulness-Based Cognitive Therapy, or Placebo, for Relapse Prophylaxis in Recurrent Depression." *Archives of General Psychiatry* 67,
no. 12 (December 2010): 1256–64; J. A. Sze, A. Gyurak, J. W. Yuan, and
R. W. Levenson. "Coherence Between Emotional Experience and Phys-
iology: Does Body Awareness Training Have an Impact?" *Emotion* 10,
no. 6 (December 2010): 803–14; Eileen Luders, Arthur W. Toga, Nata-
sha Lepore, and Christian Gaser. "The Underlying Anatomical Corre-
lates of Long-Term Meditation: Larger Hippocampal and Frontal
Volumes of Gray Matter." *NeuroImage* 45, no. 3 (April 2009): 672–78;
Kenneth Tyler, Lynda Brown-Wright, Danelle Stevens-Watkins, Deneia
Thomas, Ruby Stevens, Clarissa Roan-Belle, Nadia Gadson, and La
Toya Smith. "Linking Home-School Dissonance to School-Based Out-
comes for African American High School Students." *Journal of Black
Psychology* 36, no. 4 (November 2009): 410–25; Netta Weinstein, Kirk
W. Brown, and Richard M. Ryan. "A Multi-Method Examination of the
Effects of Mindfulness on Stress Attribution, Coping, and Emotional
Well-Being." *Journal of Research in Personality* 43, no. 3 (June 2009):
374–85; Richard J. Davidson, Jon Kabat-Zinn, Jessica Schumacher,
Melissa Rosenkranz, Daniel Muller, Saki F. Santorelli, Ferris Ur-
banowski, Anne Harrington, Katherine Bonus, and John F. Sheridan.
"Alterations in Brain and Immune Function Produced by Mindfulness
Meditation." *Psychosomatic Medicine* 65, no. 4 (July-August 2003):
564–70.

113 **And if that isn't enough** Kimberly M. Carson and Donald H. Baucom.
"Mindfulness-Based Relationship Enhancement." *Behavior Therapy* 35,
no. 3 (Summer 2004): 471–94.

Chapter 6: How to Die Happy, Giving, and Beloved

117 **But who could have foreseen** George E. Vaillant. *Triumphs of Experience: The Men of the Harvard Grant Study* (Cambridge, Mass.: Belknap
Press, 2012).

117 **People with many social connections** Robert D. Putnam. *Bowling
Alone: The Collapse and Revival of American Community* (New York:
Touchstone, 2001).

118 ***Love is our supreme emotion*** Barbara L. Fredrickson. *Love 2.0: Creating Happiness and Health in Moments of Connection* (New York:
Plume, 2013).

118 **In one study** Matthew D. Lieberman. *Social: Why Our Brains Are
Wired to Connect* (New York: Crown Publishers, 2013); G. M. Walton
and G. L. Cohen. "A Brief Social-Belonging Intervention Improves Academic and Health Outcomes of Minority Students." *Science* 331, no.
6023 (March 2011): 1447–51; Walton and Cohen. "A Question of Be-

longing: Race, Social Fit, and Achievement." *Journal of Personality and Social Psychology* 92, no. 1 (January 2007): 82–96.

118 Beyond feeling a sense Matthew D. Lieberman. *Social: Why Our Brains Are Wired to Connect* (New York: Crown Publishers, 2013); John Zenger and Joseph Folkman. *The Extraordinary Leader: Turning Good Managers into Great Leaders* (New York: McGraw-Hill, 2009).

118 Similarly, a person's social Matthew D. Lieberman. *Social: Why Our Brains Are Wired to Connect* (New York: Crown Publishers, 2013); Janet B. Kellett, Ronald H. Humphrey, and Randall G. Sleeth. "Empathy and the Emergence of Task and Relations Leaders." *The Leadership Quarterly* 17, no. 2 (April 2006): 146–62.

119 [*A lack of connection*] Barbara L. Fredrickson. *Love 2.0: Creating Happiness and Health in Moments of Connection* (New York: Plume, 2013).

119 Many, many economic studies Matthew D. Lieberman. *Social: Why Our Brains Are Wired to Connect* (New York: Crown Publishers, 2013); N. Powdthavee. "Putting a Price Tag on Friends, Relatives, and Neighbors: Using Surveys of Life Satisfaction to Value Social Relationships." *Journal of Socio-Economics* 37, no. 4 (August 2008): 1459–80; see also Andrew E. Clark and Andrew J. Oswald. "A Simple Statistical Method for Measuring How Life Events Affect Happiness." *International Journal of Epidemiology* 31, no. 6 (December 2002): 1139–44.

119 Surprised that such hard N. Powdthavee. "Putting a Price Tag on Friends, Relatives, and Neighbors: Using Surveys of Life Satisfaction to Value Social Relationships." *Journal of Socio-Economics* 37, no. 4 (August 2008): 1459–80.

120 One reason that social emotions Matthew D. Lieberman. *Social: Why Our Brains Are Wired to Connect* (New York: Crown Publishers, 2013); F. Van Overwalle. "A Dissociation Between Social Mentalizing and General Reasoning." *NeuroImage* 54, no. 2 (January 15, 2011): 1589–99; Marco Iacoboni, Matthew D. Lieberman, Barbara J. Knowlton, Istvan Molnar-Szakacs, Mark Moritz, C. Jason Throop, and Alan Page Fiske. "Watching Social Interactions Produces Dorsomedial Prefrontal and Medial Parietal BOLD fMRI Signal Increases Compared to a Resting Baseline." *NeuroImage* 21, no. 3 (March 2004): 1167–73; Jason P. Mitchell, C. Neil Macrae, and Mahzarin R. Banaji. "Encoding-Specific Effects of Social Cognition on the Neural Correlates of Subsequent Memory." *Journal of Neuroscience* 24, no. 21 (May 26, 2004): 4912–17.

121 Positivity resonance happens Barbara L. Fredrickson. *Love 2.0: Creating Happiness and Health in Moments of Connection* (New York: Plume, 2013).

121 Much fuss has been made Ibid.; Greg J. Stephens, Lauren J. Silbert, and Uri Hasson. "Speaker-Listener Neural Coupling Underlies Successful Communication." *Proceedings of the National Academy of Sciences of the United States of America* 107, no. 32 (August 10, 2010): 14425–30.

122 Understanding other people's Barbara L. Fredrickson. *Love 2.0: Creating Happiness and Health in Moments of Connection* (New York: Plume, 2013).

122 And studies show that positive emotions Ibid.

123 A half dozen new studies Elizabeth W. Dunn and Michael Norton. "Hello, Stranger." *New York Times* (April 25, 2014). http://www.nytimes.com/2014/04/26/opinion/sunday/hello-stranger.html; see also Gillian M. Sandstrom and Elizabeth W. Dunn. "Is Efficiency Overrated? Minimal Social Interactions Lead to Belonging and Positive Affect." *Social Psychological and Personality Science* 5, no. 4 (September 12, 2013): 437–42; Eric D. Wesselmann, Florencia D. Cardoso, Samantha Slater, and Kipling D. Williams. "To Be Looked at as Though Air: Civil Attention Matters." *Psychological Science* 23, no. 2 (February 2012): 166–68.

124 *Love requires tenacity* Brené Brown. "Brené Brown: 3 Ways to Improve Your Relationship." *O, The Oprah Magazine* (February 2014). http://www.oprah.com/relationships/Love-Better-Improve-Your-Relationship.

126 People who volunteer D. Oman, C. E. Thoresen, and K. McMahon. "Volunteerism and Mortality Among the Community-Dwelling Elderly." *Journal of Health Psychology* 4, no. 3 (May 1999): 301–16.

127 About half of participants J. Moll, F. Krueger, and R. Zahn. "Human Fronto–mesolimbic Networks Guide Decisions About Charitable Donation." *Proceedings of the National Academy of Sciences of the United States of America* 103, no. 42 (October 17, 2006): 15623–28; S G Post. "Altruism, Happiness, and Health: It's Good to Be Good." *International Journal of Behavioral Medicine* 12, no. 2 (June 2005): 66–77.

127 Adolescents who identify Joseph P. Allen and S. Philliber. "Preventing Teen Pregnancy and Academic Failure: Experimental Evaluation of a Developmentally Based Approach." *Child Development* 64, no. 4 (August 1997): 729–42.

127 Heart attacks and other Larry Scherwitz, R. McKelvain, C. Laman, J. Patterson, L. Dutton, S. Yusim, J. Lester, I. Kraft, D. Rochelle, and R. Leachman. "Type A Behavior, Self-Involvement, and Coronary Atherosclerosis." *Psychosomatic Medicine* 45, no. 1 (March 1983): 47–57.

128 One study showed, for example Neal Krause. "Church-Based Social Support and Mortality." *Journals of Gerontology: Series B: Psychological & Social Sciences* 61, no. 3 (May 2006): S140–46; Neal Krause, Christopher G. Ellison, and Keith M. Wulff. "Church-Based Emotional Support, Negative Interaction, and Psychological Well-Being: Findings from a National Sample of Presbyterians." *Journal for the Scientific Study of Religion* 37, no. 4 (December 1998): 725–41.

128 Another study found Michael J. Poulin, Stephanie L. Brown, Amanda J. Dillard, and Dylan M. Smith. "Giving to Others and the Association Between Stress and Mortality." *American Journal of Public Health* 103, no. 9 (September 2013): 1649–55.

128 Simply thinking about giving Neal Krause. "Church-Based Social

Support and Mortality." *Journals of Gerontology: Series B: Psychological & Social Sciences* 61, no. 3 (May 2006): S140–46.

129 Over a nine-week period Barbara L. Fredrickson. "Updated Thinking on Positivity Ratios." *American Psychologist* 68, no. 9 (December 2013): 814–22; David P. Johnson, David L. Penn, Barbara L. Fredrickson, Ann M. Kring, Piper S. Meyer, Lahnna I. Catalino, and Mary Brantley. "A Pilot Study of Loving-Kindness Meditation for the Negative Symptoms of Schizophrenia." *Schizophrenia Research* 129, no. 2–3 (2011): 137–40.

131 Gratitude letters are one Steven M. Toepfer, Kelly Cichy, and Patti Peters. "Letters of Gratitude: Further Evidence for Author Benefits." *Journal of Happiness Studies* 13, no. 1 (March 2012): 187–201; Martin E. P. Seligman, Tracy A. Steen, Nansook Park, and Christopher Peterson. "Positive Psychology Progress: Empirical Validation of Interventions." *American Psychologist* 60, no. 5 (July-August 2005): 410–21.

132 Giving love is far N. Guéguen. "Nonverbal Encouragement of Participation in a Course: The Effect of Touching." *Social Psychology of Education* 7, no. 1 (2004): 89–98.

132 The live connection B. App, D. N. McIntosh, C. L. Reed, and M. J. Hertenstein. "Nonverbal Channel Use in Communication of Emotion: How May Depend on Why." *Emotion* 11, no. 3 (June 2011): 603–17.

133 Touch soothes cardiovascular Dacher Keltner. *Born to Be Good: The Science of a Meaningful Life* (New York: W. W. Norton & Company, 2009); Darlene D. Francis and Michael J. Meaney. "Maternal Care and the Development of Stress Responses." *Current Opinion in Neurobiology* 9, no. 1 (February 1999): 128–34.

133 How about this amazing Dacher Keltner, Keith Oatley, and Jennifer M. Jenkins. *Understanding Emotions* (Hoboken, N.J.: Wiley, 2013).

133 Similarly, psychologists can Robert Kurzban. "The Social Psychophysics of Cooperation: Nonverbal Communication in a Public Goods Game." *Journal of Nonverbal Behavior* 25, no. 4 (December 2001): 241–59.

133 Premature babies Tiffany Field. "Massage Therapy for Infants and Children." *Journal of Developmental & Behavioral Pediatrics* 16, no. 2 (April 1995).

133 People who are anticipating James A. Coan, Hillary S. Schaefer, and Richard J. Davidson. "Lending a Hand: Social Regulation of the Neural Response to Threat." *Psychological Science* 17, no. 12 (December 2006): 1032–39.

133 And students whose teachers N. Guéguen. "Nonverbal Encouragement of Participation in a Course: The Effect of Touching." *Social Psychology of Education* 7, no. 1 (2004): 89–98.

134 Although cluster-giving Adam M. Grant. *Give and Take: A Revolutionary Approach to Success* (New York: Viking, 2013).

135 But asking people for favors J. Jecker. "Liking a Person as a Function of Doing Him a Favour." *Human Relations* 22, no. 4 (August 1969): 371–78.

135 Multiple sclerosis patients Carolyn E. Schwartz and Rabbi Meir

Sendor. "Helping Others Helps Oneself: Response Shift Effects in Peer Support." *Social Science & Medicine* 48, no. 11 (June 1999): 1563–75.

136 **Although we seem** Dacher Keltner, Jason Marsh, and Jeremy Adam Smith, ed. *The Compassionate Instinct: The Science of Human Goodness* (New York: W. W. Norton & Company, 2010).

136 **As Wendell Barry once said** Wendell Berry. *Conversations with Wendell Berry* (Jackson: University Press of Mississippi, 2007).

137 **Compassion is not** Gregory Boyle. *Tattoos on the Heart: The Power of Boundless Compassion* (New York: Free Press, 2011).

138 **The feeling or perception** Sendhil Mullainathan and Eldar Shafir. *Scarcity: Why Having Too Little Means So Much* (New York: Times Books, 2013).

138 **Sendhil Mullainathan** Mullainathan and Shafir. "Freeing Up Intelligence." *Scientific American Mind* (January-February 2014): 58–63.

139 **More of anything** Lynne Twist. *The Soul of Money: Reclaiming the Wealth of Our Inner Resources* (New York: W. W. Norton & Company, 2006).

139 **Our perception that** Ibid.

140 **But another study shows** E. W. Dunn, L. B. Aknin, and M. I. Norton. "Prosocial Spending and Happiness: Using Money to Benefit Others Pays Off." *Current Directions in Psychological Science* 23, no. 1 (February 2014): 41–47; Elizabeth W. Dunn, Lara B. Aknin, and Michael I. Norton. "Spending Money on Others Promotes Happiness." *Science* 319, no. 5870 (March 21, 2008): 1687–88.

140 **Spending money on other people** Elizabeth W. Dunn, Lara B. Aknin, and Michael I. Norton. "Spending Money on Others Promotes Happiness." *Science* 319, no. 5870 (March 21, 2008): 1687–88.

142 **Researchers sent people** Elizabeth W. Dunn and Michael Norton. "Hello, Stranger." *New York Times* (April 25, 2014). http://www.nytimes.com/2014/04/26/opinion/sunday/hello-stranger.html; see also Gillian M. Sandstrom and Elizabeth W. Dunn. "Is Efficiency Overrated? Minimal Social Interactions Lead to Belonging and Positive Affect." *Social Psychological and Personality Science* 5, no. 4 (September 12, 2013): 437–42.

Chapter 7: Mending Ruptures

143 **The only things** Joshua Wolf Shenk. "What Makes Us Happy?" *Atlantic* (June 1, 2009). http://www.theatlantic.com/magazine/archive/2009/06/what-makes-us-happy/307439.

143 **In *Triumphs of Experience*** George E. Vaillant. *Triumphs of Experience: The Men of the Harvard Grant Study* (Cambridge, Mass.: Harvard University Press, 2012).

145 **Shelly Turkle, an MIT sociologist** Sherry Turkle. *Alone Together: Why We Expect More from Technology and Less from Each Other* (Philadelphia: Basic Books, 2012).

147 **Practice being alone** Ibid.

151 This is something that James Baraz and Shoshana Alexander. *Awakening Joy: 10 Steps to Happiness* (Berkeley: Parallax Press, 2012).

152 Make sure that your friends Tara Parker-Pope. *For Better: The Science of a Good Marriage* (New York: Dutton, 2010); Natalya C. Maisel and Shelly L. Gable. "The Paradox of Received Social Support: The Importance of Responsiveness." *Psychological Science* 20, no. 8 (August 2009): 928–32; Shelly L. Gable, Gian C. Gonzaga, and Amy Strachman. "Will You Be There for Me When Things Go Right? Supportive Responses to Positive Event Disclosures." *Journal of Personality and Social Psychology* 91, no. 5 (November 2006): 904–17.

154 Research suggests that it is Cameron L. Gordon, Robyn A. M. Arnette, and Rachel E. Smith. "Have You Thanked Your Spouse Today? Felt and Expressed Gratitude Among Married Couples." *Personality and Individual Differences* 50, no. 3 (February 2011): 339–43.

154 But what I've learned Ibid.; Sara B. Algoe, Shelly L. Gable, and Natalya C. Maisel. "It's the Little Things: Everyday Gratitude as a Booster Shot for Romantic Relationships." *Personal Relationships* 17, no. 2 (June 2010): 217–33.

155 The key word there Sonja Lyubomirsky. *The Myths of Happiness: What Should Make You Happy, but Doesn't, What Shouldn't Make You Happy, but Does* (New York: Penguin Books, 2014); Shelly L. Gable. "Approach and Avoidance Social Motives and Goals." *Journal of Personality* 74, no. 1 (February 2006): 175–222; E. A. Impett, S. L. Gable, and L. A. Peplau. "Giving up and Giving In: The Costs and Benefits of Daily Sacrifice in Intimate Relationships." *Journal of Personality and Social Psychology* 89, no. 3 (September 2005): 327–44.

155 And although we adapt Ken M. Sheldon and S. Lyubomirsky. "Achieving Sustainable Gains in Happiness: Change Your Actions, Not Your Circumstances." *Journal of Happiness Studies* 7, no. 1 (March 2006): 55–86.

157 When researchers have couples Sonja Lyubomirsky. *The Myths of Happiness: What Should Make You Happy, but Doesn't, What Shouldn't Make You Happy, but Does* (New York: Penguin Books, 2014); Arthur Aron, Christina C. Norman, Elaine N. Aron, and Colin McKenna. "Couples' Shared Participation in Novel and Arousing Activities and Experienced Relationship Quality." *Journal of Personality and Social Psychology* 78, no. 2 (February 2000): 273–84.

158 Our brains are pattern finders Sonja Lyubomirsky. *The Myths of Happiness: What Should Make You Happy, but Doesn't, What Shouldn't Make You Happy, but Does* (New York: Penguin Books, 2014).

158 When our relationship goals Ibid.

161 This perspective is what Richard R. Powell. *Wabi Sabi Simple: Create Beauty. Value Imperfection. Live Deeply* (Avon, Mass.: Adams Media, 2014).

161 Researchers call a similar tactic Minkyung Koo, Sara B. Algoe, Timothy D. Wilson, and Daniel T. Gilbert. "It's a Wonderful Life: Mentally Subtracting Positive Events Improves People's Affective States, Contrary to Their Affective Forecasts." *Journal of Personality and Social Psychology* 95, no. 5 (November 2008): 1217–24.

161 **Accepting people** Rick Hanson. *RickHanson.net*. "Accept Them as They Are." (September 16, 2013). http://www.rickhanson.net/accept -them-as-they-are.

162 **People who receive** Robert A. Baron. "Negative Effects of Destructive Criticism: Impact on Conflict, Self-Efficacy, and Task Performance." *Journal of Applied Psychology* 73, no. 2 (May 1988): 199–207.

165 **It's more constructive** John M. Gottman. *What Predicts Divorce? The Relationship Between Marital Processes and Marital Outcomes* (New York: Psychology Press, 1994); Gottman. "The Roles of Conflict Engagement, Escalation, and Avoidance in Marital Interaction: A Longitudinal View of Five Types of Couples." *Journal of Consulting and Clinical Psychology* 61, no. 1 (February 1993): 6–15.

167 **According to Aaron Lazare** Aaron Lazare. "Making Peace through Apology." Greater Good Science Center (September 1, 2004). http:// greatergood.berkeley.edu/article/item/making_peace_through_apology.

170 **In a study of Protestants** Fred Luskin. "The Choice to Forgive." Greater Good Science Center (September 1, 2004). http://greatergood .berkeley.edu/article/item/the_choice_to_forgive.

170 **Few people fully realize** G. Bono, M. E. McCullough, and L. M. Root. "Forgiveness, Feeling Connected to Others, and Well-Being: Two Longitudinal Studies." *Personality and Social Psychology Bulletin* 34, no. 2 (February 2008): 182–95; M. E. McCullough, E. L. Worthington, and K. C. Rachal. "Interpersonal Forgiving in Close Relationships." *Journal of Personality and Social Psychology* 73, no. 2 (August 1997): 321–36.

172 **Sadly, financial wealth** Jason Marsh. "Why Inequality Is Bad for the One Percent." Greater Good Science Center (September 25, 2012). http://greatergood.berkeley.edu/article/item/why_inequality_is_bad_for _the_one_percent; Michael W. Kraus, Paul K. Piff, and Dacher Keltner. "Social Class as Culture: The Convergence of Resources and Rank in the Social Realm." *Current Directions in Psychological Science* 20, no. 4 (August 2011): 246–50; Richard Wilkinson and Kate Pickett. *The Spirit Level: Why Greater Equality Makes Societies Stronger* (New York: Bloomsbury Press, 2011).

172 **One of the most striking** Paul K. Piff, Daniel M. Stancato, Stéphane Côté, Rodolfo Mendoza-Denton, and Dacher Keltner. "Higher Social Class Predicts Increased Unethical Behavior." *Proceedings of the National Academy of Sciences of the United States of America* 109, no. 11 (March 13, 2012): 4086–91.

172 **It's worth noting** Tim Kasser. *The High Price of Materialism* (Cambridge, Mass.: MIT Press, 2002).

173 **Similarly, although research** Paul K. Piff, Daniel M. Stancato, Stéphane Côté, Rodolfo Mendoza-Denton, and Dacher Keltner. "Higher

Social Class Predicts Increased Unethical Behavior." *Proceedings of the National Academy of Sciences of the United States of America* 109, no. 11 (March 13, 2012): 4086–91; Michael W. Kraus, Paul K. Piff, and Dacher Keltner. "Social Class as Culture: The Convergence of Resources and Rank in the Social Realm." *Current Directions in Psychological Science* 20, no. 4 (August 2011): 246–50.

Chapter 8: Making Hard Things Easy

179 *The Talent Code* Daniel Coyle. *The Talent Code.* Vol. 1 (New York: Bantam, 2009).

181 Distance [is] Martin E. P. Seligman. *Flourish: A Visionary New Understanding of Happiness and Well-Being* (New York: Atria Books, 2012).

181 This is hard for most K. Anders Ericsson and Paul Ward. "Capturing the Naturally Occurring Superior Performance of Experts in the Laboratory: Toward a Science of Expert and Exceptional Performance." *Current Directions in Psychological Science* 16, no. 6 (December 2007): 346–50; K. Anders Ericsson. "The Influence of Experience and Deliberate Practice on the Development of Superior Expert Performance." In *The Cambridge Handbook of Expertise and Expert Performance* edited by K. Anders Ericcson, Neil Charness, Robert R. Hoffman, and Paul J. Feltovich (Cambridge, UK: Cambridge University Press, 2006): 685–706; K. Anders Ericsson, Ralf T. Krampe, Clemens Tesch-Römer, Catherine Ashworth, Gregory Carey, Janet Grassia, Reid Hastie, et al. "The Role of Deliberate Practice in the Acquisition of Expert Performance." *Psychological Review* 100, no. 3 (July 1993): 363–406.

182 Ericsson says that "A New Theory of Elite Performance." Greater Good Science Center (August 26, 2013). http://greatergood.berkeley.edu/raising_happiness/post/a_new_theory_of_elite_performance.

182 True masters gain Malcolm Gladwell. *Outliers: The Story of Success* (New York: Back Bay Books, 2011).

183 Why does mastery require so much effort? For a thorough and entertaining guide to myelination and deep practice, see Daniel Coyle. *The Talent Code.* (New York: Bantam, 2009).

184 Does this mean Ibid.

185 Consider that 75 percent Stephen Joseph. *What Doesn't Kill Us: The New Psychology of Posttraumatic Growth* (Philadelphia: Basic Books, 2013).

188 One study showed that when Stanford American Academy of Sleep Medicine. "Extra Sleep Improves Athletic Performance." *Science Daily* (June 10, 2008). http://www.sciencedaily.com/releases/2008/06/080609071106.htm.

190 It isn't just brain function Jane E. Brody. "Cheating Ourselves of Sleep." *New York Times* (June 17, 2013). http://well.blogs.nytimes.com/2013/06/17/cheating-ourselves-of-sleep/.

191 From a stress-management Clay Risen. "Quitting Can Be Good for

You." *New York Times Magazine.* (December 9, 2007). http://www.nytimes .com/2007/12/09/magazine/09quit.html.

192 **Rosenthal and Jacobson** Robert Rosenthal and Lenore Jacobson. "Pygmalion in the Classroom." *Urban Review* 3, no. 1 (September 1968): 16–20.

193 **But high self-esteem** Kristin Neff. *Self-Compassion: The Proven Power of Being Kind to Yourself* (New York: William Morrow, 2011).

193 **Believe it or not** R. F. Baumeister, J. D. Campbell, J. I. Krueger, and K. D. Vohs. "Does High Self-Esteem Cause Better Performance, Inter-personal Success, Happiness, or Healthier Lifestyles?" *Psychological Science in the Public Interest* 4, no. 1 (May 2003): 1–44.

193 **Kristin Neff, a prominent** Kristin Neff. "Why Self-Compassion Trumps Self-Esteem." Greater Good Science Center (May 27, 2011). http://greatergood.berkeley.edu/article/item/try_selfcompassion.

194 **Self-affirmation comes** Sharon Begley. "To Love You Is to Know You." *Mindful* (June 2013).

194 **Self-affirmation also makes** Lisa Legault, Timour Al-Khindi, and Mi-chael Inzlicht. "Preserving Integrity in the Face of Performance Threat: Self-Affirmation Enhances Neurophysiological Responsiveness to Er-rors." *Psychological Science* 23, no. 12 (December 2012): 1455–60.

195 **Perfectionism is the dark side** Petra H. Wirtz, Sigrid Elsenbruch, Luljeta Emini, Katharina Rüdisüli, Sara Groessbauer, and Ulrike Ehlert. "Perfectionism and the Cortisol Response to Psychosocial Stress in Men." *Psychosomatic Medicine* 69, no. 3 (April 2007): 249–55; Kath-leen Y. Kawamura and S. L. Hunt. "Perfectionism, Anxiety, and Depres-sion: Are the Relationships Independent?" *Cognitive Therapy and Research* 25, no. 3 (June 2001): 291–301.

195 **All that fear diverts** Ibid.

197 **Perfectionism is** Julia Cameron. *The Artist's Way* (New York: Jeremy P. Tarcher/Putnam, 2002).

198 **The ability to** Shauna Shapiro and Chris White. *Mindful Discipline: A Loving Approach to Setting Limits and Raising an Emotionally Intelligent Child* (Oakland, Calif.: New Harbinger Publications, 2014).

Chapter 9: How to Be Divergent

199 **Becoming fearless isn't the point** Roth, Veronica. *Divergent.* (New York: Katherine Tegan Books, 2011).

202 **Brené Brown, author of** Brené Brown. *Daring Greatly: How the Courage to Be Vulnerable Transforms the Way We Live, Love, Parent, and Lead* (New York: Gotham, 2012).

204 **What we can't do** Ibid.

205 ***Long experience*** Martha Beck. "Ready . . . Aim . . . Oh, Well: Why You Need to Embrace Imperfection." *O, The Oprah Magazine*, (July 2003). Emphasis mine.

205 **As Maria Shriver writes** Maria Shriver. *And One More Thing Before You Go . . .* (New York: Free Press, 2008).

205 *Our deepest fear* Marianne Williamson. *A Return to Love: Reflections on the Principles of "A Course in Miracles"* (New York: HarperOne, 1996).

210 Consider the old experiment Daniel M. Wegner, David J. Schneider, Samuel R. Carter III, and Teri L. White. "Paradoxical Effects of Thought Suppression." *Journal of Personality and Social Psychology* 53, no. 1 (July 1987): 5–13.

212 Researchers have found J. P. Jamieson, W. B. Mendes, and M. K. Nock. "Improving Acute Stress Responses: The Power of Reappraisal." *Current Directions in Psychological Science* 22, no. 1 (February 2013): 51–56; see also Kelly McGonigal's fantastic TED talk, "How to make stress your friend," on this line of research: Kelly McGonigal. "How to Make Stress Your Friend" (June 2013), *TED.com*. http://www.ted.com/talks/kelly_mcgonigal_how_to_make_stress_your_friend.

Chapter 10: A Short Guide to Getting Your Groove Back

213 The setbacks we face This section is about dealing with everyday hard knocks rather than moving through full-fledged trauma or post-traumatic stress. If you are suffering from post-traumatic stress syndrome, please find a professional to support you for example by using this database: http://www.nacbt.org/searchfortherapists.asp. (There are also some great new books dedicated just to trauma recovery; see, for example, Linda Graham's *Bouncing Back* and Stephen Joseph's *What Doesn't Kill Us.*

214 As Omid Kordestani Omid Kordestani. "Omid Kordestani Graduation Speech—Video & Transcript." *Graduation Speeches* (May 26, 2007). http://gradspeeches.com/2007/2007/omid-kordestan.

214 Even though it Jill Bolte Taylor. *My Stroke of Insight: A Brain Scientist's Personal Journey* (New York: Plume, 2009).

216 Susan David, a Harvard psychologist Susan David and Christina Congleton. "Emotional Agility: How Effective Leaders Manage Their Negative Thoughts and Feelings." *Harvard Business Review* 91, no. 11 (November 2013): 125–29.

217 When we acknowledge Ibid.

218 *Self-criticism is very* Jason Marsh. "The Power of Self-Compassion." Greater Good Science Center (March 14, 2012). http://greatergood.berkeley.edu/article/item/the_power_of_self_compassion.

218 subconscious pulls Ibid.

219 Neff's research demonstrates Ibid.

219 Neff herself was Ibid.

219 In one study, Neff Kristin D. Neff and Pittman McGehee. "Self-Compassion and Psychological Resilience Among Adolescents and Young Adults." *Self and Identity* 9, no. 3 (July 2010): 225–40.

219 Contrary to what you Kristin Neff. *Self-Compassion: The Proven Power of Being Kind to Yourself* (New York: William Morrow, 2011).

220 One thing Neff Neff made this important point at a "Science of a

Meaningful Life" conference on March 8, 2013, hosted by UC Berkeley's Greater Good Science Center. I often think of this point—that we
practice compassion not to feel better but because we feel pain—when
I'm comforting my children or a friend who is suffering. My kindness
and compassion and simple presence is a response to their suffering,
but it doesn't intend to change or negate what they are feeling.

223 **As South African** Boyd Varty. *Cathedral of the Wild: An African Journey Home* (New York: Random House, 2014).

Conclusion: Making the Final Shift

228 **Compelling research indicates** Psychologist Roy Baumeister and
his colleagues have taken pains to distinguish between lives high on
happiness and lives full of *meaning*—as well as their causes and consequences. See Roy Baumeister, Kathleen Vohs, Jennifer Lynn Aaker, and
Emily N. Garbinsky. "Some Key Differences Between a Happy Life and
a Meaningful Life." Stanford Graduate School of Business research
paper no. 2119. Social Science Research Network. (October 1, 2012).
http://ssrn.com/abstract=2168436.

228 **Social psychologists define** Emily Esfahani Smith and Jennifer L.
Aaker. "Millennial Searchers." *New York Times* (November 30, 2013).
http://www.nytimes.com/2013/12/01/opinion/sunday/millennial
-searchers.html.

228 **Consider that 42 percent** S. Blakeslee. "Placebos Prove so Powerful
Even Experts Are Surprised; New Studies Explore the Brain's Triumph
over Reality." *New York Times* (October 13, 1998). http://www.nytimes
.com/1998/10/13/science/placebos-prove-so-powerful-even-experts-are
-surprised-new-studies-explore-brain.html; Ilian Bandaranayake and
Paradi Mirmirani. "Hair Loss Remedies—Separating Fact from Fiction." *Cutis* 73, no. 2 (February 2004): 107–14.

228 **Or that when researchers rubbed** S. Blakeslee. "Placebos Prove so
Powerful Even Experts Are Surprised; New Studies Explore the Brain's
Triumph over Reality." *New York Times* (October 13, 1998). http://www
.nytimes.com/1998/10/13/science/placebos-prove-so-powerful-even
-experts-are-surprised-new-studies-explore-brain.html.

229 **Physician Lissa Rankin** Lissa Rankin. *Mind Over Medicine: Scientific Proof That You Can Heal Yourself* (Calsbad, Calif.: Hay House, Inc.,
2013).

229 **Although we don't know** Steve Stewart-Williams and John Podd.
"The Placebo Effect: Dissolving the Expectancy versus Conditioning
Debate." *Psychological Bulletin* 130, no. 2 (March 2004): 324–40.

230 **Placebo effects aren't confined** Alia J. Crum and Ellen J. Langer.
"Mind-Set Matters: Exercise and the Placebo Effect." *Psychological Science* 18, no. 2 (February 2007): 165–71.

231 **For example, Dweck's research team** Carol S. Dweck. *Mindset:
The New Psychology of Success* (New York: Ballantine Books, 2007); Andrew J. Elliot and Carol S. Dweck. *Handbook of Competence and Moti-*

vation (New York: The Guilford Press, 2007); Melissa L. Kamins and Carol S. Dweck. "Person versus Process Praise and Criticism: Implications for Contingent Self-Worth and Coping." *Developmental Psychology* 35, no. 3 (May 1999): 835–47.

232 **In Dweck's study** Carol S. Dweck. "Caution—Praise Can Be Dangerous." In *Educational Psychology in Context: Readings for Future Teachers*, edited by Bruce A. Marlowe and Alan S. Canestrari (Thousand Oaks, Calif.: Sage Publications, 2006): 206–17; 299; Melissa L. Kamins and Carol S. Dweck. "Person versus Process Praise and Criticism: Implications for Contingent Self-Worth and Coping." *Developmental Psychology* 35, no. 3 (May 1999): 835–47; Claudia M. Mueller and Carol S. Dweck. "Praise for Intelligence Can Undermine Children's Motivation and Performance." *Journal of Personality and Social Psychology* 75, no. 1 (July 1998): 33–52.

232 **For example, managers** Peter A. Heslin, Don VandeWalle, and Gary P. Latham. "The Effect of Implicit Person Theory on Performance Appraisals." *Journal of Applied Psychology* 90, no. 5 (September 2005): 842–56.

232 **Because people with** Lara K. Kammrath and Carol S. Dweck. "Voicing Conflict: Preferred Conflict Strategies Among Incremental and Entity Theorists." *Personality and Social Psychology Bulletin* 32, no. 11 (November 2006): 1497–508.

234 **In an effort to see** Adam M. Grant, Elizabeth M. Campbell, Grace Chen, Keenan Cottone, David Lapedis, and Karen Lee. "Impact and the Art of Motivation Maintenance: The Effects of Contact with Beneficiaries on Persistence Behavior." *Organizational Behavior and Human Decision Processes* 103, no. 1 (May 2007): 53–67.

234 **In another study, Grant** Adam M. Grant. "The Significance of Task Significance: Job Performance Effects, Relational Mechanisms, and Boundary Conditions." *Journal of Applied Psychology* 93, no. 1 (January 2008): 108–24.

234 **Grant replicated his call-center studies** Ibid.

235 **Long-term studies of grandparents** Sara M. Moorman and Jeffrey E. Stokes. "Does Solidarity in the Grandparent/Grandchild Relationship Protect Against Depressive Symptoms?" Paper presented at the Annual Meeting of the American Sociological Association, New York, N.Y. (August 12, 2013); Daniel Fowler. "Strong Grandparent–Adult Grandchild Relationships Reduce Depression for Both." American Sociological Association (August 12, 2013). http://www.asanet.org/press/strong_grandparent_grandchild_relationships_reduce_depression_for_both.cfm.

235 **As Viktor Frankl wrote** Viktor E. Frankl. *Man's Search for Meaning* (Boston: Beacon Press, 2006).

237 **Tibetan meditators** Jill Bolte Taylor. *My Stroke of Insight: A Brain Scientist's Personal Journey* (New York: Plume, 2009).

237 **Researchers were able to identify** Andrew Newberg, Eugene

D'Aquili, and Vince Rause. *Why God Won't Go Away: Brain Science and the Biology of Belief* (New York: Ballantine Books, 2002).

237 **Feelings of profound meaning** Jill Bolte Taylor. *My Stroke of Insight: A Brain Scientist's Personal Journey* (New York: Plume, 2009).

238 **Beck teaches practices** Martha Beck. *Finding Your Way in a Wild New World: Reclaim Your True Nature to Create the Life You Want* (New York: Atria Books, 2013).

239 **This year at Wisdom 2.0** Arianna Huffington. *Thrive: The Third Metric to Redefining Success and Creating a Life of Well-Being, Wisdom, and Wonder* (New York: Harmony, 2014).

240 **One study found** Amy Wrzesniewski, Clark McCauley, Paul Rozin, and Barry Schwartz. "Jobs, Careers, and Callings: People's Relations to Their Work." *Journal of Research in Personality* 31, no. 1 (March 1997): 21–33.

BIBLIOGRAPHY

"A New Theory of Elite Performance." Greater Good Science Center (August 26, 2013). http://greatergood.berkeley.edu/raising_happiness/post/a_new_theory_of_elite_performance.

Algoe, Sara B., Shelly L. Gable, and Natalya C. Maisel. "It's the Little Things: Everyday Gratitude as a Booster Shot for Romantic Relationships." *Personal Relationships* 17, no. 2 (June 2010): 217–33.

Alcorn, Katrina. "Letter from Baltimore." (December 1, 2010). *Working Moms Break.* http://www.workingmomsbreak.com/2010/12/01/letter-from-baltimore/.

Allen, Joseph P., and S. Philliber. "Preventing Teen Pregnancy and Academic Failure: Experimental Evaluation of a Developmentally Based Approach." *Child Development* 64, no. 4 (August 1997): 729–42.

American Academy of Sleep Medicine. "Extra Sleep Improves Athletic Performance." *ScienceDaily* (June 10, 2008). http://www.sciencedaily.com/releases/2008/06/080609071106.htm.

American Psychological Association. "Stress in America 2009."

Anderson, Adam K., Kalina Christoff, David Panitz, Eve De Rosa, and John D. E. Gabrieli. "Neural Correlates of the Automatic Processing of Threat Facial Signals." *Journal of Neuroscience* 23, no. 13 (July 2, 2003): 5627–33.

Anderson, Adam K., Peter E. Wais, and John D. E. Gabrieli. "Emotion Enhances Remembrance of Neutral Events Past." *Proceedings of the National Academy of Sciences of the United States of America* 103, no. 5 (January 31, 2006): 1599–1604.

App, B., D. N. McIntosh, C. L. Reed, and M. J. Hertenstein. "Nonverbal Channel Use in Communication of Emotion: How May Depend on Why." *Emotion* 11, no. 3 (November 2011): 603–17.

Aron, Arthur, Christina C. Norman, Elaine N. Aron, Colin McKenna, and Richard E. Heyman. "Couples' Shared Participation in Novel and Arousing Activities and Experienced Relationship Quality." *Journal of Personality and Social Psychology* 78, no. 2 (February 2000): 273–84.

Ashton, Kevin. "Creative People Say No." *Medium: Thoughts on Creativity.* (March 18, 2013). https://medium.com/thoughts-on-creativity/bad7c34842a2.

Auerbach, Stephen M. "Trait-State Anxiety and Adjustment to Surgery." *Journal of Consulting and Clinical Psychology* 40, no. 2 (1973): 264–71.

Bandaranayake, Ilian, and Paradi Mirmirani. "Hair Loss Remedies—Separating Fact from Fiction." *Cutis* 73, no. 2 (February 2004): 107–14.

Baraz, James, and Shoshana Alexander. *Awakening Joy: 10 Steps to Happiness.* Berkeley: Parallax Press, 2012.

Baron, Robert A. "Negative Effects of Destructive Criticism: Impact on Conflict, Self-Efficacy, and Task Performance." *Journal of Applied Psychology* 73, no. 2 (May 1988): 199–207.

Barrett, Bruce. "Meditation or Exercise for Preventing Acute Respiratory Infection: A Randomized Controlled Trial." *Annals of Family Medicine* 10, no. 4 (July-August 2012): 337–46.

Baumeister, R. F., J. D. Campbell, J. I. Krueger, and K. D. Vohs. "Does High Self-Esteem Cause Better Performance, Interpersonal Success, Happiness, or Healthier Lifestyles?" *Psychological Science in the Public Interest* 4, no. 1 (May 2003): 1–44.

Baumeister, Roy, Kathleen Vohs, Jennifer Lynn Aaker, and Emily N. Garbinsky. "Some Key Differences Between a Happy Life and a Meaningful Life." Stanford Graduate School of Business research paper no. 2119. Social Science Research Network. (October 1, 2012). http://ssrn.com/abstract=2168436.

Beck, Martha. *Finding Your Own North Star: Claiming the Life You Were Meant to Live.* New York: Harmony, 2002.

————. *Finding Your Way in a Wild New World: Reclaim Your True Nature to Create the Life You Want.* New York: Atria Books, 2013.

————. "Ready . . . Aim . . . Oh, Well: Why You Need to Embrace Imperfection." *O, The Oprah Magazine* (July 2003).

Begley, Sharon. "To Love You Is to Know You." *Mindful* (June 2013).

Bennett, Mary Payne, and Cecile Lengacher. "Humor and Laughter May Influence Health: III. Laughter and Health Outcomes." *Evidence-Based Complementary and Alternative Medicine* 5, no. 1 (March 2008): 37–40.

————. "Humor and Laughter May Influence Health: IV. Humor and Immune Function." *Evidence-Based Complementary and Alternative Medicine* 6, no. 2 (June 2009): 159–64.

Berns, Gregory S., Jonathan Chappelow, Caroline F. Zink, Giuseppe Pagnoni, Megan E. Martin-Skurski, and Jim Richards. "Neurobiological Correlates of Social Conformity and Independence During Mental Rotation." *Biological Psychiatry* 58, no. 3 (August 2005): 245–53.

Berry, Wendell. *Conversations with Wendell Berry.* Jackson: University Press of Mississippi, 2007.

Blakeslee, S. "Placebos Prove so Powerful Even Experts Are Surprised; New Studies Explore the Brain's Triumph over Reality." *New York Times* (October 13, 1998). http://www.nytimes.com/1998/10/13/science/placebos-prove-so-powerful-even-experts-are-surprised-new-studies-explore-brain.html.

Bono, G., M. E. McCullough, and L. M. Root. "Forgiveness, Feeling Connected to Others, and Well-Being: Two Longitudinal Studies." *Personality and Social Psychology Bulletin* 34, no. 2 (February 2008): 182–95.

Boyle, Gregory. *Tattoos on the Heart: The Power of Boundless Compassion.* Free Press, 2011.

Bregman, Peter. *18 Minutes: Find Your Focus, Master Distraction, and Get the Right Things Done.* London: Hachette UK, 2011.

Brody, Jane E. "Cheating Ourselves of Sleep." *New York Times* (June 17, 2013). http://well.blogs.nytimes.com/2013/06/17/cheating-ourselves-of-sleep.

Brown, Brené. "Brené Brown: 3 Ways to Improve Your Relationship." *O, The Oprah Magazine* (February 2014). http://www.oprah.com/relationships/Love-Better-Improve-Your-Relationship.

————. *Daring Greatly: How the Courage to Be Vulnerable Transforms the Way We Live, Love, Parent, and Lead.* New York: Gotham, 2012.

Bryant, Fred B., and Joseph Veroff. *Savoring: A New Model of Positive Experience.* Mahwah, N.J.: Lawrence Erlbaum Associates, 2007.

Cameron, Julia. *The Artist's Way.* New York: Jeremy P. Tarcher/Putnam, 2002.

Carney, Dana R., Amy J. C. Cuddy, and Andy J. Yap. "Power Posing: Brief Nonverbal Displays Affect Neuroendocrine Levels and Risk Tolerance." *Psychological Science* 21, no. 10 (October 2010): 1363–68.

Carson, Kimberly M., and Donald H. Baucom. "Mindfulness-Based Relationship Enhancement." *Behavior Therapy* 35, no. 3 (Summer 2004): 471–94.

Christakis, Nicholas A., and James H. Fowler. *The Surprising Power of Our Social Networks and How They Shape Our Lives.* New York: Little, Brown, and Company, 2009.

Clark, Andrew E., and Andrew J. Oswald. "A Simple Statistical Method for Measuring How Life Events Affect Happiness." *International Journal of Epidemiology* 31, no. 6 (December 2002): 1139–44.

Coan, James A., Hillary S. Schaefer, and Richard J. Davidson. "Lending a Hand: Social Regulation of the Neural Response to Threat." *Psychological Science* 17, no. 12 (December 2006): 1032–39.

Collins, Jim, and Morten T. Hansen. *Great by Choice: Uncertainty, Chaos and Luck—Why Some Thrive Despite Them All.* New York: Random House, 2011.

"Contamination of Mobile Phones and Hands Revealed for Global Handwashing Day." London School of Hygiene & Tropical Medicine (October 14, 2011). http://www.lshtm.ac.uk/newsevents/news/2011/global_handwashing_day_2011.html.

Coyle, Daniel. *The Talent Code.* New York: Bantam, 2009.

Crum, Alia J., and Ellen J. Langer. "Mind-Set Matters: Exercise and the Placebo Effect." *Psychological Science* 18, no. 2 (February 2007): 165–71.

Csikszentmihalyi, Mihaly. *Flow: The Classic Work on How to Achieve Happiness.* London: Rider, 2002.

Cuddy, Amy J. C., Caroline Ashley Wilmuth, and Dana R. Carney. "The Benefit of Power Posing before a High-Stakes Social Evaluation." Harvard Business School working paper no. 13-027 (September 2012).

David, Susan, and Christina Congleton. "Emotional Agility: How Effective Leaders Manage Their Negative Thoughts and Feelings." *Harvard Business Review* 91, no. 11 (November 2013): 125–29.

Davidson, Richard J., Jon Kabat-Zinn, Jessica Schumacher, Melissa Rosenkranz, Daniel Muller, Saki F. Santorelli, Ferris Urbanowski, Anne Harrington, Katherine Bonus, and John F. Sheridan. "Alterations in Brain and Immune Function Produced by Mindfulness Meditation." *Psychosomatic Medicine* 65, no. 4 (July-August 2003): 564–70.

Dhabhar, Firdaus S., William B. Malarkey, Eric Neri, and Bruce S. McEwen. "Stress-Induced Redistribution of Immune Cells—from Barracks to Boulevards to Battlefields: A Tale of Three Hormones—Curt Richter Award Winner." *Psychoneuroendocrinology* 37, no. 9 (September 2012): 1345–68.

Dickinson, A. "Appetitive-Aversive Interactions: Superconditioning of Fear by an Appetitive CS." *Quarterly Journal of Experimental Psychology* 29, no. 1 (1977): 71–83.

Dijksterhuis, Ap. "Think Different: The Merits of Unconscious Thought in Preference Development and Decision Making." *Journal of Personality and Social Psychology* 87, no. 5 (November 2004): 586–98.

DiPietro, Janet A., Matthew F. S. X. Novak, Kathleen A. Costigan, Lara D. Atella, and Sarah P. Reusing. "Maternal Psychological Distress During Pregnancy in Relation to Child Development at Age Two." *Child Development* 77, no. 3 (May-June 2006): 573–87.

Drouin, Michelle, Daren H. Kaiser, and Daniel A. Miller. "Phantom Vibrations Among Undergraduates: Prevalence and Associated Psychological Characteristics." *Computers in Human Behavior* 28, no. 4 (July 2012): 1490–96.

Duhigg, Charles. *The Power of Habit: Why We Do What We Do in Life and Business.* New York: Random House, 2012.

Dunn, E. W., L. B. Aknin, and M. I. Norton. "Prosocial Spending and Happiness: Using Money to Benefit Others Pays Off." *Current Directions in Psychological Science* 23, no. 1 (February 2014): 41–47.

———. "Spending Money on Others Promotes Happiness." *Science* 319, no. 5870 (March 21, 2008): 1687–88.

Dunn, Elizabeth W., and Michael Norton. "Hello, Stranger." *New York Times* (April 25, 2014). http://www.nytimes.com/2014/04/26/opinion/sunday/hello-stranger.html.

Dweck, Carol S. "Caution—Praise Can Be Dangerous." In *Educational Psychology in Context: Readings for Future Teachers*, edited by Bruce A. Marlowe and Alan S. Canestrari. (Thousand Oaks, Calif.: Sage Publications, 2006: 206–17.

———. *Mindset: The New Psychology of Success.* New York: Ballantine Books, 2007.

"E-Mails 'Hurt IQ More Than Pot.'" CNN (April 22, 2005). http://www.cnn.com/2005 /WORLD/europe/04/22/text.iq.

Ekman, Paul, and Wallace V. Friesen. "Nonverbal Leakage and Clues to Deception." *Psychiatry* 32, no. 1 (February 1969): 88–106.

Elliot, Andrew J., and Carol S. Dweck, editors. *Handbook of Competence and Motivation.* New York: The Guilford Press, 2007.

Epstein, Robert. "Fight the Frazzled Mind: Proactive Steps Manage Stress." *Scientific American* (October 2011). http://www.scientificamerican.com/article/fight-the-frazzled-mind.

Ericsson, K. Anders. "The Influence of Experience and Deliberate Practice on the Development of Superior Expert Performance." In *The Cambridge Handbook of Expertise and Expert Performance*, edited by K. Anders Ericcson, Neil Charness, Robert R. Hoffman, and Paul J. Feltovich (Cambridge, UK: Cambridge University Press, 2006): 685–706.

Ericsson, K. Anders, Ralf T. Krampe, Clemens Tesch-Römer, Catherine Ashworth, Gregory Carey, Janet Grassia, Reid Hastie, et al. 1993. "The Role of Deliberate Practice in the Acquisition of Expert Performance." *Psychological Review* 100, no. 3 (July 1993): 363–406.

Ericsson, K. Anders, and Paul Ward. "Capturing the Naturally Occurring Superior Performance of Experts in the Laboratory: Toward a Science of Expert and Exceptional Performance." *Current Directions in Psychological Science* 16, no. 6 (December 2007): 346–50.

Ferster, Charles B., Burrhus Frederic Skinner, and Carl D. Cheney. *Schedules of Reinforcement.* Acton, Mass.: Copley Publishing Group, 1997.

Field, Tiffany. "Massage Therapy for Infants and Children." *Journal of Developmental & Behavioral Pediatrics* 16, no. 2 (December 1995).

Fortney, Luke, and Molly Taylor. "Meditation in Medical Practice: A Review of the Evidence and Practice." *Primary Care: Clinics in Office Practice* 37, no. 1 (March 2010): 81–90.

Fowler, Daniel. "Strong Grandparent–Adult Grandchild Relationships Reduce Depression for Both." American Sociological Association, August 12, 2013. http://www.asanet.org/press/strong _grandparent_grandchild_relationships_reduce_depression_for_both.cfm.

Francis, Darlene D., and Michael J. Meaney. "Maternal Care and the Development of Stress Responses." *Current Opinion in Neurobiology* 9, no. 1 (February 1999): 128–34.

Frankl, Viktor E. *Man's Search for Meaning.* Boston: Beacon Press, 2006.

Fredrickson, Barbara. "Are You Getting Enough Positivity in Your Diet?" Greater Good Science Center (June 21, 2011). http://greatergood.berkeley.edu/article/item/are_you_getting _enough_positivity_in_your_diet#.

———. "The Broaden-and-Build Theory of Positive Emotions." *Philosophical Transactions of the Royal Society of London. Series B, Biological Sciences* 359, no. 1449 (September 29, 2004): 1367–78.

———. *Love 2.0: Creating Happiness and Health in Moments of Connection.* New York: Plume, 2013.

———. *Positivity: Top-Notch Research Reveals the 3-to-1 Ratio That Will Change Your Life.* New York: Three Rivers Press, 2009.

———. "The Role of Positive Emotions in Positive Psychology: The Broaden-and-Build Theory of Positive Emotions." *American Psychologist* 56, no. 3 (March 2001): 218–26.

———. "Updated Thinking on Positivity Ratios." *American Psychologist* 68, no. 9 (December 2013): 814–22.

Fredrickson, Barbara L., and Christine Branigan. "Positive Emotions Broaden the Scope of Attention and Thought-Action Repertoires." *Cognition & Emotion* 19, no. 3 (May 1, 2005): 313–32.

Fredrickson, Barbara L., and Robert W. Levenson. "Positive Emotions Speed Recovery from the Cardiovascular Sequelae of Negative Emotions." *Cognition & Emotion* 12, no. 2 (1998): 191–220.

Fredrickson, Barbara L., Roberta A. Mancuso, Christine Branigan, and Michele M. Tugade. "The Undoing Effect of Positive Emotions." *Motivation and Emotion* 24, no. 4 (December 2000): 237–58.

Frias, Araceli, Philip C. Watkins, Amy C. Webber, and Jeffrey J. Froh. "Death and Gratitude: Death Reflection Enhances Gratitude." *Journal of Positive Psychology* 6, no. 2 (March 2011): 154–62.

Gable, Shelly L. "Approach and Avoidance Social Motives and Goals." *Journal of Personality* 74, no. 1 (February 2006): 175–222.

Gable, Shelly L., Gian C. Gonzaga, and Amy Strachman. "Will You Be There for Me When Things Go Right? Supportive Responses to Positive Event Disclosures." *Journal of Personality and Social Psychology* 91, no. 5 (November 2006): 904–17.

Gilbert, Daniel Todd. *Stumbling on Happiness.* New York: Alfred A. Knopf, 2006.

———. "The Surprising Science of Happiness." (February 2004). *TED.com.* http://www.ted .com/talks/dan_gilbert_asks_why_are_we_happy.html.

Gilbert, Daniel T., and Jane E. J. Ebert. "Decisions and Revisions: The Affective Forecasting of Changeable Outcomes." *Journal of Personality and Social Psychology* 82, no. 4 (April 2002): 503–14.

Gilbert, Paul. "How to Turn Your Brain from Anger to Compassion." Greater Good Science Center (September 4, 2013). http://greatergood.berkeley.edu/article/item/how_to_turn_brain_anger _compassion.

Gladwell, Malcolm. *Outliers: The Story of Success.* New York: Back Bay Books, 2011.

Goleman, Daniel. *Focus: The Hidden Driver of Excellence.* New York: Harper, 2013.

Goleman, Daniel, Bruce H. Lipton, Gary Small, Jeanne Achterberg, Lynne McTaggart, and Daniel J. Siegel. *Measuring the Immeasurable: The Scientific Case for Spirituality.* Louisville, Ky.: Sounds True, 2008.

Gollwitzer, Peter M., and Paschal Sheeran. "Implementation Intentions and Goal Achievement: A Meta-Analysis of Effects and Processes." *Advances in Experimental Social Psychology* 38 (2006): 69–119.

Bibliography

Gopinathan, P. M. "Role of Dehydration in Heat Stress–Induced Variations in Mental Performance." *Archives of Environmental Health* 43, no. 1 (January-February 1988): 15–17.

Gordon, Cameron L., Robyn A. M. Arnette, and Rachel E. Smith. "Have You Thanked Your Spouse Today? Felt and Expressed Gratitude Among Married Couples." *Personality and Individual Differences* 50, no. 3 (February 2011): 339–43.

Gottman, John M. "The Roles of Conflict Engagement, Escalation, and Avoidance in Marital Interaction: A Longitudinal View of Five Types of Couples." *Journal of Consulting and Clinical Psychology* 61, no. 1 (February 1993): 6–15.

———. *What Predicts Divorce? The Relationship Between Marital Processes and Marital Outcomes.* New York: Psychology Press, 1994.

Grandey, Alicia A. "When 'The Show Must Go On': Surface Acting and Deep Acting as Determinants of Emotional Exhaustion and Peer-Rated Service Delivery." *Academy of Management Journal* 46, no. 1 (February 2003): 86–96.

Grant, Adam M. *Give and Take: A Revolutionary Approach to Success.* New York: Viking, 2013.

———. "The Significance of Task Significance: Job Performance Effects, Relational Mechanisms, and Boundary Conditions." *Journal of Applied Psychology* 93, no. 1 (January 2008): 108–24.

Grant, Adam M., Elizabeth M. Campbell, Grace Chen, Keenan Cottone, David Lapedis, and Karen Lee. "Impact and the Art of Motivation Maintenance: The Effects of Contact with Beneficiaries on Persistence Behavior." *Organizational Behavior and Human Decision Processes* 103, no. 1 (May 2007): 53–67.

Guéguen, N. "Nonverbal Encouragement of Participation in a Course: The Effect of Touching." *Social Psychology of Education* 7, no. 1 (2004): 89–98.

Haidt, Jonathan. *The Happiness Hypothesis: Finding Modern Truth in Ancient Wisdom.* New York: Basic Books, 2006.

Halvorson, Heidi Grant. 2012. "Nine Ways Successful People Defeat Stress." *Dr. Heidi Grant Halvorson* (December 13, 2012). http://www.heidigranthalvorson.com/2012/12/nine-ways-successful-people-defeat.html.

Hamer, Mark, Romano Endrighi, Shreenidhi M. Venuraju, Avijit Lahiri, and Andrew Steptoe. "Cortisol Responses to Mental Stress and the Progression of Coronary Artery Calcification in Healthy Men and Women." *PloS One* 7, no. 2 (January 2012): e31356.

Hanson, Rick. *RickHanson.net.* "Accept Them as They Are." (September 16, 2013). http://www.rickhanson.net/accept-them-as-they-are.

———. *Buddha's Brain: The Practical Neuroscience of Happiness, Love, and Wisdom.* Oakland, Calif.: New Harbinger Publications, 2009.

———. *Hardwiring Happiness: The New Brain Science of Contentment, Calm, and Confidence.* New York: Harmony, 2013.

Harmon, Katherine. "Rare Genetic Mutation Lets Some People Function with Less Sleep." *Scientific American* (August 13, 2009). http://www.scientificamerican.com/article/genetic-mutation-sleep-less.

Heath, Chip, and Dan Heath. *Switch: How to Change Things When Change Is Hard.* New York: Broadway Books, 2010.

Heslin, Peter A., Don VandeWalle, and Gary P. Latham. "The Effect of Implicit Person Theory on Performance Appraisals." *Journal of Applied Psychology* 90, no. 5 (September 2005): 842–56.

Hilário, Monica R. F., and Rui M Costa. "High on Habits." *Frontiers in Neuroscience* 2, no. 2 (2008): 208–17.

Hochschild, Arlie Russell. *The Time Bind: When Work Becomes Home and Home Becomes Work.* Vol. 2. New York: Holt Paperbacks, 2001.

Holland, P. C. "Differential Effects of Reinforcement of an Inhibitory Feature After Serial and Simultaneous Feature Negative Discrimination Training." *Journal of Experimental Psychology: Animal Behavior Processes* 10, no. 4 (1984): 461–75.

Hölzel, Britta K., James Carmody, Mark Vangel, Christina Congleton, Sita M. Yerramsetti, Tim Gard, and Sara W. Lazar. "Mindfulness Practice Leads to Increases in Regional Brain Gray Matter Density." *Psychiatry Research* 191, no. 1 (January 30, 2011): 36–43.

Houston, Thomas K., and Jeroan J. Allison. "Culturally Appropriate Storytelling to Improve

Blood Pressure: A Randomized Trial." *Annals of Internal Medicine* 154, no. 2 (January 18, 2011): 77–84.

Huffington, Arianna. *Thrive: The Third Metric to Redefining Success and Creating a Life of Well-Being, Wisdom, and Wonder.* New York: Harmony, 2014.

Iacoboni, Marco, Matthew D. Lieberman, Barbara J. Knowlton, Istvan Molnar-Szakacs, Mark Moritz, C. Jason Throop, and Alan Page Fiske. "Watching Social Interactions Produces Dorsomedial Prefrontal and Medial Parietal BOLD fMRI Signal Increases Compared to a Resting Baseline." *NeuroImage* 21, no. 3 (March 2004): 1167–73.

Impett, E. A., S. L. Gable, and L. A. Peplau. "Giving up and Giving In: The Costs and Benefits of Daily Sacrifice in Intimate Relationships." *Journal of Personality and Social Psychology* 89, no. 3 (September 2005): 327–44.

Iyengar, Sheena S., and Mark R. Lepper. "When Choice Is Demotivating: Can One Desire Too Much of a Good Thing?" *Journal of Personality and Social Psychology* 79, no. 6 (December 2000): 995–1006.

Iyengar, Sheena S., Rachael E. Wells, and Barry Schwartz. "Doing Better but Feeling Worse: Looking for the 'Best' Job Undermines Satisfaction." *Psychological Science* 17, no. 2 (February 2006): 143–50.

Jamieson, J. P., W. B. Mendes, and M. K. Nock. "Improving Acute Stress Responses: The Power of Reappraisal." *Current Directions in Psychological Science* 22, no. 1 (February 2013): 51–56.

Jecker, J. "Liking a Person as a Function of Doing Him a Favour." *Human Relations* 22, no. 4 (August 1969): 371–78.

Johnson, David P., David L. Penn, Barbara L. Fredrickson, Ann M. Kring, Piper S. Meyer, Lahnna I. Catalino, and Mary Brantley. "A Pilot Study of Loving-Kindness Meditation for the Negative Symptoms of Schizophrenia." *Schizophrenia Research* 129, no. 2–3 (2011): 137–40.

Joseph, Stephen. *What Doesn't Kill Us: The New Psychology of Posttraumatic Growth.* Philadelphia Basic Books, 2013.

Kamins, Melissa L., and Carol S. Dweck. "Person versus Process Praise and Criticism: Implications for Contingent Self-Worth and Coping." *Developmental Psychology* 35, no. 3 (May 1999): 835–47.

Kammrath, Lara K., and Carol S. Dweck. "Voicing Conflict: Preferred Conflict Strategies Among Incremental and Entity Theorists." *Personality and Social Psychology Bulletin* 32, no. 11 (November 2006): 1497–508.

Kasser, Tim. *The High Price of Materialism.* Cambridge, Mass.: MIT Press, 2002.

Kawamura, Kathleen Y., and S L Hunt. "Perfectionism, Anxiety, and Depression: Are the Relationships Independent?" *Cognitive Therapy and Research* 25, no. 3 (June 2001): 291–301.

Kellett, Janet B., Ronald H. Humphrey, and Randall G. Sleeth. "Empathy and the Emergence of Task and Relations Leaders." *Leadership Quarterly* 17, no. 2 (April 2006): 146–62.

Keltner, Dacher. *Born to Be Good: The Science of a Meaningful Life.* New York: W. W. Norton & Company, 2009.

Keltner, Dacher, Keith Oatley, and Jennifer M. Jenkins. *Understanding Emotions.* Hoboken, N.J.: Wiley, 2013.

Keltner, Dacher, Jason Marsh, and Jeremy Adam Smith, ed. *The Compassionate Instinct: The Science of Human Goodness.* New York: W. W. Norton & Company, 2010.

Keng, Shian-Ling, Moria J. Smoski, and Clive J. Robins. "Effects of Mindfulness on Psychological Health: A Review of Empirical Studies." *Clinical Psychology Review* 31, no. 6 (August 2011): 1041–56.

Kennelly, Stacey. "Can Awe Buy You More Time and Happiness?" Greater Good Science Center (August 17, 2012). http://greatergood.berkeley.edu/article/item/can_awe_buy_you_more_time_and_happiness.

———. "10 Steps to Savoring the Good Things in Life." Greater Good Science Center (July 23, 2012). http://greatergood.berkeley.edu/article/item/10_steps_to_savoring_the_good_things_in_life.

Kerr, C. E., S. R. Jones, and Q. Wan. "Effects of Mindfulness Meditation Training on Anticipatory Alpha Modulation in Primary Somatosensory Cortex." *Brain Research Bulletin* 85, nos. 3–4 (May 30, 2011).

Keyes, Corey L. M. "The Mental Health Continuum: From Languishing to Flourishing in Life." *Journal of Health and Social Behavior* 43, no. 2 (June 2002): 207–22.

Khalfa, Stephanie, Simone Dalla Bella, Mathieu Roy, Isabelle Peretz, and Sonia J. Lupien. "Effects of Relaxing Music on Salivary Cortisol Level after Psychological Stress." *Annals of the New York Academy of Sciences* 999 (November 2003): 374–76.

King, Laura A. "The Health Benefits of Writing About Life Goals." *Personality and Social Psychology Bulletin* 27, no. 7 (July 1, 2001): 798–807.

Kirby, Elizabeth D., Sandra E. Muroy, Wayne G. Sun, David Covarrubias, Megan J. Leong, Laurel A. Barchas, and Daniela Kaufer. "Acute Stress Enhances Adult Rat Hippocampal Neurogenesis and Activation of Newborn Neurons via Secreted Astrocytic FGF2." *eLife* 2 (e00362) (April 16, 2013): 1–23.

Koo, Minkyung, Sara B. Algoe, Timothy D. Wilson, and Daniel T. Gilbert. "It's a Wonderful Life: Mentally Subtracting Positive Events Improves People's Affective States, Contrary to Their Affective Forecasts." *Journal of Personality and Social Psychology* 95, no. 5 (November 2008): 1217–24.

Koolhaas, J. M., S. M. Korte, S. F. De Boer, B. J. Van Der Vegt, C. G. Van Reenen, H. Hopster, I. C. De Jong, M. A. Ruis, and H. J. Blokhuis. "Coping Styles in Animals: Current Status in Behavior and Stress-Physiology." *Neuroscience and Biobehavioral Reviews* 23, no. 7 (November 1999): 925–35.

Kordestani, Omid. "Omid Kordestani Graduation Speech—Video & Transcript." *Graduation Speeches* (May 26, 2007). http://gradspeeches.com/2007/2007/omid-kordestan.

Kozasa, Elisa H., João R. Sato, Shirley S. Lacerda, Maria A. M. Barreiros, João Radvany, Tamara A. Russell, Liana G. Sanches, Luiz E. A. M. Mello, and Edson Amaro. "Meditation Training Increases Brain Efficiency in an Attention Task." *NeuroImage* 59, no. 1 (January 2, 2012): 745–49.

Kraus, Michael W., Paul K. Piff, and Dacher Keltner. "Social Class as Culture: The Convergence of Resources and Rank in the Social Realm." *Current Directions in Psychological Science* 20, no. 4 (August 2011): 246–50.

Krause, Neal. "Church-Based Social Support and Mortality." *Journals of Gerontology: Series B: Psychological & Social Sciences* 61, no. 3 (May 2006): S140–46.

Krause, Neal, Christopher G. Ellison, and Keith M. Wulff. "Church-Based Emotional Support, Negative Interaction, and Psychological Well-Being: Findings from a National Sample of Presbyterians." *Journal for the Scientific Study of Religion* 37, no. 4 (December 1998): 725–41.

Kurzban, Robert. "The Social Psychophysics of Cooperation: Nonverbal Communication in a Public Goods Game." *Journal of Nonverbal Behavior* 25, no. 4 (December 2001): 241–59.

Lally, Phillippa, Cornelia H. M. Van Jaarsveld, Henry W. W. Potts, and Jane Wardle. "How Are Habits Formed: Modelling Habit Formation in the Real World." *European Journal of Social Psychology* 40, no. 6 (October 2010): 998–1009.

Lamarre, J., and P. C. Holland. "Transfer of Inhibition After Serial Feature Negative Discrimination Training." *Learning and Motivation* 18, no. 4 (1987): 319–42.

Landau, Elizabeth. "Why so Many Minds Think Alike." CNN (January 15, 2009). http://www.cnn.com/2009/HEALTH/01/15/social.conformity.brain.

Lashley, Karl Spencer. "Basic Neural Mechanisms in Behavior." *Psychological Review* 37, no. 1 (January 1930): 1–24.

Lazare, Aaron. "Making Peace Through Apology." Greater Good Science Center (September 1, 2004). http://greatergood.berkeley.edu/article/item/making_peace_through_apology.

Legault, Lisa, Timour Al-Khindi, and Michael Inzlicht. "Preserving Integrity in the Face of Performance Threat: Self-Affirmation Enhances Neurophysiological Responsiveness to Errors." *Psychological Science* 23, no. 12 (December 2012): 1455–60.

Lehrer, Jonah. "Blame It on the Brain." *Wall Street Journal* (December 26, 2009). http://online.wsj.com/articles/SB10001424052748703478704574612052322122442.

Levenson, Robert W., Paul Ekman, and Wallace V. Friesen. "Voluntary Facial Action Generates Emotion-Specific Autonomic Nervous System Activity." *Psychophysiology* 27, no. 4 (July 1990): 363–84.

Lieberman, Matthew D. *Social: Why Our Brains Are Wired to Connect.* New York: Crown Publishers, 2013.

Lieberman, Matthew D., Kevin N. Ochsner, Daniel T. Gilbert, and Daniel L. Schacter. "Do Amnesics Exhibit Cognitive Dissonance Reduction? The Role of Explicit Memory and Attention in Attitude Change." *Psychological Science* 12, no. 2 (March 1, 2001): 135–40.

Lipsenthal, Lee. *Enjoy Every Sandwich: Living Each Day as If It Were Your Last.* New York: Harmony, 2011.

Luders, Eileen, Arthur W. Toga, Natasha Lepore, and Christian Gaser. 2009. "The Underlying Anatomical Correlates of Long-Term Meditation: Larger Hippocampal and Frontal Volumes of Gray Matter." *NeuroImage* 45, no. 3 (April 2009): 672–78.

Luskin, Fred. "The Choice to Forgive." Greater Good Science Center (September 1, 2004). http://greatergood.berkeley.edu/article/item/the_choice_to_forgive.

Lyubomirsky, Sonja. *The How of Happiness: A New Approach to Getting the Life You Want.* New York: Penguin Press, 2008.

———. *The Myths of Happiness: What Should Make You Happy, but Doesn't, What Shouldn't Make You Happy, but Does.* New York: Penguin Books, 2014.

Lyubomirsky, Sonja, Laura King, and Ed Diener. "The Benefits of Frequent Positive Affect: Does Happiness Lead to Success?" *Psychological Bulletin* 131, no. 6 (November 2005): 803–55.

Maisel, Natalya C., and Shelly L. Gable. "The Paradox of Received Social Support: The Importance of Responsiveness." *Psychological Science* 20, no. 8 (August 2009): 928–32.

Marlatt, G. Alan, and Judith R. Gordon. "Determinants of Relapse: Implications for the Maintenance of Behavior Change." In *Behavioral Medicine: Changing Health Lifestyles,* edited by Park O. Davidson and Sheena M. Davidson. New York: Brunner/Mazel, 1980: 410–52.

Marsh, Jason. "A Little Meditation Goes a Long Way." Greater Good Science Center (February 9, 2011). http://greatergood.berkeley.edu/article/item/a_little_meditation_goes_a_long_way/.

———. "The Power of Self-Compassion." Greater Good Science Center (March 14, 2012). http://greatergood.berkeley.edu/article/item/the_power_of_self_compassion.

———. "Why Inequality Is Bad for the One Percent." Greater Good Science Center (September 25, 2012). http://greatergood.berkeley.edu/article/item/why_inequality_is_bad_for_the_one_percent.

"The Marvelous Properties of Gamma Brain Waves." *OmHarmonics* (April 15, 2012). http://www.omharmonics.com/blog/gamma-brain-waves.

Mazar, Nina, and Chen-Bo Zhong. "Do Green Products Make Us Better People?" *Psychological Science* 21, no. 4 (April 2010): 494–98.

McCullough, M. E., E. L. Worthington, and K. C. Rachal. "Interpersonal Forgiving in Close Relationships." *Journal of Person* 73, no. 2 (August 1997): 321–36.

McGonigal, Kelly. "How to Make Stress Your Friend" (June 2013). *TED.com.* http://www.ted.com/talks/kelly_mcgonigal_how_to_make_stress_your_friend.

———. *The Willpower Instinct: How Self-Control Works, Why It Matters, and What You Can Do To Get More of It.* New York: Avery, 2011.

Mischel, Walter. "Processes in Delay of Gratification." In *Advances in Experimental Social Psychology,* edited by Leonard Berkowitz. Vol. 7 (New York: Academic Press, 1974): 249–92.

Mitchell, Jason P., C. Neil Macrae, and Mahzarin R. Banaji. "Encoding-Specific Effects of Social Cognition on the Neural Correlates of Subsequent Memory." *Journal of Neuroscience:* 24, no. 21 (May 26, 2004): 4912–17.

Moll, J., F. Krueger, and R. Zahn. "Human Fronto–mesolimbic Networks Guide Decisions About Charitable Donation." *Proceedings of the National Academy of Sciences of the United States of America* 103, no. 42 (October 17, 2006): 15623–28.

Moore, Adam, Thomas Gruber, Jennifer Derose, and Peter Malinowski. "Regular, Brief Mindfulness Meditation Practice Improves Electrophysiological Markers of Attentional Control." *Frontiers in Human Neuroscience* 6 (January 2012): 18.

Moorman, Sara M., and Jeffrey E. Stokes. "Does Solidarity in the Grandparent/Grandchild Relationship Protect Against Depressive Symptoms?" Paper presented at the Annual Meeting of the American Sociological Association, New York, N.Y. (August 12, 2013).

Morhenn, V., L. E. Beavin, and P. J. Zak. "Massage Increases Oxytocin and Reduces Adrenocorticotropin Hormone in Humans." *Alternative Therapies in Health and Medicine* 18, no. 6 (November-December 2012): 11–18.

Mueller, Claudia M., and Carol S. Dweck. "Praise for Intelligence Can Undermine Children's Motivation and Performance." *Journal of Personality and Social Psychology* 75, no. 1 (July 1998): 33–52.

Mullainathan, Sendhil, and Eldar Shafir. "Freeing Up Intelligence." *Scientific American Mind* (January-February 2014): 58–63.

———. *Scarcity: Why Having Too Little Means So Much.* New York: Times Books, 2013.

Muller, Wayne. *A Life of Being, Having, and Doing Enough.* New York: Harmony, 2011.

———. *Sabbath: Finding Rest, Renewal, and Delight in Our Busy Lives.* New York: Bantam, 2000.

Neal, David T., and Wendy Wood. "Automaticity in Situ: Direct Context Cuing of Habits in Daily Life." In *Psychology of Action (Vol. 2): Mechanisms of Human Action,* edited by P. M. Gollwitzer, E. Morsella, and J. A. Bargh. Oxford: Oxford University Press, 2009.

Neff, Kristin. *Self-Compassion: The Proven Power of Being Kind to Yourself.* New York: William Morrow, 2011.

———. "Why Self-Compassion Trumps Self-Esteem." Greater Good Science Center (May 27, 2011). http://greatergood.berkeley.edu/article/item/try_selfcompassion.

Neff, Kristin D., and Pittman McGehee. "Self-Compassion and Psychological Resilience Among Adolescents and Young Adults." *Self and Identity* 9, no. 3 (July 2010): 225–40.

Nelson, Leif D., Tom Meyvis, and Jeff Galak. "Enhancing the Television-Viewing Experience through Commercial Interruptions." *Journal of Consumer Research* 36, no. 2 (August 2009): 160–72.

Newberg, Andrew, Eugene D'Aquili, and Vince Rause. *Why God Won't Go Away: Brain Science and the Biology of Belief.* New York: Ballantine Books, 2002.

Nishiyama, Katsuo, and Jeffrey V. Johnson. "Karoshi—Death from Overwork: Occupational Health Consequences of Japanese Production Management." *International Journal of Health Services* 27, no. 4 (1997): 625–41.

Oliver, Mary. "The Summer Day." In *New and Selected Poems, Vol. 1.* Boston: Beacon Press, 1992.

Oman, D., C. E. Thoresen, and K. McMahon. "Volunteerism and Mortality Among the Community-Dwelling Elderly." *Journal of Health Psychology* 4, no. 3 (May 1999): 301–16.

Orbell, Sheina, and Paschal Sheeran. "Motivational and Volitional Processes in Action Initiation: A Field Study of the Role of Implementation Intentions." *Journal of Applied Social Psychology* 30, no. 4 (April 2000): 780–97.

Overwalle, F. Van. "A Dissociation Between Social Mentalizing and General Reasoning." *NeuroImage* 54, no. 2 (January 15, 2011): 1589–99.

Parker-Pope, Tara. *For Better: The Science of a Good Marriage.* New York: Dutton, 2010.

Peper, Erik, and I-Mei Lin. "Increase or Decrease Depression: How Body Postures Influence Your Energy Level." *Biofeedback* 40, no. 3 (2012): 125–30.

Perlow, Leslie A. *Sleeping with Your Smartphone: How to Break the 24/7 Habit and Change the Way You Work.* Boston: Harvard Business Review Press, 2012.

Pickett, Kate, and Richard Wilkinson. *The Spirit Level: Why Greater Equality Makes Societies Stronger.* New York: Bloomsbury Press, 2011.

Piff, Paul K., Daniel M. Stancato, Stéphane Côté, Rodolfo Mendoza-Denton, and Dacher Keltner. "Higher Social Class Predicts Increased Unethical Behavior." *Proceedings of the National Academy of Sciences of the United States of America* 109, no. 11 (March 13, 2012): 4086–91.

Pink, Daniel. *Drive: The Surprising Truth About What Motivates Us.* New York: Riverhead Books, 2009.

Post, S. G. "Altruism, Happiness, and Health: It's Good to Be Good." *International Journal of Behavioral Medicine* 12, no. 2 (June 2005): 66–77.

Poulin, Michael J., Stephanie L. Brown, Amanda J. Dillard, and Dylan M. Smith. "Giving to Others and the Association Between Stress and Mortality." *American Journal of Public Health* 103, no. 9 (September 2013): 1649–55.

Powdthavee, N. "Putting a Price Tag on Friends, Relatives, and Neighbours: Using Surveys of Life Satisfaction to Value Social Relationships." *Journal of Socio-Economics* 37, no. 4 (August 2008): 1459–80.

Powell, Richard R. *Wabi Sabi Simple: Create Beauty. Value Imperfection. Live Deeply.* Avon, Mass.: Adams Media, 2004.

Putnam, Robert D. *Bowling Alone: The Collapse and Revival of American Community.* New York: Touchstone Books by Simon & Schuster, 2001.

Quoidbach, Jordi, Elizabeth W. Dunn, K. V. Petrides, and Moïra Mikolajczak. "Money Giveth, Money Taketh Away: The Dual Effect of Wealth on Happiness." *Psychological Science* 21, no. 6 (May 2010): 759–63.

Rankin, Lissa. *Mind Over Medicine: Scientific Proof That You Can Heal Yourself.* Calsbad, Calif.: Hay House, Inc., 2013.

Rindfuss, Ronald R., Elizabeth C. Cooksey, and Rebecca L. Sutterlin. "Young Adult Occupational Achievement: Early Expectations versus Behavioral Reality." *Work and Occupations* 26, no. 2 (1999): 220–63.

Risen, Clay. "Quitting Can Be Good for You." *New York Times Magazine* (December 9, 2007). http://www.nytimes.com/2007/12/09/magazine/09quit.html.

Robinson, Sara. "Why We Have to Go Back to a 40-Hour Work Week to Keep Our Sanity." *AlterNet,* March 13, 2012. http://www.alternet.org/story/154518/why_we_have_to_go_back_to _a_40-hour_work_week_to_keep_our_sanity.

Rosenthal, Robert, and Lenore Jacobson. "Pygmalion in the Classroom." *Urban Review* 3, no. 1 (September 1968): 16–20.

Roth, Veronica. *Divergent.* New York: Katherine Tegan Books, 2011.

Rudd, Melanie, Kathleen D. Vohs, and Jennifer Aaker. "Awe Expands People's Perception of Time, Alters Decision Making, and Enhances Well-Being." *Psychological Science* 23, no. 10 (October 2012): 1130–36.

Sandstrom, Gillian M., and Elizabeth W. Dunn. "Is Efficiency Overrated?: Minimal Social Interactions Lead to Belonging and Positive Affect." *Social Psychological and Personality Science* 5, no. 4 (September 12, 2013): 437–42.

Sapolsky, Robert M. *Why Zebras Don't Get Ulcers.* 3rd ed. New York: Holt Paperbacks, 2004.

Scherwitz, Larry, R. McKelvain, C. Laman, J. Patterson, L. Dutton, S. Yusim, J. Lester, I. Kraft, D. Rochelle, and R. Leachman. "Type A Behavior, Self-Involvement, and Coronary Atherosclerosis." *Psychosomatic Medicine* 45, no. 1 (March 1983): 47–57.

Schulte, Brigid. *Overwhelmed: Work, Love and Play When No One Has the Time.* London: Bloomsbury Publishing, 2014.

Schwartz, Barry. *The Paradox of Choice: Why More Is Less.* New York: Ecco, 2004.

Schwartz, Barry, Andrew Ward, John Monterosso, Sonja Lyubomirsky, Katherine White, and Darrin R. Lehman. "Maximizing versus Satisficing: Happiness Is a Matter of Choice." *Journal of Personality and Social Psychology* 83, no. 5 (November 2002): 1178–97.

Schwartz, Carolyn E., and Rabbi Meir Sendor. "Helping Others Helps Oneself: Response Shift Effects in Peer Support." *Social Science & Medicine* 48, no. 11 (1999): 1563–75.

Schwartz, Tony, and Catherine McCarthy. "Manage Your Energy, Not Your Time." *Harvard Business Review* 85, no. 10 (October 2007): 63–73.

Segal, Zindel V., Peter Bieling, Trevor Young, Glenda MacQueen, Robert Cooke, Lawrence Martin, Richard Bloch, and Robert D. Levitan. "Antidepressant Monotherapy vs Sequential Pharmacotherapy and Mindfulness-Based Cognitive Therapy, or Placebo, for Relapse Prophylaxis in Recurrent Depression." *Archives of General Psychiatry* 67, no. 12 (December 2010): 1256–64.

Seligman, Martin E. P. *Flourish: A Visionary New Understanding of Happiness and Well-Being.* New York: Atria Books, 2012.

Seligman, Martin E. P., Tracy A. Steen, Nansook Park, and Christopher Peterson. "Positive Psychology Progress: Empirical Validation of Interventions." *American Psychologist* 60, no. 5 (July-August 2005): 410–21.

Shapiro, Shauna, and Chris White. *Mindful Discipline: A Loving Approach to Setting Limits and Raising an Emotionally Intelligent Child.* Oakland, Calif.: New Harbinger Publications, 2014.

Sheldon, Ken M., and S. Lyubomirsky. "Achieving Sustainable Gains in Happiness: Change Your Actions, Not Your Circumstances." *Journal of Happiness Studies* 7, no. 1 (March 2006): 55–86.

Shenk, Joshua Wolf. "What Makes Us Happy?" *Atlantic* (June 1, 2009). http://www.theatlantic .com/magazine/archive/2009/06/what-makes-us-happy/307439.

Shriver, Maria. *And One More Thing Before You Go . . .* New York: Free Press, 2008.

Simon-Thomas, Emiliana R. "A 'Thnx' a Day Keeps the Doctor Away." Greater Good Science

Center (December 19, 2012). http://greatergood.berkeley.edu/article/item/a_thnx_a_day_keeps _the_doctor_away.

Smith, Emily Esfahani, and Jennifer L. Aaker. "Millennial Searchers." *New York Times* (2013). http://www.nytimes.com/2013/12/01/opinion/sunday/millennial-searchers.html.

Stephens, Greg J., Lauren J. Silbert, and Uri Hasson. "Speaker-Listener Neural Coupling Underlies Successful Communication." *Proceedings of the National Academy of Sciences of the United States of America* 107, no. 32 (August 10, 2010): 14425–30.

Stephens, Thomas. "Physical Activity and Mental Health in the United States and Canada: Evidence from Four Population Surveys." *Preventive Medicine* 17, no. 1 (January 1988): 35–47.

Stevenson, Betsey, and Justin Wolfers. "The Paradox of Declining Female Happiness." *American Economic Journal: Economic Policy* 1, no. 2 (2009): 190–225.

Stewart-Williams, Steve, and John Podd. "The Placebo Effect: Dissolving the Expectancy versus Conditioning Debate." *Psychological Bulletin* 130, no. 2 (March 2004): 324–40.

Surakka, V., and J. K. Hietanen. "Facial and Emotional Reactions to Duchenne and Non-Duchenne Smiles." *International Journal of Psychophysiology* 29, no. 1 (June 1998): 23–33.

Sze, J. A., A. Gyurak, J. W. Yuan, and R. W. Levenson. "Coherence Between Emotional Experience and Physiology: Does Body Awareness Training Have an Impact?" *Emotion* 10, no. 6 (December 2010): 803–14.

Taylor, Jill Bolte. *My Stroke of Insight: A Brain Scientist's Personal Journey.* New York: Plume, 2009.

Toepfer, Steven M., Kelly Cichy, and Patti Peters. "Letters of Gratitude: Further Evidence for Author Benefits." *Journal of Happiness Studies* 13, no. 1 (March 2012): 187–201.

Turkle, Sherry. *Alone Together: Why We Expect More from Technology and Less from Each Other.* Philadelphia: Basic Books, 2012.

Twist, Lynne. *Soul of Money: Reclaiming the Wealth of Our Inner Resources.* New York: W. W. Norton & Company, 2006.

Tyler, Kenneth, Lynda Brown-Wright, Danelle Stevens-Watkins, Deneia Thomas, Ruby Stevens, Clarissa Roan-Belle, Nadia Gadson, and La Toya Smith. "Linking Home-School Dissonance to School-Based Outcomes for African American High School Students." *Journal of Black Psychology* 36, no. 4 (November 2009): 410–25.

Vaillant, George E. *Triumphs of Experience: The Men of the Harvard Grant Study.* Cambridge, Mass.: Belknap Press, 2012.

Van Cappellen, Patty, and Vasslis Saroglou. "Awe Activates Religious and Spiritual Feelings and Behavioral Intentions." *Psychology of Religion and Spirituality* 4, no. 3 (August 2012): 223–36.

Van Ogtrop, Kristin. *Just Let Me Lie Down: Necessary Terms for the Half-insane Working Mom.* (New York: Little, Brown, and Company, 2010).

Varty, Boyd. *Cathedral of the Wild: An African Journey Home.* New York: Random House, 2014.

Verplanken, Bas, and Wendy Wood. "Interventions to Break and Create Consumer Habits." *Journal of Public Policy & Marketing* 25, no. 1 (Spring 2006): 90–103.

Wallace, Robert Keith. "Physiological Effects of Transcendental Meditation." *Science* 167, no. 3926 (March 1970): 1751–54.

Walton, G. M., and G. L. Cohen. 2011. "A Brief Social-Belonging Intervention Improves Academic and Health Outcomes of Minority Students." *Science* 331, no. 6023 (March 2011): 1447–51.

———. "A Question of Belonging: Race, Social Fit, and Achievement." *Journal of Personality and Social Psychology* 92, no. 1 (January 2007): 82–96.

Weaver, Jane. "Can Stress Actually Be Good for You?" (December 20, 2006). NBC News. http://www.nbcnews.com/id/15818153/ns/health-mental_health/t/can-stress-actually-be-good-you.

Wegner, Daniel M., David J. Schneider, Samuel R. Carter III, and Teri L. White. "Paradoxical Effects of Thought Suppression." *Journal of Personality and Social Psychology* 53, no. 1 (July 1987): 5–13.

Weinstein, Netta, Kirk W. Brown, and Richard M. Ryan. "A Multi-Method Examination of the Effects of Mindfulness on Stress Attribution, Coping, and Emotional Well-Being." *Journal of Research in Personality* 43, no. 3 (June 2009): 374–85.

Wesselmann, Eric D., Florencia D. Cardoso, Samantha Slater, and Kipling D. Williams. "To

Be Looked at as Though Air: Civil Attention Matters." *Psychological Science* 23, no. 2 (February 2012): 166–68.

Williamson, Marianne. *A Return to Love: Reflections on the Principles of "A Course in Miracles."* New York: HarperOne, 1996.

Wirtz, Petra H., Sigrid Elsenbruch, Luljeta Emini, Katharina Rüdisüli, Sara Groessbauer, and Ulrike Ehlert. "Perfectionism and the Cortisol Response to Psychosocial Stress in Men." *Psychosomatic Medicine* 69, no. 3 (April 2007): 249–55.

Wrzesniewski, Amy, Clark McCauley, Paul Rozin, and Barry Schwartz. "Jobs, Careers, and Callings: People's Relations to Their Work." *Journal of Research in Personality* 31, no. 1 (March 1997): 21–33.

Zenger, John, and Joseph Folkman. *The Extraordinary Leader: Turning Good Managers into Great Leaders.* New York: McGraw-Hill, 2009.

INDEX

9 WAYS TO EASE OVERWHELM

1. Make your bed. There is something true about the adage that the state of your bed is the state of your head.

2. Set your phone to automatically go into silent mode an hour before your bedtime. Enjoy the peace and quiet.

3. Develop a way to "give good no." As in: *"Thank you so much for asking, but that isn't going to work out for me right now."*

4. Turn off your TV unless you intend to watch something specific. Never watch commercials—record your show and skip through them.

5. Eat at least one meal a day without doing anything else at the same time. No driving, reading, or responding to email.

6. Make decisions about routine things once. Buy the same brands at the grocery store every time; get the same outfit in different colors so you don't have to decide what to wear every morning; prepare the same basic meals most week days.

7. Clean out one drawer or shelf a day. Eventually, everything in your home will have a place, and this will make it easy to find what you need when you need it.

8. Establish "predictable time off" with your colleagues and family. When will you commit to *not* working? Start with dinnertime, work up to weekends.

9. Stop multi-tasking. It makes you error prone, and even though you think you're getting more done, it's actually quite inefficient.

7 EASY THINGS YOU CAN DO TO ENJOY TODAY (AND TOMORROW) MORE

1. Take a good old-fashioned recess in the middle of the day. For every 60 to 90 minutes that you focus, take a 10 to 15 minute break. Go outside and play! Or at least sit inside and daydream.

2. Increase your ratio of positive to negative emotions by watching a silly YouTube video, expressing gratitude to someone, or reading something inspiring. (Yes, you get credit for watching funny animal videos!)

3. Establish a tiny time-saving habit. Put your keys by the door where you will be sure to find them. Set up your coffee machine at night. Sometimes a small effort today can have a big impact tomorrow! Allow yourself to feel gleeful when you succeed.

4. Establish a happiness habit. Do a daily crossword puzzle if that does it for you. Read a favorite magazine at lunchtime. Throw the ball for your dog every morning. What would make *you* really happy if you did it every day?

5. Take 10 minutes to do nothing. Unplug from your phones and computer. Sit down in a room where you can be alone. Stare into space. It's fine if you feel bored— you'll be more productive later.

6. Smile at the barista and strike up a short conversation. Or with the people sharing your elevator. Or with the crossing guard.

7. Repair a minor crack in an important relationship. Call your mom and invite her to lunch, even though your last conversation with her was tense. Find something nice to say to your spouse, even though he can be frustrating.

7 WAYS TO FEEL MORE LOVED AND CONNECTED

1. Celebrate other people's success. The people we love feel closer to us when we actively rejoice with them. When they succeed, whoop and holler like a cheerleader, bring them cupcakes, or pop open a bottle of champagne.

2. Consciously practice gratitude. Everyday, express appreciation to a friend or family member.

3. Allow yourself to be vulnerable. Vulnerability can be uncomfortable, but it allows trust and intimacy to develop.

4. Accept that people are often annoying. Love them anyway.

5. Learn how to apologize effectively. We all make mistakes; the trick is knowing how to repair them.

6. Forgive people. Forgiveness is not about erasing the original hurt; it is about choosing positive emotions over negative ones.

7. Stop thinking about yourself so much. Turn your attention to the things that you can do to make *other people* happy.

Would you rather not destroy your book?
Go to www.christinecarter.com to download this
and other helpful printable lists.

CHRISTINE CARTER, PH.D., is a sociologist and senior fellow at UC Berkeley's Greater Good Science Center, an interdisciplinary research center that "translates" the study of happiness, resilience, and emotional intelligence for the public. The author of the bestselling *Raising Happiness,* Dr. Carter blogs regularly for *Greater Good, The Huffington Post, U.S. News and World Report,* and *Psychology Today.* She has appeared on *The Oprah Winfrey Show, The Dr. Oz Show, The Rachael Ray Show, The Daily Show with Jon Stewart,* the *Today* show, and NPR, and has helped thousands of people lead happier and more productive lives through her lectures and online classes. Her e-newsletters have more than 50,000 subscribers. She lives with her husband, children, and dog, Buster, near San Francisco.

christinecarter.com

ABOUT THE TYPE

This book was set in Fairfield, the first typeface from the hand of the distinguished American artist and engraver Rudolph Ruzicka (1883–1978). Ruzicka was born in Bohemia (in the present-day Czech Republic) and came to America in 1894. He set up his own shop, devoted to wood engraving and printing, in New York in 1913 after a varied career working as a wood engraver, in photoengraving and banknote printing plants, and as an art director and freelance artist. He designed and illustrated many books, and was the creator of a considerable list of individual prints—wood engravings, line engravings on copper, and aquatints.

Praise for *The Sweet Spot*

"When you are living in your sweet spot you feel both calm and energetic, accomplished and joyful, strong and at ease. Dr. Christine Carter's *The Sweet Spot* illuminates the simple and sustainable path toward this precious and happy balance." —DEEPAK CHOPRA, M.D.

"Timely, lively, and vital, *The Sweet Spot* is an immediately useful must-read. Carter gets to the heart of how to pursue happiness in a busy world, without sacrificing excellence. This book spoke to me."

—SHAWN ACHOR, *New York Times*
bestselling author of *The Happiness Advantage*

"Finally, an accessible guide to being more productive (and happier!). Dr. Carter is an acclaimed scholar and her advice is derived from data, studies, and proven methods, yet her readable, conversational style makes us think she's an old friend. *The Sweet Spot* is a must-read for every overworked executive, overwrought parent, or overscheduled human being."

—JENNIFER GRANHOLM, governor of Michigan, 2003–11;
distinguished adjunct professor, UC Berkeley School of
Law & Goldman School of Public Policy

"My copy of Christine Carter's *The Sweet Spot* is underlined, scribbled on, and dog-eared because of all the pages I want to come back to. Filled with evidence-based research, helpful, practical advice, and her own warm, generous, and funny stories, *The Sweet Spot* is a gift, like a good friend drawing a personal road map out of the crazy busy swirl of our overloaded lives toward the sweet spot of a happier and more meaningful one."

—BRIGID SCHULTE, author of *Overwhelmed,* and
Pulitzer Prize–winning *Washington Post* staff writer

"I sat down to read Christine Carter's *The Sweet Spot* on a particularly busy day, and oddly found that as I read, I could see a better way through obligations. In other words, this book did something I thought was impossible: It seemed to *give me more time*. In this age of overstuffed schedules, that's about as good as self-help advice can get. Thank you, Christine!"

—MARTHA BECK, author of *Finding Your Way in a Wild New World* and *Expecting Adam*

"You can read stacks of the best books on stress management and well-being, sign up for classes about resiliency, and hire a personal coach to help you find true happiness or you can just pick up a copy of *The Sweet Spot*. Refreshing, timely, and inspiring, it will help you experience a new way of being: calm, energized, and free to focus on what really matters most."

—RENÉE PETERSON TRUDEAU, life balance coach and author of *The Mother's Guide to Self-Renewal*

"If it isn't hard it isn't work, right? Carter turns this assumption on its head by showing us how to be stronger and make life easier, both through her own experience and new research. The Sweet Spot is worth finding, and she teaches us how."

—LUCY DANZIGER, *New York Times* bestselling co-author of *The Nine Rooms of Happiness*

"*The Sweet Spot* has inspired me to make immediate changes that have increased my productivity and lowered my stress. I've also shared Dr. Carter's research-backed ideas with my executive coaching clients— men and women eager to up their game—and I know it will help them manage their teams to better results, too."

—DAN MULHERN, Haas School of Business, UC Berkeley

"Funny, intimately honest, and so practical—Dr. Carter pulls pure gold out of studies on the brain and happiness. Her book reads like a page-turning thriller full of proven ways to have the life you want."

—RICK HANSON, PH.D., author of *Hardwiring Happiness*

"In this compelling and practical book, you will learn not only the latest research about how to wire your brain and body for your *sweet spot*, you will learn exactly how to use this information right now to create a much sweeter life!"   —CHRISTIANE NORTHRUP, M.D.

"I have a rich and full life, but I sometimes find myself bowled over by the waves of everyday life. Reading this book is like being given a surfboard and surfing lessons. It is full to the brim with research-based tips and tricks for living in flow. Adopting even a few of them will profoundly improve your quality of life."
                —CASSANDRA VIETEN, PH.D., president and CEO, Institute of
                Noetic Sciences, and co-author of *Living Deeply*

"Finally, the author of my favorite book on parenting has written a book on work-life balance. Christine Carter has once again created the perfect blend of science and story to give us practical tools for combating the overwhelm that seems to pervade modern life."
                —KATRINA ALCORN, author of *Maxed Out:
                American Moms on the Brink*

"Filled with science-informed wisdom, touching and humorous stories, and practical suggestions, this inspiring guide will help you create a life of connection and purpose, ease and well-being, no matter your age or background. Read and enjoy!"
                —DANIEL J. SIEGEL, MD, *New York Times* bestselling author of
                Brainstorm, No-Drama Discipline, and *The Whole-Brain Child*

"Like a wise friend you can depend on, Christine Carter takes you by the hand and, with gentle encouragement, shows you step by step how to create true well-being in your life. Honest, playful, unpretentious, and chock-full of wisdom, *The Sweet Spot* just might convince you to do what's really good for you and enjoy the process. I love this book!"
                –JAMES BARAZ, co-author of *Awakening Joy* and
                co-founding teacher of Spirit Rock Meditation Center

by christine carter, ph.d.

raising happiness
the sweet spot
the other side of silence